T0385051

I SAW WATER

ITHELL COLQUHOUN

Edited, with an introduction and notes,
by Richard Shillitoe and Mark S. Morrisson

I SAW WATER

AN OCCULT NOVEL AND OTHER
SELECTED WRITINGS

The Pennsylvania State University Press
University Park, Pennsylvania

Library of Congress Cataloging-in-Publication Data
Colquhoun, Ithell, 1906–1988, author.
I saw water : an occult novel and other selected writings /
Ithell Colquhoun ; edited, with an introduction and
notes, by Richard Shillitoe and Mark S. Morrisson
pages   cm
Summary: "The first publication of I Saw Water, the second
novel by the surrealist artist, writer, and occultist Ithell
Colquhoun (1906–1988). Also included is a selection
of her writings and images"—Provided by publisher.
Includes bibliographical references and index.
ISBN 978-0-271-06423-9 (cloth : alk. paper)
1. Nuns—Fiction.
2. Convents—Fiction.
3. Future life—Fiction.
I. Shillitoe, R. W. (Richard W.), 1950– , editor.
II. Morrisson, Mark S., editor.
III. Title.

PR6053.O434I17 2014
823'.914z—dc23
2014015845

CONTENTS

ILLUSTRATIONS

ACKNOWLEDGMENTS

The editors gratefully acknowledge the support and assistance that made this first publication of Colquhoun's novel possible. Staff at the Hyman Kreitman Research Centre, Tate Britain, London, provided professional facilities, information, and advice with their customary courtesy throughout the preparation of this book. D.A.S. provided the first-named editor with domestic facilities, information, and advice with her customary courtesy throughout the same period. Laura Reed-Morrisson contributed her sustaining encouragement, shrewd scholarly feedback, and ongoing patience from start to finish. The College of the Liberal Arts at The Pennsylvania State University provided financial support for the research and publication of this edition. Finally, we thank Eleanor Goodman for shepherding this project from its earliest conception through its final publication and Julie Schoelles for her thoughtful and expert copyediting.

NOTE ON THE TEXTS

Drafts of *I Saw Water* are to be found in twelve thick folders (TGA 929/2/1/31) in the Colquhoun archive, housed in the Hyman Kreitman Research Centre, Tate Britain, London. The folders also contain Colquhoun's contemporaneous dated transcripts of many of the dreams that she incorporated into the novel and some that she considered for inclusion but did not use, notes containing alternative schemes for the novel's structure and possible names for the characters, calendars of saint's days, and other related documents. From the evidence of Colquhoun's letters to publishers, the final typescript on which we have based this first published edition dates to around 1967. It is very clean, with only the occasional autograph correction. We have retained the author's punctuation (including her use of quotation marks) and British English spelling.

With regard to the previously unpublished essays and poems included in this volume, drafts and typescripts are also housed in the Hyman Kreitman Research Centre. Several drafts often exist for the items we have selected, but the author's final intentions are always clear. For the published pieces, we have kept to the texts as published. Every reasonable effort has been made to contact the copyright holders of the texts printed here. The editors wish to thank *Quest* for permission to reprint "The Openings of the Body"; the *Hermetic Journal* for permission to reprint "The Zodiac and the Flashing Colours"; and Peter Owen Publishers for permission to reprint "Love-Charm II."

EDITORS' INTRODUCTION

The centerpiece of this book is the previously unpublished novel *I Saw Water*. Written by the author and artist Ithell Colquhoun (1906–1988), it is set on the island of Ménec, where Sister Brigid inhabits the Ianua Vitae Convent. She is an unconventional nun, but it is soon revealed that the convent itself has an unconventional mission. It belongs to the Parthenogenesist Order, ostensibly Roman Catholic, but whose purpose is more reminiscent of certain schools of alchemy than of Catholicism. Its aim is the unification of the separated genders, the achievement of which will signal the transmutation of fallen, sinful humanity to a state of spiritual perfection, restore nature's equilibrium, and confirm the unity of the hermetic cosmos. In tandem with this alchemical undercurrent, many aspects of conventual and ritual life on Ménec have more in common with pagan nature worship than with Christianity. Ménec itself is an unusual island. It is the Island of the Dead, and all the inhabitants, nuns and laity alike, have died and are now in transit, working their way toward their second death. The concept of the second death presented in this novel differs from that of Judeo-Christian eschatology. It has no place in Catholic theology, being more associated with Eastern spiritualities that would have likely reached Colquhoun through the teachings of the Theosophical Society.

Sister Brigid's cousin, Charlotte, is also on the island, having just taken her own life. Before her suicide, she was the mistreated wife of a homosexual husband. Despite the personal vulnerabilities that she carries with her, she is as much a spiritual guide to Brigid as are the convent mistresses. Another influence on Brigid is a local landowner and heir named Nikolaz, who bears strong similarities to Adonis, the mythological vegetation god. He entices Brigid from the convent but dies by drowning (inevitably, as it will come to be understood) before they can leave the island together. Nonetheless, eventually Sister Brigid is able to cast off her personality and human emotions and achieve a state of disembodied peace. *I Saw Water* is narrated in a matter-of-fact style that recounts as commonplace a remarkable series of events, including an encounter with a subhuman baboon girl, rituals dedicated to sacred wells, a pagan snake dance, the circulation of a powerful heirloom, the touch of an ectoplasmic hand, and even a demonstration of the power of bilocation by the convent's novice mistress. Naturalistic passages are juxtaposed with lengthy sequences derived from dreams, resulting in dislocations of time, place, and logic.

As this brief summary shows, the novel is not mainstream fiction. It is forgivable that in the mid 1960s, when it was written, no publisher felt confident enough to add it to their list, especially as Colquhoun required that each chapter be printed on color-coded paper to evoke its occult structure. Today, with more widespread knowledge of the spiritual traditions of East and West, deeper appreciation of dreams and their imagery, and greater awareness of the importance of the occult in modernism, some of the surface strangeness has mellowed. Even so, there is still much to challenge the nonspecialist reader. One purpose of our introduction and notes is to explain concepts and terms that occur within the novel and might be unfamiliar. Another is to suggest important lines of analysis.

Although Colquhoun is well known to two groups of people—those interested in the history of surrealism in England in the years leading up to World War II and those interested in ceremonial magic in the mid-twentieth century—outside of these groups (neither of which is extensive) she remains almost entirely unknown. Much of her written work is unpublished or appeared in "little" magazines that can be difficult to access. Similarly, her artwork is largely in private ownership or stored in archives and is rarely seen in public. So, in order to place the novel in the context of her work and to show how it fits within wider historical influences, we have included a small but representative sample of her images and other writings. Through this book we hope to bring her extraordinary work into wider knowledge and appreciation.

BIOGRAPHY

Margaret Ithell Colquhoun was born to British parents in Assam, India, where her father held a senior position in the Indian Civil Service. She was brought to England as a young child, the family eventually settling in Cheltenham. There she attended a well-known private school, Cheltenham Ladies College, and the local college of art, and then moved to London in October 1927 to study at the Slade School of Art, at that time the foremost art school in England. The Slade had been instrumental in the nascence of modern art in pre-WWI London. It had taught such painters as Augustus John—known for his espousal of postimpressionism—and a younger generation that included Mark Gertler, Christopher Nevinson, and Paul Nash. The important Bloomsbury painters

Duncan Grant and Dora Carrington enrolled at the Slade, as did the vorticist artists Wyndham Lewis, Edward Wadsworth, and David Bomberg, who published their anti-Bloomsbury and anti-Victorian little magazine *Blast* just a month before the outbreak of war. Colquhoun entered the Slade during the interwar period, only a few years after Eileen Agar had left it for Paris. As a measure of her skill and potential, Colquhoun shared the school's prestigious Summer Composition Prize in 1929. She graduated at a time when, as it had been shortly before World War I, British art was being revitalized by its engagement with continental art movements, to which it had initially been slow to respond.

In the 1930s, the intellectual and artistic movement that left the greatest mark on the British scene was surrealism. Its watershed event in London was the International Surrealist Exhibition at the New Burlington Galleries. From June 11 to July 4, 1936, it attracted some one thousand spectators per day. The exhibition featured works by the major continental surrealists, supplemented by a program of talks and readings. Colquhoun attended a lecture by Salvador Dalí, during which, while bolted into a deep-sea diving suit, he very nearly suffocated. The poet and essayist André Breton, the movement's leading figure, spoke to a crowded house. A young Dylan Thomas wandered about the gallery serving cups of boiled string.

Colquhoun was drawn to surrealism by the work of visual artists such as Dalí, but more importantly by the writings of Breton. Breton elaborated a theoretical framework for surrealism in which automatism, poetry, psychoanalytic theory, trances, and the study of dreams were used to challenge accepted notions of reality. Believing that the contradictions between apparent opposites such as the conscious and the unconscious, or dream and wakeful thought, could be resolved by such methods, surrealism aimed at a higher reality. As Breton had put it in 1924, "I believe in the future resolution of these two states, dream and reality, which are seemingly so contradictory, into a kind of absolute reality, a surreality, if one may so speak."[1]

The appeal of such ideas for Colquhoun is not hard to fathom. During her youth, she had developed a lasting interest in magic, acquiring a wide range and depth of occult knowledge. This was ably demonstrated by her first publication, an article entitled "The Prose of Alchemy," which was written while she was still a student and published in 1930 in G. R. S. Mead's influential journal of Gnosticism and esotericism, *The Quest*.[2] Mead had been part of Theosophical Society founder H. P. Blavatsky's inner circle in the 1880s, even editing the key theosophical publication *Lucifer* with Annie Besant after Blavatsky's death. But internal scandals that tore rifts in the Theosophical Society led Mead to resign from it in

1909. He then founded the Quest Society, whose lectures at Kensington Town Hall were attended by, among others, W. B. Yeats, Ezra Pound, T. E. Hulme, Martin Buber, Jessie Weston (author of *From Ritual to Romance,* a major influence on T. S. Eliot's *The Waste Land*), and the young Ithell Colquhoun. Mead published works by several of these authors in *The Quest.* So, while many of Colquhoun's subsequent publications would appear in journals tied to surrealism, she was equally engaged in the circles and journals of occult London.

To the continental surrealists, the link between the surreal and the hermetic was clear and uncontentious. In the *Second Surrealist Manifesto* (1929), Breton made the bond between alchemy and surrealism explicit.[3] His "union of opposites" would have been a familiar idea to a woman steeped in alchemy; indeed, an important alchemical motto is *conjunctio oppositorum* (the conjunction of opposites).[4] The impact of occult ideas and alchemical imagery on the work of visual artists associated with surrealism has long been recognized, and recent scholarship, such as the work of Urszula Szulakowska (2011) and Camelia Darie (2012), continually redraws and extends these boundaries.[5]

In England, however, the situation was very different. When, in 1940, Colquhoun refused to curtail her magical activities, she was expelled from the London surrealist group. The group's leader, E. L. T. Mesens, undoubtedly had a strong and unwavering personal mistrust of the occult. His motives, however, may have been mixed: it is said that his antipathy to Colquhoun was heightened by a powerful sexual jealousy.[6] The consequences for Colquhoun were profound. On the cover of the June 15, 1939, issue of the *London Bulletin,* one of the most progressive British art publications of its day, she had shared the bill with such figures as René Magritte, Pablo Picasso, Man Ray, and the Marquis de Sade.[7] Her photograph had been taken by Man Ray (fig. 1).[8] She had recently visited Breton in Paris, exchanging horoscopes with him (both had Neptune in the House of Death), before spending time in Chemillieu with a number of other artists engaged in reevaluating the role of automatism in surrealist painting. To all appearances, her star was rising. In fact, it had reached its zenith. World War II was about to change the intellectual climate of Europe and the United Kingdom. Surrealism, whose promise of intellectual and personal freedom had clearly failed, became the voice of the discredited past. Colquhoun's exclusion from the London group, the bitterness surrounding her disastrous and short-lived marriage to surrealist artist and writer Toni del Renzio, her failure to find a publisher for her alchemical novel *Goose of Hermogenes,* and two commercially unsuccessful shows at the prestigious Mayor Gallery in Mayfair all made the 1940s a testing decade for her.

Colquhoun spent increasing periods of time away from London, in Cornwall, moving there permanently in 1956. For the last three decades of her life, she lived in a village near Penzance on the Land's End peninsula. Eventually, in physical isolation from the London-based art world and the capital's magical societies, she achieved a measure of recognition, more from her writing than from her painting. *Goose of Hermogenes* finally appeared in print in 1961, following the publication of Colquhoun's idiosyncratic and highly imaginative travel books on Ireland and Cornwall.[9] It was here in Cornwall, with its rich traditions of myth and folklore, as well as its profusion of prehistoric monuments, that she spent much of her time developing and diversifying her occult knowledge and skills. Her final prose book, *Sword of Wisdom*,[10] remains the authoritative account of MacGregor Mathers, a key figure in late nineteenth-century magic and a founder of the Hermetic Order of the Golden Dawn, a society whose teachings and rituals are still influential today. It was also in Cornwall that Colquhoun wrote *I Saw Water*.

THE SPIRITUAL FRAMEWORK OF *I SAW WATER*

In this book, we use the words "occult," "magical," "hermetic," and "esoteric" to indicate aspects of a worldview that has its roots in antiquity and which, in today's world, offers a description of the universe that differs markedly from those proposed by materialist sciences and monotheistic religions. It numbers among its diverse sources Egyptian and Greek mystery texts, as well as writings by pre-Socratic philosophers, Gnostics, and medieval Jewish mystics. It is sufficiently flexible to incorporate aspects of Eastern religion within a generally Christian framework. It includes the practical arts of alchemy, divination, and the casting of spells. It frequently claims that all things are related through a series of correspondences and regards the cosmos not only as living but as perpetually regenerating and reconstituting itself.[11] As a serious explanation of how the universe works, occultism suffered major reversals at the hands of the Enlightenment but never received a knockout blow. In fact, Colquhoun came of age when Britain, Western Europe, and the United States were experiencing a decades-long resurgence of interest in magic that has loosely been styled the "occult revival." As a result of spiritualist séances, magical orders (such as the Golden Dawn), explorations of Eastern and Western esoteric traditions by the Theosophical Society, alchemical experiments, and a broad popular interest in subjects ranging from poltergeists to the Gothic, Britain witnessed a proliferation of print culture (books, periodicals, posters, and artwork) and what might

now be termed "new religious movements." These offered alternative spiritualities, together with social and cultural opportunities for participation.

Colquhoun herself was as completely at home with the Qabalah, the system
of magical study derived from medieval Jewish mysticism,[12] as she was with
Eastern traditions such as Tantra. She would, in her maturity, be drawn to contemporary developments such as Wicca, neo-Druidism, and Goddess religions.
At various times in her adult life, she was a member of two Golden Dawn–
inspired organizations (the Ordo Templi Orientis and the Order of the Pyramid
and the Sphinx), the somewhat similar Order of the Keltic Cross, several Co-
Masonic lodges, English and French Druidical orders, the Theosophical Society
of England, and the Fellowship of Isis, this last being an association dedicated
to honoring the divine mother Goddess.

As a magician, then, Colquhoun adopted a highly syncretic approach. That
is, she valued diversity and attempted to make a harmonious whole out of fragments taken from different spiritual traditions, each of which, she believed,
contained hidden aspects of the greater truth.[13] Among these influences, Colquhoun's roots in her own Christian background remain readily apparent. Hers,
however, was a heterodox Christianity. Her lasting interest, for example, in the
loss of androgyny that allegedly occurred at the Fall, and the consequent need
for gender reintegration, places her much closer to the ideas of mystical thinkers
such as Jacob Böhme, Emanuel Swedenborg, and William Blake than to conventional Christian doctrines.

In keeping with Colquhoun's personal spiritual landscape, *I Saw Water* is
a syncretic novel: within its pages ceremonial magic, alchemy, pagan nature
worship, and theosophical teachings all happily rub shoulders with Roman
Catholicism. In fact, as was the case with Colquhoun's earlier novel *Goose of
Hermogenes*, the hermetic is embedded in the novel's structure. In *Goose of Hermogenes*, progress through the chapters reflected the heroine's progress through
the stages of alchemical transformation. In *I Saw Water*, Colquhoun originally
intended to represent the heroine's spiritual advancement by ascending, chapter
by chapter, through the sephiroth of the Qabalistic Tree of Life, from Malkuth in
chapter 1 to Kether in the final chapter. Her notes show that she also considered
associating the chapters with a Christian journey: progression along the Stations
of the Cross or the Mysteries of the Rosary. In the final scheme, however, she
rejected both the Qabalistic and the Christian paths, choosing instead to name
each chapter after one or another of the geomantic figures.

Geomancy is a traditional technique of divination believed to have originated in
the Middle East at some uncertain time in the past. It achieved some popularity in

the twentieth century thanks largely to its advocacy by Golden Dawn–influenced magicians, but never to the extent achieved by another divinatory technique: Tarot readings. In geomancy, the inquirer generally makes a series of marks upon a sheet of paper, renouncing all conscious control. The resulting pattern is then classified according to a formula to produce one of a number of standard figures. Each of the geomantic figures is known by a Latin name and has a range of meanings, derived in part from its planetary and zodiacal associations.[14] So, for example, the figure Laetitia, which Colquhoun translates as "Joy," governs chapter 13 and signifies progression and happiness. For the chapter in which the heroine finally achieves complete separation from all her earthbound concerns, its relevance is clear.

Colquhoun's adoption of the geomantic figures was a late decision, made after the basic structure of the novel had been determined. According to Israel Regardie, geomancy and other methods of divination are not used primarily to predict what is to come. Instead, they are used to facilitate the expression and growth of inner psychospiritual abilities by placing practitioners in contact with internal or external forces of which they are unaware.[15] Colquhoun uses the figures, therefore, not to prefigure what might lie ahead, but as a commentary on the psychological state of her characters, their development, and their circumstances.

Despite these structural changes, the idea of a journey remains central to the novel, as all the characters are progressing, in their individual ways, toward their second death. The second death is a construct popularized in the West by the teachings of the Theosophical Society. Members of the society draw distinctions between a person's physical body, their astral body, their mental body, and the immortal soul. There is no such thing as the finality of death as it is ordinarily understood; death is merely the laying aside of the physical body. The emotions and passions generated during life on earth continue to live on in the astral body until, with time, they become exhausted and fade away. When this process has finished, the second death takes place, but the soul survives and will later occupy another physical body. Over the course of many such cycles of reincarnation, the soul evolves until, ultimately, it dispenses with material phases altogether, existing only in a world of thought-forms.[16]

Sister Brigid, Charlotte, Dr. Wiseacre, Roli, and the novel's other characters are in a dynamic state of disequilibrium and do not necessarily understand what is happening (some readers may share the feeling). This is because, although they are physically dead, their personalities are still active in the astral body and they continue to see, hear, think, and feel. But gradually the fact that physical death has occurred becomes inescapable. It is then that the second death can occur. This is the journey that the heroine makes during the course of *I Saw Water*.

Arriving at Ménec as Ella de Maine, she becomes Sister Brigid for the duration of her stay at the convent. Once she has moved beyond the convent, she finally loses all sense of personal identity. Name and personality are attributes that, along with her possessions, she casts aside: "Everything is free and I am free of everything," she says in her culminating insight (page 134).

THE PHYSICAL SETTING OF I SAW WATER

The place where people live their lives influences the nature of the lives they lead. In turn, those lives leave their mark upon the place. This is as true of inner, spiritual lives as it is of outer, practical ones. Religious beliefs and activities have a reciprocal interaction with the locality. Beliefs may be inspired or strengthened by natural features, and, conversely, beliefs and observances leave their imprint on the landscape—for instance, in the placement of devotional buildings and funerary monuments. As beliefs change over time, their history may be read in the archaeological record and in place names. There can be few places in Europe that demonstrate this more convincingly than Brittany, where the events in I Saw Water take place.[17]

Brittany is a region of northwestern France. It is a peninsula, jutting out from the mainland into the Atlantic Ocean. Its remoteness has led to cultural as well as physical isolation. Brittany has, for example, retained its own language, folklore, and musical traditions. Archaeologically, it is a highly ritualized landscape, containing prehistoric stone circles, megalithic tombs, and stone avenues in abundance. It was Christianized by missionaries from Wales in the sixth century and still possesses a rich diversity of saints and religious communities. Christian worship has left its physical mark in the erection of churches and the adaptation of pagan tombs. The Pardon—the celebration of a saint's feast day, involving a procession, Mass, and feasting—is a uniquely Breton carnival.

For I Saw Water, Colquhoun drew heavily upon her personal knowledge of Brittany—its places, customs, and festivals. At the time when she was writing her novel, she was an active member of the British Druid Order. As a fellow Druid visiting from Cornwall, she was able to take part in the rites of a Breton Gorsedd (a large gathering devoted to spiritual, poetic, and musical celebrations) and attend at least one religious pardon in 1961.

Many of the place names in the novel are authentic locations in Brittany, although Colquhoun often adapts them for her own purposes. The novel is set on the island of Ménec, which Colquhoun identifies with the Island of the Dead. In reality, Ménec is not an island but the mainland site of vast prehistoric avenues of standing stones (fig. 2). Although the purpose of these enigmatic stone rows is largely obscure, their connection with Neolithic funeral rituals and beliefs is not in doubt. They, and many dolmens, are orientated according to astronomical events concerning the movements of the sun and moon. One of the most extensive of these alignments, containing more than one thousand stones and extending over four thousand feet in length, is known locally as the House of the Dead. In light of this, Colquhoun's poetic identification of Ménec with the Island of the Dead is easily understood. Similarly, Cruz-Moquen, the name Colquhoun gives to a neighboring island, in reality is not an island either, but the site of a prehistoric dolmen that has been Christianized by the erection of a Calvary cross on top of its capstone (fig. 3). By adopting and adapting these locations, Colquhoun is indicating that they are sacred spaces of lasting spiritual significance. She locates the novel's action in places that have been associated with worship, death, and rebirth since prehistory. Religious beliefs and ceremonies may change with the passage of time—pagan, Catholic, or neo-Druidic—but the sequence of changing observances over millennia provides a sense of continuity and natural order. More than that, because of their astronomical alignments, these places are tied to solar and lunar rhythms that predate and will outlast human presence.

From the outset, Colquhoun is at pains to emphasize the rhythms of nature. Sister Brigid, whose very name recalls the Celtic triple goddess, devotes her time to seasonal pastoral activities and to animal husbandry. References to holy wells, tree lore, herbal remedies, and the celebration of the equinoxes establish connections between nature, an ancient past, and present-day Druidic revivals. Worship at the Ianua Vitae Convent, although Roman Catholic, contains many pre-Christian, pagan elements. Vestiges of the ancient religion of the Celts are everywhere, in the land, the place names, and the monuments.

Colquhoun's choice of personal names reflects Breton history. Several of the characters, such as Sister Gildas, are named after historical figures, frequently saints, who have connections with Brittany. Colquhoun chose names with one eye to the saint's feast day in the Breton religious calendar and the other to the internal chronology of the novel, thereby linking the two. Some characters, such as Mother Ste. Barbe, have names taken from local place names, thus locking the individuals into the fabric of the locality.

NATURE-BASED SPIRITUALITY IN *I SAW WATER*

Shortly after Charlotte arrives unexpectedly on Ménec, Sister Brigid offers some surprising advice to her troubled cousin: "Springs, trees and rocks have a self-acting power: they're not interested in your faith. Just follow the rites, and the virtue will come through" (page 54). These words, coming from the mouth of a Catholic nun, are heretical. By claiming that natural objects—including those normally regarded as inanimate—contain a life force that can be engaged through the observance of ritual, she is placing her personal experience above doctrine and gnosis above faith.

However, had Brigid not been a nun but, say, a New Age neo-pagan or Druid, her words would have been entirely uncontentious. To followers of such spiritualities as these, a belief in the healing powers of natural objects and places is fundamental. Repeatedly in *I Saw Water*, Brigid and her mentor, Sister Paracelsus, are portrayed as practically and spiritually in tune with Nature in a manner that places them at odds with conventional Catholic doctrine. In fact, there are times when the rituals and beliefs of nature worship—carried out at such places as the Shrine of the Triple Well and the Well-Meadow—seem just as important as Catholic liturgy and dogma.

Today's pagan spiritualities exhibit a postmodern attitude toward truth, authority, and objectivity. They are characterized by an openness to personal interpretation and development in ways that dogmatic (in the literal sense of based on officially sanctioned belief) theologies are not. It is instructive in this regard to compare the Celtic figure of Brigid, in her emerging twentieth-century form, with the Roman Catholic figure of the Virgin Mary to see how the main models of female spirituality in *I Saw Water* differ. Mary, of course, is not a goddess, but she is the nearest thing that Christianity has to a female deity. As an intercessor for women and for the weak and powerless, she takes a subservient role to the all-powerful male deity (not to mention an authoritative all-male clergy). The Celtic Brigid, however, does not carry this burden of oppression by a male deity. Her "pre-Christian status allows her to function within the guiding mythology of neo-pagan ritual as representative of an ancient earth-centred and woman-centred spirituality."[18] Just as the increasing importance of women in occult societies had mirrored the increasing independence of women in Victorian society, so too did the development of pagan and goddess spiritualities in the mid-twentieth century reflect the increased secularization of Western society, coupled with a suspicion of institutional religions and a steady decline in their authority. The Druid Order, for example, encouraged its members (including Colquhoun) to discover their own individual relationship with the divine, however it was revealed—through God, Goddess, Great Spirit, or some other source. The Fellowship of Isis (of which Colquhoun was also a member) has always simply required members to love the Goddess, irrespective of any other beliefs or affiliations they might hold.[19]

We have already noted the importance of personal and place names in establishing the spiritual context of the novel. Sister Paracelsus, the novice mistress, is particularly important in this regard, because one of the ways in which Colquhoun distinguishes the spirituality of the Ianua Vitae Convent from that of Catholic orthodoxy is through her name. Sister Paracelsus is known in the vicinity of the convent as "La Druidesse." Through her name, ancient knowledge, and practical skills, she maintains a link between pagan beliefs and Christianity. The religion of the Gauls (and ancient Britons) is said to have been Druidism. Meeting in sacred groves, the Druids forged a close partnership with the powers of the earth and developed a deep understanding of the healing properties of herbs, trees, and plants. The extent to which this picture is historically accurate is open to doubt. Where apologists see an unbroken tradition, scholars see a fantasy construction originating with eighteenth-century antiquarians that has little connection to historical reality.[20] In its mid-twentieth-century form, Druidism owed a good deal of its popularity to Robert Graves, whose book *The White Goddess* (1948) proposed the existence of a tripartite deity, the White Goddess, who presided over Birth, Love, and Death.[21] Colquhoun's own indebtedness to Graves is clear throughout *I Saw Water,* not least in the person of Brigid.

Several years after the completion of *I Saw Water,* the influence of Graves remained strong. Colquhoun explicitly expressed her debt to him when, in 1972, she dedicated her illustrated poetry volume *Grimoire of the Entangled Thicket* to "The White Goddess." In the title, Colquhoun couples "grimoire," an archaic word for a textbook of magical practice, with "the entangled thicket," a phrase from the *Hanes Taliesin,* a traditional Welsh poem about a shape-shifting hero named Taliesin. Deciphering the meaning of this poem (at least to his own satisfaction) was central to Graves's understanding of Celtic mythology. In *The White Goddess,* Graves also wrote about the Celtic tree calendar and the tree alphabet, in which the name of each letter in the Ogham alphabet (an early script used in parts of Ireland and Britain and, allegedly, for secret communications by the Druids) is also the name of a tree or plant, linked through the flow of its sap to a month of the lunar year. One drawing from the *Grimoire,* entitled *Beth-Luis-Nion on Trilithon* (fig. 4), shows how the Ogham letters can be nicked on the stones that form the classic Stonehenge trilithon. This allowed Graves to relate each letter to its appropriate tree and to construct the complete Beth-Luis-Nion (Birch, Rowan, Ash) calendar. Each poem in Colquhoun's collection was inspired by one of the months or festivals of the pagan calendar. So, for example, the poem "Muin" relates to September, the month of the vine tree.

Colquhoun, whose interest in covert forms of communication is evident in a number of passages in *I Saw Water*, returned to the tree alphabets in an unpublished essay written in 1966, "The Tree Alphabets and the Tree of Life." The *Barddas* referred to in the essay is a collection of Welsh writings, ostensibly medieval but largely written by Edward Williams (1747–1826) and published posthumously under his bardic name, Iolo Morganwg. It contains a mixture of mystical Christianity, Arthurian legend, and an entirely invented system of writing, the "Coelbren y Beirdd," or "bardic alphabet," supposedly the alphabet of the ancient Druids. It also proposes a cosmic system of emanations, or rings of existence, that has similarities with the Qabalistic Tree of Life and which was of particular interest to Colquhoun. She undoubtedly knew of the false provenance of the writings but must have felt that they contained authentic insights into ancient lore and scripts, important enough for her to tease out their meanings and associations.[22]

As a member of both English and French Druidical orders, Colquhoun's engagement with Druidry was practical as well as theoretical. In 1961 she traveled to France with Ross Nichols, one of the leading lights of British Druidry. They were joined there by Robert MacGregor-Reid, the chief of the Druid Order.[23] Modern Druidry has close associations with heterodox Christianity, and during the visit Colquhoun was ordained a deaconess in the Saint Église Celtique en Bretagne—the Ancient Celtic Church.[24] After the celebrations, she and Nichols toured Brittany visiting churches, holy wells, and prehistoric sites. Some of the material she collected at this time was incorporated into *I Saw Water*.[25] Nichols split from the British Druid Order in 1964 to form the separate Order of Bards, Ovates, and Druids, named for the supposed three elements of ancient Druidry: bards (poets and singers), ovates (masters of occult lore), and druids (philosophers and thinkers). Colquhoun, while attempting to reconcile the two factions, continued her formal allegiance with the old British Druid Order, taking part in a number of its regular equinox ceremonies.

Colquhoun's own belief in an earth power that can be detected at a local level, such as the one that can be experienced at the Ianua Vitae Convent's Well-Meadow or the nearby Hill of Tan, finds expression throughout her writings and in several paintings. Although the force is felt locally, she understood such manifestations not as separate, isolated, or self-contained, but as part of a global power that girdles the earth. Places where the earth force is particularly strong become places of worship: Neolithic stone circle; Druidic grove;

holy well or Christian church. At these places, Colquhoun envisaged streams of energy, generated within the earth, emerging or erupting as geysers. She shows this clearly in the oil painting *Dance of the Nine Opals* (1942; fig. 5), which features the Nine Maidens, a stone circle in Cornwall. The energy stream wells up from a subterranean source, and glowing stones are joined by encircling lines of force. Colquhoun summarized the complexity of the painting's symbolism in an explanatory note (pages 165–66).

In a much later text entitled "Pilgrimage," published in 1979, she declares that this spiritual power spouts from the body of Hecate, the Great Earth Goddess. The identification of the earth force as specifically female is an ancient belief that can be traced back at least as far as the Chaldean Oracles. It was discouraged by patriarchal monotheistic religions for their own obvious reasons, but interest in Her was rekindled in the late eighteenth century by Romantic writers who initiated a nostalgia harking back to supposed goddess-worshipping and women-centered societies of the ancient Middle East. It became a popular trope in the nineteenth century among utopian social reformers and Victorian occult societies. It influenced twentieth-century occultists, in particular Colquhoun's mentor in occult matters, Kenneth Grant, with whom she studied in the early 1950s. It is found in Gardnerian Wicca, Druidism, and feminist neo-paganism. In other contemporary manifestations, it has been incorporated into certain strands of radical environmentalism. At its most extreme, it is a theory of nature that not only casts divisions within the human world as false, but also seeks to blur or even deny distinctions between the animal, vegetable, and mineral kingdoms.

Such a belief in an animating force that is present throughout all nature is, of course, roundly rejected by mainstream scientists. But it has never been confined simply to minority spiritual groups. In the twentieth century, it attracted panpsychically inclined philosophers, psychoanalysts, and others who rejected post-Enlightenment materialism.[26] Colquhoun tried to keep a foot in both camps and did not believe that the scientific and the spiritual were necessarily incompatible. In her essay "The Night Side of Nature" (1953), she attempted a reconciliation between contemporary sciences and the apparently discredited old worldview. Drawing on ideas derived from modern psychiatry and biology, she claimed that not only are all things in nature linked but, consequently, the forces that shape human nature are to be found throughout the natural world.[27] The skeptic will point out that her psychiatry is outmoded, her biology is confused, and her argument that friable rocks exhibit the same process that accounts for the splitting of the human personality is merely fanciful. Yet her claim that human characteristics reflect universal processes is no more than a contemporary expression of the traditional occult dictum "as above, so below." Similarly, her remarks about the importance of overcoming duality in nature, as evidenced by splits in the psyche, splintered rocks, and the divided genders, can be regarded as examples of the alchemical search for *conjunctio*.

OCCULT GENDER IN *I SAW WATER*

Through its name alone, the Parthenogenesist Order takes the reader not into the world of reproductive biology but into the very different world of hermetic gender. In biology, parthenogenesis refers to asexual reproduction, but Colquhoun is dealing with the route to spiritual perfection. This is not an inappropriate mission for a religious order, but in the hands of the nuns at the Ianua Vitae Convent, it cannot be said to represent mainstream theology.

In Western esoteric traditions, certain writings of many different groups, including Qabalists, Gnostics, Neoplatonists, Swedenborgians, and Theosophists, assert that male and female properties were originally contained within one and the same body.[28] It is claimed that Adam was an androgynous being whose fall from grace in the Garden of Eden was signified by his splitting into the two separate genders that exist today. Redemption will occur when the duality of gender is transcended and male and female are reunited in wholeness and completion. Colquhoun further believed that, since Adam was originally hermaphrodite, then God, in whose image Adam was created, was also hermaphrodite. She nurtured a deeply held suspicion that the translators of the Bible deliberately suppressed God's feminine aspects. For Colquhoun, as for other advocates of this viewpoint, spiritual advancement lies in overcoming the polarities of the separated genders and the achievement once again of the hermaphrodite or androgynous whole. (It is never entirely clear whether the united genders will have the secondary sexual characteristics of both or neither; ultimately, Colquhoun thinks, it does not matter, since we will evolve beyond materiality and exist only as thought-forms.)[29]

The use of gender-conflating names in *I Saw Water* reflects this pursuit of spiritual perfection through unification. Examples include Mary Fursey, Mary Paracelsus, and the place name Kervin-Brigitte. Widening the focus beyond *I Saw Water*, we might also consider Colquhoun's painting *Linked Islands II* (1947; fig. 6). It is one of a series of works painted to elucidate the poetic sequence "The Myth of Santa Warna," in which she also explored the theme of gender unification, together with the nature of a sexualized landscape.[30] The watercolor was painted using an automatic technique known as decalcomania, which allows the artist to capitalize on apparently chance effects. *Linked Islands II* presents an aerial view of St. Agnes, one of the Scilly Isles that lie off the coast of Cornwall. It interprets St. Agnes, with two of its ancient monuments, as a sexualized landscape. Depending on the state of the tide, St. Agnes is two in one. At low tide it is one island, and at high tide it becomes separated into two smaller land masses, linked only by a slender sand bar. Each islet has its own gender identity. St. Agnes is the site of a holy well, shown on the left of the painting. Water, as always in Colquhoun's work, symbolizes the female force. The islet of Gugh on the right, with its prehistoric phallic menhir known locally as the Old Man, is the male counterpart. When, at low tide, the two are united in *conjunctio,* they become the "hermaphrodite whole" of the alchemists.

Colquhoun's interest in the byways of Christian mysticism led her to the writings of the seventeenth-century Flemish mystic Antoinette Bourignon. If the separation of the genders at the Fall is an idea shared by many writers, Bourignon's account of the creation of Jesus appears to be unique to her. Her vision was illustrated by Colquhoun in the watercolor *Second Adam* (ca. 1942; fig. 7). According to Bourignon, before Eve was created, Adam wished for a companion to join with him in prayer and the glorification of God. He set out to make one. Inside his abdomen, in place of intestines, Colquhoun's Adam has what looks suspiciously like an alchemist's furnace and retort, in which he brews the second Adam.[31] After he is born, God looks after the young Adam and, in due course, implants him in Mary. In this way, the firstborn of the androgynous Adam became Christ.

DREAMS AND *I SAW WATER*

Throughout her entire adult life, when she woke from dreaming sleep, it was Colquhoun's practice to make an immediate written record of the dream and jot down other features that struck her as relevant, such as her mood on awakening. She would sometimes supplement these records with small sketches of objects or people she had encountered during the dream. As she worked on *I Saw Water* during the 1960s, she combed through her diaries, selected recent dreams as well as others extending back over some twenty years, "cut and pasted" them together, and linked them with consciously composed narrative passages (see fig. 8). She also provided the Breton setting for the events and added appropriate place and character names, as we have earlier discussed. Any changes that she made to the dream material itself were minimal.

Colquhoun assigned such great importance to her dreams that they provided the source material for virtually all of her imaginative prose, much of her poetry, and a number of her paintings. Although the extent to which she relied on dreams for her raw material was unusual, the very fact of doing so was not: dreams have inspired artists and writers for centuries. However, during her lifetime, a revolution in the understanding of dreams took place. It is a legitimate question, therefore, to ask what she understood herself to be doing when recording and making use of her dreams in this way. When she dreamed, did she suppose that she was delving into her personal past and that her dreams could help her understand her fears and insecurities? Did she perhaps imagine that she was tapping into shared ancestral memories? Did she think that she was receiving spiritual illumination, maybe opening up channels of communication between physical and incorporeal worlds? Did she believe that she was traveling into ethereal territories, using faculties that were unavailable to her in the waking state? It is unlikely that she would have made use of her dreams in the ways she did had she thought that they held no intrinsic meaning—if they were, say, merely a by-product of her brain cells performing routine maintenance tasks while she slept, or if they were caused by indigestion. In this section, we discuss the reasons why her dreams assumed such significance in her life.

The primary reason was that she considered dreams to be an important method of acquiring occult knowledge. Such a view is not new. For the first four thousand years of recorded history, most people believed that dreams contained messages from the gods. Philosophers and skeptics might have quibbled or debated the details, but for the majority, dreams contained divine guidance and should, if possible, be acted upon. It is true that some dreams are so bizarre that one might wonder whether they came from demons rather than gods, and it is also true that some dreams, when acted upon, have led to personal, political, or military disasters, but this merely points to difficulties of interpretation. To mitigate this, priestly guidance was always available.[32]

During the Enlightenment, the growth of rationalism led to the decline of supernatural explanations for dreams. These were now condemned as superstition. It fell to occultists and astrologers to keep belief in the external origin of dreams and their prophetic nature alive. In fact, in the face of growing scientific opposition, occultists hardened their position, coming to define dreaming sleep as a privileged state. Rationality, it was claimed, was at its weakest during sleep. Sleep, therefore, is the time when we are closest to the gods and most receptive to godly messages.[33]

By the end of the nineteenth century, diverse theories about dreams were in circulation. The cultural environment of the Victorian period was sufficiently rich to support the rise of science and secularization while, at the same time, hosting a resurgence of magic and spiritualism. The intellectual context was the complex interface between established sciences such as physics; emerging sciences such as psychology; marginal sciences such as mesmerism; and supernatural and occult traditions. Some empirical scientists studied the role of memory, emotion, and sensory stimuli on dream content and rejected occult explanations. Others, such as those associated with the London-based Society for Psychical Research (founded in 1882 and numbering eminent physicists, philosophers, and psychologists among its members), while often rigorously skeptical by the standards of the day and even agnostic, were more prepared to accept the existence of telepathic and precognitive dreams, and even to undertake practical experiments with mediums in the hope of making contact with spirits.[34] As far as the mechanisms underlying telepathic phenomena were concerned, new explanations represented little advance on the proposal first made in classical Greece that happenings in one place may be transmitted to another location by vibrations. Rather than "vibration," however, Victorian theories were couched in contemporary vocabularies of electricity and magnetism and the ether physics that had dominated since Thomas Young demonstrated the wave properties of light in the early nineteenth century. Many noteworthy scientists of the Victorian period, such as Peter G. Tait and Balfour Stewart in their popular book *The Unseen Universe; or, Physical Speculations on a Future State* (1875), ascribed spiritual and mysterious properties to the ether. The former president of the Society for Psychical Research and eminent scientist Sir Oliver Lodge, author of the classic *The Ether of Space* (1909), continued to argue for the ether hypothesis well into the 1930s, after it had been abandoned by most physicists.

At the more magical end of the spectrum, members of the Theosophical Society and the Hermetic Order of the Golden Dawn either remained largely untouched by mainstream developments in the physical sciences or turned to them to justify their occult convictions.[35] These were the two most important occult societies established during the second half of the nineteenth century. The Theosophical Society was formed in New York in 1876 under the leadership of the Russian émigré H. P. Blavatsky and the American lawyer Colonel Henry Steel Olcott, who had distinguished himself as a member of the three-man commission charged with investigating the assassination of Abraham Lincoln. The Golden Dawn, founded twelve years later, was based in London but also had temples elsewhere in the United Kingdom and in the United States and France. Members of these occult groups attempted to capitalize on the cognitive authority of science by quantifying and systematizing their learning in ways that resembled those of science. But most of them were opposed to scientific materialism, focusing instead on strictly nonrational methods of surrendering the self to occult forces. Freed from the physical body during sleep, they argued, the spirit is free to travel in nonmaterial, astral planes, meeting and conversing with other spirits. When the sleeper awakes, these journeys are remembered as dreams. This claim opened up the possibility that astral travel can be developed and taught. Perhaps astral meetings between two sleeping occultists could be prearranged, resulting in a shared dream. The Golden Dawn provided magicians with detailed instructions on "scrying in the spirit vision," as they termed such practices. The astral meetings between two Golden Dawn initiates, W. B. Yeats and Maud Gonne, had the result that "their famous love affair, frustrated at mundane level, achieved a hidden consummation."[36]

As a member of the Theosophical Society and one-time applicant to the Golden Dawn, Colquhoun absorbed these teachings. In the early 1950s, while studying for advancement in a Golden Dawn successor organization, the Ordo Templi Orientis, she summarized the multiple ways in which she believed the practicing magician might acquire magical knowledge during dreaming:

> The night dream, when suitable, can be used for definite magical aims, either through the information it gives in symbolic terms[,] thereby helping to clarify the magical will, or through the initiation it confers [and] which gives the desire to know more. Guidance ([the] solving of problems [is] not perhaps definitely magical enough). [Other examples are] the pre-cognitive dream, the shared dream, the telepathic dream [and] the directed dream (induced by objects under the pillow). Suggestions taken from a dream can be used in magical ritual.[37]

Today, these ideas appear eccentric, but had Colquhoun been living in Babylon at the time of Gilgamesh, and had she inscribed her words in cuneiform on tablets of clay, they would not have raised an eyebrow. Her recommendation of placing an object under the pillow in order to influence the content of a dream derived directly from the technique of "dream incubation," which was widely practiced in ancient Mesopotamia.[38] Similarly, when she mentioned the "gates of horn" in her poem "Muin," she was referring to the ancient Greek belief that predictive dreams can be distinguished from false or deceptive dreams by their mode of delivery to the dreamer, through one or the other of the two Gates of Hypnos.

A dream, as a channel for occult revelation or communication, while providing the dreamer with a route into the spirit world, also opens a channel in the reverse direction. The result may be more than the dreamer bargained for: spirits or demons may visit him or her, whether invited or not, and leave a mark of their presence on the dreamer's astral body. This subsequently becomes imprinted on the physical body. The poem "Wedding of Shades" relates one of Colquhoun's own experiences of this sort.

Contact, however, was more often verbal than physical. The name of the Parthenogenesist Order and the nature of its mission were revealed to Colquhoun in a dream of May 8/9, 1956. In a dream several years earlier, in 1942, she had heard a disembodied voice saying, "This is the grotto of the sun and moon, Nicaragua." So strong was the impact of this message that she reflected upon its meaning for the remainder of her life. It inspired her to research the topography and archaeology of Nicaragua, where the dream grotto was evidently located, and it became the subject of the oil painting *Grotto of the Sun and Moon* (1952). She finally concluded that "the Grotto was an occult centre used by an eponymous order which existed in the past or still exists, either in that state of being commonly recognised as reality today, or else in regions variously called the Higher Worlds or the Inner Planes." For some reason, she had been granted a glimpse of this mysterious center: "And now if I receive an idea or perception which does not seem to be a direct result of anything I have read, heard or thought, I take it to be a message from the Order."[39]

The publication of Sigmund Freud's *The Interpretation of Dreams* in 1899 marked the beginning of a revolution in the study of dreams.[40] Although Freud continued to recognize the traditional standpoint that dreams could provide helpful guidance for the dreamer, his reason for doing so was anything but traditional. In his view, it was not because of any divine source, the possibility of which he categorically rejected, but because dreams revealed the dreamer's hidden fears, hopes, and desires. The information contained within the dream, however, was coded, disguised by subconscious censorship. This was why dreams were largely unintelligible to the dreamer. The expertise of a skilled interpreter was still required to understand them. This function was no longer to be fulfilled by a priest, as of old, but rather a psychoanalyst.

Freud's materialistic view of the world explains his rejection of the existence of prophetic dreams and the spirit world, although he was still prepared to accept—even at the height of his professional eminence and albeit hesitantly—the possibility of telepathic dreams.[41] His core belief that dreams were firmly rooted in an individual's unconscious also caused him to reject the dramatic assertion by his colleague Carl Jung that some aspects of the unconscious are shared and common to all humanity. According to Jung, some dreams come from a region of the mind termed the "collective unconscious," a depository of memories, images, and mythologies from the ancient past. Although they are largely forgotten at a conscious level by modern civilized Europeans, they may be accessible during sleep, when rationality is suspended. They reflect a natural wisdom deep within the human unconscious. They connect the dreamer with the past and provide insights that can give guidance along the path of self-development.

It is hardly surprising that some of Jung's ideas, including suspended rationality and the shared unconscious, which he frequently expressed using the language and concepts of alchemy, found a receptive audience among many occultists. For several years during the 1950s, Colquhoun herself was associated with the London-based Buck Research Unit in Psychodynamics, run by Alice Buck, a Jungian psychotherapist. Although its duration is unclear, Colquhoun also underwent a period of psychotherapy with Dr. Buck, who was prepared to analyze her dreams by letter in addition to meeting with her in group therapy sessions. The Jungian context of the research unit is clear from Colquhoun's brief account of its activities, "Divination Up-to-Date." The research interests of the group included the extent to which shared dreams could be analyzed and used to predict natural or man-made disasters. Buck disagreed with occultists on some points and regarded shared dreams (which might include clairvoyant content) as instances not of astral travel but of two individuals "inter dreaming"—that is, simultaneously accessing an aspect of the shared unconscious. In 1950, Colquhoun and Buck experienced one such shared dream, consisting of geometrical forms, which were later used as the design for the dust wrapper of the book in which Buck gave her own account of the research unit's activities.[42]

For his part, André Breton had no doubt as to the central role of dreams in the surrealist quest for truth. Basing many of surrealism's investigatory methods on Freud and contemporary psychiatry (including the study of dreams and hallucinations, and the use of automatic writing and free association), Breton regarded it as a fundamental truth that the world of dreams and the waking world are but one; both are of equal importance, and each is as incomplete as the other. In place of the traditional viewpoint that treats dreaming and the waking state as opposites, Breton wanted to substitute reciprocity—hence the metaphor of communicating vessels that he developed in *Les vases communicants* (1932), the book that contains his most detailed discussion of dreams.[43] Breton imagined existence as two interconnected containers, one being the dream state and the other the waking state. Because they are constantly connected to each other, they are in a state of equilibrium and material can flow freely in either direction.

Despite the enthusiasm that the surrealists showed for his work, Freud regarded some of Breton's ideas as an almost unintelligible distortion of his own. For example, in an assertion that put him completely at odds with Freud's position, Breton tried to show that space, time, and causality are identical in both dreams and reality. In other words, they are both objective states, rather than one (the dream) being no more than a subjective mental process. If Breton's view is accepted, one consequence is that traditional views of time must be rejected. In material reality, anticipation of historic time is an impossibility. In psychic time, however, knowledge of the future in the present—or, indeed, multiple futures in multiple presents—is perfectly possible. Some Jungians also disagreed with Freud on this point. Alice Buck, for example, when attempting to explain predictive dreams, was content to accept that paranormal events occur outside of time as it is ordinarily understood. She believed that conventional linear time is a creation of consciousness that can be escaped during dreaming. In its place, she adopted the concept of "serial time," in which the "future" in our three-dimensional world is simply the "now" viewed from elsewhere in a multidimensional world with infinite planes of existence.[44]

Time, as Breton put it, contains "the perfect continuity of the possible with the impossible."[45] Further, if there is no difference between dreamed representations and real perceptions, then the imaginary and the real are one and the same thing. The realization that the one-way flow of time is an illusion is a consequence of this. Ultimately, we can no longer tell which came first, as the difference is artificial. Additionally, it cannot matter at what rate, or in what order, images that are later seen to be connected are released into consciousness—nor, indeed, whether they are first perceived in the dreaming state, the waking state, or some combination of the two. It is this that makes it possible for certain dreams to prefigure episodes in waking life. It is this that allowed Breton to claim that his poem "Sunflower" was an accurate description of a person he had yet to meet (and whom he subsequently married),[46] and Colquhoun, in *I Saw Water*, to compose a sequential narrative in which the constituent dreams had occurred over a period of many years and in no logical or temporal sequence. The novel was dreamed episodically, like a serial in a magazine, but a serial in which the episodes were published in no discernible order, with no *ex-ante* structure and at apparently random intervals.

AUTHOR OR MIDWIFE: WHO WROTE *I SAW WATER*?

Colquhoun's method raises questions about authorship and originality: Who, exactly, wrote *I Saw Water*? Colquhoun undoubtedly had the dreams, wrote them down, and ordered them, but if she saw herself as a channel through which a hidden intelligence, or intelligences, communicated, then her task was more that of editor than author. The principles that governed her selection of which dreams to include in the final text are nowhere explicitly stated, but the evidence suggests that she regarded each of the dreams she included as a fragment of a greater whole, and that her task was to piece together a hidden, but gradually revealed, original. Examination of her dream diaries shows that during the period of active composition, she was adding dreams to the narrative as they occurred. In a footnote to one transcription, written when the novel was nearly finished, Colquhoun ruefully added that if the dream had to be included, this would entail a great deal of revision (see fig. 8). She clearly felt that she had limited personal choice in selection, but, in the end, the dream was not required.

One way of approaching the question of authorship is to ask whether *I Saw Water* is an automatic text. Automatism lay at the heart of surrealism. Indeed, Breton had originally defined surrealism as "psychic automatism in the pure state."[47] In other words, by writing rapidly and without pause or reflection, by drawing or applying paint in a spontaneous, unplanned, and unregulated manner, it was hoped to bypass the mind's critical faculties and so provide access to deeper, more fundamental levels of the psyche. Some surrealists were happy to accept dreams as automatic phenomena. The argument in favor is clear: to put it at its simplest, conscious and critical control, by definition, cannot be exerted during dreaming sleep. Others were skeptical. The act of translating dream images into words, the unavoidable period of transition from dream state to waking state, and the inevitable passage of time between dream and transcript all increased the likelihood of conscious selection, memory failure, and the imposition of a structure that the original dream may not have possessed.

Approaching the problem from a slightly different angle, *I Saw Water,* composed almost entirely of material assembled from dreams, is a collage novel. As M. E. Warlick noted in relation to Max Ernst's collage novels, because of the way in which this kind of text transforms its materials to give birth to a new creation, it is a form of alchemy.[48] Ernst's novels used engravings and woodcuts as their source material, but Warlick's argument applies equally well to *I Saw Water.* Colquhoun's dreams form the *prima materia* with which the work commences. They are taken apart, recombined, and fused, not by fire in the alchemist's furnace, nor by adhesive in Ernst's gluepot, but by Colquhoun's imposition of a narrative structure. Colquhoun had no doubt that collage, using either words or images, was an automatic technique. To her, it was on equal footing with the "found object," another surrealist method for stripping an article from its manifest meaning. "Surely," she wrote, "such objects are found through the use of the automatic faculty."[49] Further, she might have added, the juxtaposition of apparently unrelated objects, which brings out hidden affinities between them, is not far removed from the pursuit of correspondences in occult research. Indeed, the discovery of hidden links is the very stuff of magic.

If we allow that dream transcription is a species of automatism, the problem still remains: where does automatically generated material actually come from? At first, the answer seemed clear: it came from the unconscious. Automatic writing was just like taking dictation from the lower reaches of the mind. As Max Ernst expressed it, the use of automatic methods led to the author being revealed as "a mere spectator at the birth of the work."[50] It was noted, however, that during the surrealists' early experimental sessions with automatic writing, the participants sometimes entered a trance state, recalling the practice of spiritualists and mediums who claimed to be in communication with the dead. Over time, the explanations for automatically produced material ranged from the occult at one extreme to contemporary physical science, including particle physics, at the other.[51]

All of this amounted to what Nicolas Calas termed a "crisis of automatism," leading some to turn away from automatism entirely.[52] For Colquhoun, the nature of automatism was clear and unproblematic. She drew out the similarities between surrealist automatism and the attempts of spiritualists to contact noncorporeal entities: "It would seem that the only significant difference in method between the two types of automatism is the fact that the surrealist is his own 'medium.'"[53] In other words, the source of the material is external, but another person is not required as an intermediary in order to make contact with the source. If this explanation is accepted, it shifts us away from a narrow consideration of a person's relationship with their unconscious to a much broader, mystical consideration of humankind's relationship to nature.[54]

In fact, some surrealists, including Breton, had always displayed mystical leanings. For a time, this seemed to be the direction that surrealist painting might take, were it not for the disruption of World War II. In the summer of 1939, shortly before the outbreak of war, Colquhoun took part in theoretical discussions with some of the younger surrealist painters in the Rhône Valley, where they had rented the Chateau de Chemillieu. The participants included Roberto Matta, Wolfgang Paalen, and Gordon Onslow Ford, who were developing a style of automatic painting that has become known as "psychological morphology." The existence of these debates is well known, but Colquhoun's participation in them, however fleeting, has almost been forgotten. When Matta and Onslow

Ford fled to New York at the outbreak of World War II, their ideas and methods helped influence a generation of American artists at the birth of the movement now known as abstract expressionism.[55]

The paintings produced under the influence of psychological morphology, in particular those of Matta, with their multiple perspectives and deep pools of color, often appear to conquer the limits of space and time. Beings or *personages* appear that seem to belong not to the known world but to worlds that lie beyond our experience and understanding.[56] Perhaps, said Breton, we share the planet with other creatures that, through camouflage or some other means, are able to escape discovery. We cannot begin to imagine the nature of these beings, whose behavior may be as strange to us as ours is "to the mayfly or the whale."[57]

Colquhoun responded to Breton's remarks about the invisible ones with the automatic watercolor *Un grand invisible* (ca. 1943; fig. 9) and the poem "Les Grandes Transparentes." In the final line of the poem, "And if they should call, can we answer?," we hear the voice of the practicing occultist. Establishing contact with spirits, elementals, and other entities is a major aim of the magician. It would be a mistake, however, to assume that all such beings are benign: as Colquhoun recounted in "Wedding of Shades," they might bite. Through the use of appropriate containing and banishing rituals at the onset and conclusion of their ceremonies, magicians seek to ensure their personal safety. Colquhoun was always alert to the dangers of unwary or unskilled magicians unleashing malign forces that were beyond their competence to contain. She was critical of those surrealists who investigated automatic or occult phenomena from a position of comparative ignorance. They were dipping their toes in dangerous waters. By not paying due regard to protective ceremonies, many paid a great price: "The movement's approach to esoteric study and experiment was too diffuse and sporadic to impress a naturally sceptical world. From the human angle, it may be added that the high proportion of suicides and other tragedies among its adherents is characteristic of psychic exploration without adequate safeguard."[58]

COLQUHOUN THE MAGICIAN

Colquhoun's position as a female occultist in the mid-twentieth century was, in some ways, privileged, but in others problematic. Historically, she was one of the first generation of women who took part in ceremonial magic as of right and as equals to men. Prior to the pioneering work of women such as H. P. Blavatsky (1831–1891), Anna Kingsford (1846–1888), and Moïna Mathers (1865–1928), the occult had been an all-male preserve. These women exerted a lasting influence on the occult scene, paving the way for influential female near-contemporaries of Colquhoun, such as Dion Fortune (born Violet Mary Firth; 1890–1946), whose Society of the Inner Light rejected Colquhoun as a member in 1956, and Tamara Bourkhoun (1911–1990), whose Order of the Pyramid and the Sphinx accepted Colquhoun as a member in the 1970s. The new status of women, not just as participants in occult activity but as founders and leaders of hermetic societies, was, in part, a consequence of changing social conditions, but it also owed much to the concurrent development of a specifically female spirituality.

One of the key figures in the latter process was the Frenchman Alphonse Constant, better known today as Eliphas Lévi (1810–1875). Lévi, whose influence on occultism in France and England is still felt, closely identified Woman with the powers of nature: she was an elemental energy, a prophetess, a transforming life force. In the words of Moïna Mathers, "Woman is the magician born of nature by reason of her great natural sensibility, and of her instinctive sympathy with such subtle energies as these intelligent inhabitants of the air, the earth, fire and water."[59]

Emotional and sexual attachment to a woman, then, is to achieve proximity to elemental powers. Lévi's views helped form those of André Breton, for whom love and desire occupied a central place in surrealist transformation. The glorification of the power of desire and its capacity to challenge conventional moral and social constraints formed part of the surrealist program, in the belief that it would lead to social as well as sexual revolution. However, while surrealist language and imagery eroticized the female body, it did so, paradoxically, by treating it destructively through distortion and dismemberment or by treating it as a passive object of male desire. It was a contradiction that was never resolved: most male surrealists were quite unable to live up to their revolutionary precepts. Their treatment of women remained a projection of traditional male fantasies; women were revered but simultaneously feared, objectified, and debased.

For the women who were drawn to surrealism, this represented a challenge that was both personal and philosophical. Some resigned themselves, more or less unwillingly, to the role imposed upon them as muse. Some, such as the artists Toyen and Claude Cahun, rejected gender stereotypes, in life as well as in art, each living a life of gender ambiguity. Others made use of Lévi's recently established links between the hermetic tradition and women's creative powers. If recognition of their unique spiritual powers offered nineteenth-century women a way forward from their social, biological, and reproductive bondage, the same might be hoped for by women attracted to surrealism.[60] Leonora Carrington, for instance, often used alchemical symbols in her art and writings, while Remedios Varo frequently depicted the paraphernalia of magic: crystal balls, alchemical laboratories, retorts, alembics, and ritualistic activities. What sets these artists apart from Colquhoun, however, is that for all their theoretical knowledge and occasional practical ventures—Varo, for example, is known to have consulted the *I Ching* before making important decisions[61]—they were primarily consumers of magic rather than contributors to the development of magical knowledge. They drew upon established traditions, but more as a source of pictorial imagery than inspiration for their own research. Unlike Colquhoun, they did not develop or modify ritual practices or make magical discoveries of their own. Further, the playful whimsicality and theatricality that frequently suffused their work is entirely absent from that of Colquhoun, whose attitude toward magic was always studious and respectful.

In the popular imagination, magic and divination are associated with the use of a crystal ball. However, this is not mandatory and, in practice, any reflective surface will do. As many magicians had done before her, Colquhoun used a mirror for divination. Hers was nineteen inches in diameter, with an ornate hand-beaten copper frame that she had made by a local craftsperson. When not in use, to keep it from prying eyes and preserve its accumulated magical powers, she kept it wrapped in a lace shawl, knotted with three double knots, to harmonize with three knot-work bosses on the copper frame (fig. 10). The knots were then wrapped round with a yellow rope, which she called "Um," short for "umbilicus." When using the mirror, Colquhoun would wrap one end of the rope around her waist, connecting the other to the mirror. With the shawl over her head and enclosing the mirror, she linked herself to her image in the mirror via "Um." Identifying her mirror image with her astral body, she projected her consciousness into it and traveled in astral realms.[62]

In a rare excursion into esoteric Islam, *Torso* (1981; fig. 11), Colquhoun applies a Western sensibility to an Eastern theme. It concerns the *lataif-e-sitta,* the six subtleties, or suprasensory organs said by Sufis to be part of the spiritual self, in the way that biological organs are part of the physical body. Sufic development involves the awakening of these dormant spiritual centers in a set order. The lataif are, in sequence, Nafs (blue: ego), Qalb (yellow: mind), Ruh (red: spirit), Sirr (white: consciousness), Khafi (black: intuition), and Ikhfa (green: deep perception). The angular connecting arrow in Colquhoun's painting indicates the order of awakening, commencing with Nafs, the pale blue background. Many readers will notice the similarity between the subtleties and, in other traditions, the chakras and the sephiroth. Additionally, those familiar with the Golden Dawn will realize that Colquhoun's method of indicating the sequence derives from the Golden Dawn technique of spelling out an angelic name on a magic square.

Notwithstanding the diversity of Colquhoun's hermetic interests, a constant focus in her magical life was the Qabalah. Central to this school of Jewish mysticism is the quest to understand the interconnections between all things in the created cosmos. The search is undertaken largely through the study of correspondences. Because Hebrew letters are also numbers, every word can be converted to a number and connected to all other words that share the same number. In this way, slowly and incrementally, God's plan may be understood.[63] The magical practitioner who wishes to construct a ritual with a specific purpose in mind will take great pains to make use of this accumulated knowledge and surround himself or herself with objects that are related to one another and associated with the magical end. For example, as part of her study program with the Ordo Templi Orientis in 1952, Colquhoun developed a ritual to be used by a woman to capture the affections of a man she loved. In other words, it was a good old-fashioned spell. We have quoted at length from the ritual below and published an associated poem to make the point that—aside from all the details concerning the setting, the magical implements, and the appropriate symbols, all chosen for their links with Venus, the goddess of love—a magical ritual is a sensory experience. The magician tries to involve as many senses as possible in pursuit of the desired outcome:

> The oratory is hung with silk curtains of bright rose colour rayed with pale green; a circle fourteen feet in diameter is painted on the floor in emerald green, and immediately within it a seven-pointed star in pale green. At each point of the star a light is burning in a copper lamp. In the centre of the star is a heptagonal altar hung with emerald green silk upon which stands a copper chalice containing in liquid form the drug damiana surrounded by a cerise-coloured girdle. To the left of this is a vase made of turquoise holding roses; to the right is a copper censer burning sandalwood, in front a silken pantacle engraved with a beautiful naked woman, the names Kedemel and Hagiel, the sigil of Venus and the Hexagram with the planetary symbol of ♀ in the right lower point. In front of this again is a large emerald engraved with the name Hagith, and a wand made of a myrtle branch.
>
> The operator wears a robe of sky-blue silk, a pendant in the shape of a Pentagram of copper set with emeralds, and cerise slippers. Standing to face the altar, she takes up the myrtle branch and makes with it the invoking pentagram of fire.[64]

Then, concentrating on the man she desires, she begins to intone the words of the spell. The poem "Love-Charm II" is based on the words of invocation that Colquhoun composed to be spoken at the climax of the rite. Whether she created the ritual for purely educational purposes or with one eye to its practical application is unknown, but why not? Why waste a perfectly good spell?

Magic is, at heart, a practical, experiential, and therefore sensory activity. Although some theoretical knowledge is required, occult advancement is largely acquired through initiation, ritual, and meditation. Colquhoun's own personal experiences of ritual clearly inform several episodes in *I Saw Water*. She was undoubtedly expressing her personal view when, during the healing service at the chapel in the Well-Meadow, Sister Brigid remarks that the effect of the music in a religious service is that "the discursive mind is lulled or entranced while 'the high dream' takes over." Although the bishop conducting the service would be unlikely to express it in the following terms, to the ceremonial magician sound is important because the vibrations of the voice are felt on the astral plane and facilitate contact with hidden powers. Similarly, at the height of the ceremony of the Snake Dance (page 57), when Brigid and Charlotte "obtained the Light," the transforming effect is dependent upon a combination of sound and rhythm.

The importance of sound is further illustrated by the poem "Red Stone." It is one of a series of eleven poems composed circa 1971 that together make up Colquhoun's "Anthology of Incantations." The sequence as a whole is a celebration of the richness of alchemical language and imagery. Each poem consists entirely of synonyms—which may be descriptive, poetical, or allegorical—that have been assigned to a substance or process used in the creation of the philosopher's stone, the objective of the alchemist's quest.[65] "Red Stone" is a verbatim transcription of a section of the eighteenth-century alchemical text *Treatise on the Great Art*, with the line lengths adjusted.[66] As such, it is a found poem, which Colquhoun regarded as another form of automatism. As the name of the series indicates, the poems are surely intended to be declaimed aloud in order to achieve maximum potency.

The importance that Colquhoun gives to another sensory modality—vision, and especially color—is evident throughout her writings and artwork. Where possible, she chose colors for their magical associations as much as for their descriptive qualities. In *I Saw Water*, for example, during her stay on Ménec, Charlotte has an affair with her physician. At one point his wife, Gertrud, hands her some letters. Charlotte "saw that there was an enclosure in one of them which was written in red ink on yellowish paper, the rest being in blue on white" (page 80). These colors are not chosen fortuitously. In alchemical usage they signify the two genders. Red (elemental fire) combined with yellow (its spiritual equivalent, philosophical sulfur) indicates the male principle. Blue (elemental water) combined with white (philosophical mercury) indicates the female principle. Using these color combinations, Gertrud signals that she knows exactly what Charlotte and her husband are up to.

Colquhoun frequently used the written word and the visual image in tandem, to illuminate or explicate each other. We have already given the example of the oil painting *Dance of the Nine Opals* and its accompanying explanatory essay, and referred to the poetic suite "The Myth of Santa Warna" in relation to the painting *Linked Islands II*. Another example is the watercolor *The Thirteen Streams of Magnificent Oil* (ca. 1940; fig. 12) and its associated text "The Openings of the Body" (1970).[67] The inspiration of this pairing is part Qabalistic and part theosophical. Colquhoun drew upon *The Kabbalah Unveiled* (1887), a volume of translations by MacGregor Mathers of a number of books in the *Zohar*, key works of Jewish mysticism.[68] It deals at length with the nature and attributes of the Supreme Being, also known by many other names, including Macroprosopus. Of particular significance is the beard, divided into thirteen parts, from which there is a continuous stream of divine light (represented by oil) that illuminates the manifest world below. The Supreme Being is androgynous, but the recipient of the divine light, Microprosopus, is separated into male and female components. *The Kabbalah Unveiled* does not specify how the divine light enters Microprosopus, simply stating that it "pours forth" or "flows down" via "gateways." Colquhoun depicts it as entering a female body through apertures, which include the eyes, nostrils, mouth, nipples, navel, anus, and genitals.[69] These orifices reflect Colquhoun's understanding of the gateways alluded to by Mathers and which, according to Blavatsky, correspond to the thirteen openings in the female body. Colquhoun expands on this in "The Openings of the Body," which includes her own unique reason for suggesting that women are more evolved than men.

Of great importance to Qabalah-inspired magicians—indeed, to the teachings of the majority of Western hermetic societies since the Victorian period—is the glyph known as the Tree of Life. It consists of ten spheres, the sephiroth, and twenty-two connecting paths. The spheres symbolize levels of existence and, taken with the paths, cosmic relationships. The Tree of Life is frequently used as a focus for meditation and as a source when devising ceremonies.[70] It was also the inspiration for a further example of the alliance between word and image in Colquhoun's work. "The Decad of Intelligence" (1979) is a series of ten poems, each one focusing on one of the sephiroth of the Tree of Life, that accompanies a corresponding series of images of the ten sephiroth.

The poem we have selected from the "Decad," entitled "Sanctifying Intelligence," evokes some of the attributions of Binah, the third sephirah. These include, among others, the path to wisdom, element, mineral, perfume, geometrical figures, and angelic order. Taken together, these correspondences build a picture of the nature of the sphere, for use in personal meditation. The image *Binah* (1979; fig. 13) serves a similar and complimentary function. Each sephirah is said to exist in four worlds, or stages of manifestation, and each is associated with its own color. Colquhoun's simultaneous depiction of the worlds through broadly concentric bands of color is unique to her. As she explained in her essay "The Zodiac and the Flashing Colours," appropriately colored magical images, when meditated upon, can have perceptual consequences that might be, by implication, magical as well as physiological.

The culmination of Colquhoun's use of color to explore magical relationships was undoubtedly the full set of seventy-eight Taro cards that she painted in 1977. In her designs, an example of which is shown in fig. 14, she applied Golden Dawn color theory in order to explore the magical relationships between the cards. Once again she published an accompanying essay, "The Taro as Colour," in which she explained the principles underlying her color combinations. Although her vocabulary may be initially unfamiliar, her explanations are coherent and her method logical.[71] It is only necessary to compare Colquhoun's designs with other prominent twentieth-century packs to gauge the extent of her originality. The best-known pack with Golden Dawn affinities is the one illustrated by Pamela Colman Smith under the instruction of A. E. Waite. Colquhoun regarded Waite's pack as corrupt. In particular, she accused him of introducing a gender imbalance into the court cards by substituting Knaves for Princesses.[72] As was her practice by this time, the cards in her series were not signed with her name but with a glyph derived from her magical motto: the initials S and V superimposed and contained within an encircling oval. The motto, chosen to indicate her personal magical purpose, was "Splendidior Vitro," meaning "more sparkling than crystal" and signifying her pursuit of purity and clarity. By signing her work with her motto, Colquhoun implied that, for her, art and magic had become one and indistinguishable. Despite the frustrations of her personal life, what better outcome could she have wished?

As artist, writer, and occultist, Colquhoun sought to enter and explore a consciousness beyond the personal, to transcend all divisions and to achieve a state of completion and harmony with the universe. She was at ease with a complicated mixture of esoteric traditions from the past and other cultures while remaining responsive to contemporary spiritualities. To the end, she described herself as a surrealist. The majority of her beliefs are rejected by established religions as deviant and by scientists as irrational. Nonetheless, she was part of a tradition that can be traced from the Neoplatonists through medieval hermetic philosophers and alchemists to theosophy and the teachings of the Golden Dawn. She was closer to the interpersonal world of Jung than to the materialist world of Freud. Hers was a pantheistic worldview in which the divine, the human, and the natural were all fused together in a unity that underlay its surface diversity.

NOTES

1. See André Breton, *Manifestos of Surrealism,* trans. R. Seaver and H. R. Lane (Ann Arbor: University of Michigan Press, 1967), 14.

2. Ithell Colquhoun, "The Prose of Alchemy," *The Quest* 21, no. 3 (April 1930): 294–303.

3. Breton, *Manifestos of Surrealism,* 173–79.

4. There are obvious parallels, too, with Carl Jung's theory of "individuation": that through psychotherapy people can learn to recognize the polar opposites inherent in their personality and bring them into balance and harmony. Jung was only the best known among other early twentieth-century psychoanalysts who explored alchemy's contributions to psychotherapy. They included Herbert Silberer, who influenced Max Ernst; Elizabeth Severn; and, slightly later, Israel Regardie, who published the papers of the Hermetic Order of the Golden Dawn.

5. Urszula Szulakowska, *Alchemy in Contemporary Art* (Burlington, Vt.: Ashgate, 2011), esp. chaps. 2 and 8; Camelia Darie, "Victor Brauner and the Surrealist Interest in the Occult" (Ph.D. thesis, University of Manchester, 2012). See also M. E. Warlick, *Max Ernst and Alchemy: A Magician in Search of Myth* (Austin: University of Texas Press, 2001), and Susan L. Aberth, *Leonora Carrington: Surrealism, Alchemy, and Art* (Aldershot, U.K.: Lund Humphries, 2004). For more broadly focused accounts, see Nadia Choucha, *Surrealism and the Occult: Shamanism, Magic, Alchemy, and the Birth of an Artistic Movement* (Rochester, Vt.: Destiny Books, 1992), and Celia Rabinovitch, *Surrealism and the Sacred: Power, Eros, and the Occult in Modern Art* (Boulder, Colo.: Westview Press, 2004).

6. See Silvano Levy, "The Del Renzio Affair: A Leadership Struggle in Wartime Surrealism," *Papers of Surrealism* 3 (Spring 2005), http://www.surrealismcentre.ac.uk/papersofsurrealism/journal3/.

7. Michel Remy explains that, after its sixth issue, the *London Bulletin* became a prominent locus of the international art world, connecting the British group to the international surrealist movement. See Michel Remy, *Surrealism in Britain* (Aldershot, U.K.: Ashgate, 1999), 155–56.

8. The negative is located at the Centre Pompidou in Paris. Though dated ca. 1932, correspondence and chronology suggest that the photo was likely taken in 1939.

9. Ithell Colquhoun, *The Crying of the Wind: Ireland* (London: Peter Owen, 1955); *The Living Stones: Cornwall* (London: Peter Owen, 1957); *Goose of Hermogenes* (London: Peter Owen, 1961).

10. Ithell Colquhoun, *Sword of Wisdom: MacGregor Mathers and "The Golden Dawn"* (London: Spearman, 1975). Colquhoun's known publications include some fifty poems in magazines; almost seventy articles, essays, and short prose works; and translations of writers such as Stéphane Mallarmé, André Breton, Romain Weingarten, and Édouard Glissant. Her unpublished texts include many other poems, essays, and short stories; work on other travel books; one additional unpublished novel (perhaps not complete) entitled *Destination Limbo;* many dream diaries; occult notes and diagrams; and a voluminous correspondence. Colquhoun's visual artwork was more substantial than her literary efforts and certainly exceeds the 928 works catalogued to date. See Richard Shillitoe, *Ithell Colquhoun: Magician Born of*

Nature, 2nd ed. (Raleigh, N.C.: Lulu, 2010), for a comprehensive catalogue of the currently known artworks.

11. Scholarly and detailed accounts of these components may be found in Antoine Faivre, *Access to Western Esotericism* (Albany: State University of New York Press, 1994); Nicholas Goodrick-Clarke, *The Western Esoteric Traditions: A Historical Introduction* (Oxford: Oxford University Press, 2008); and Henrik Bogdan, *Western Esotericism and Rituals of Initiation* (Albany: State University of New York Press, 2007).

12. "Qabalah" is Colquhoun's preferred spelling, being more consistent, in her view, with the Hebrew writing of the word than common alternatives such as "Kabbalah," "Kabala," or "Cabbala."

13. Colquhoun's syncretic project owed a debt to the nineteenth-century French occult writings of Eliphas Lévi and to the Hermetic Order of the Golden Dawn, which based itself in part upon Levi's work. It evokes the perennialism popularized by H. P. Blavatsky's and Annie Besant's theosophical writings as the "Ancient Wisdom," and by Aldous Huxley's highly influential book *The Perennial Philosophy* (New York: Harper and Brothers, 1945).

14. Each figure is also linked with one of the traditional elements—air, water, fire, and earth—each of which has an associated color. This is why Colquhoun intended each chapter to be printed on the appropriately colored paper.

15. Israel Regardie, *A Practical Guide to Geomantic Divination* (London: Aquarian Press, 1972).

16. This is a simplified account of a complex doctrine. Those who wish to discover more can turn to Charles W. Leadbeater's nontechnical book *The Life After Death,* first published in 1912, available at http://www.archive.org/details/lifeafterdeathan020962mbp.

17. One exception might be Cornwall. Like Brittany, it is an isolated peninsula with its own folklore and religious traditions. Cornish, the language of old Cornwall, is closely related to Breton, the language of old Brittany. The district of West Penwith, where Colquhoun lived, has the greatest concentration of prehistoric funerary monuments in mainland United Kingdom.

18. Geoffrey Samuel, "The Effectiveness of Goddesses, or How Ritual Works," *Anthropological Forum* 11, no. 1 (2001): 87.

19. "The Fellowship of Isis Manifesto," http://www.fellowshipofisis.com/manifesto.html. For recent scholarship on the fellowship, see Catherine Maignant, "Irish Base, Global Religion: The Fellowship of Isis," in *Ireland's New Religious Movements,* ed. Olivia Cosgrove, Laurence Cox, Carmen Kuhling, and Peter Mulholland (Newcastle, U.K.: Cambridge Scholars, 2011): 262–80.

20. For details, see Ronald Hutton, *The Druids* (London: Hambledon Continuum, 2007). See also Adam Stout, *Creating Prehistory: Druids, Ley Hunters, and Archaeologists in Pre-war Britain* (Malden, Mass.: Blackwell, 2008).

21. Robert Graves, *The White Goddess* (London: Faber and Faber, 1948), esp. chap. 22.

22. Though Morganwg had essentially made up many of these texts and histories of the "ancient" bards and druids, his achievements resonated with Romanticism and the Celtic revival. As Ronald Hutton puts it, Morganwg "revealed to the world a ceremony, a liturgy and a body of moral and religious teachings that had been handed down to the medieval Welsh poets and scholars by the ancient Druids, and a history to explain and support these. A central feature of this system was that it perfectly reconciled the figures of the bard and the Druid." Hutton, *Druids,* 22.

23. Also known as the British Circle of the Universal Bond and as An Druidh Uileach Braithrearchas.

24. Druidry's links with occult societies are explored by Colquhoun in *Sword of Wisdom,* 125–30. MacGregor-Reid's father, a previous chief Druid, adopted the name MacGregor to honor MacGregor Mathers, a founder of the Golden Dawn.

25. Colquhoun kept a diary of this trip, now in a private collection. Some of the details have been published by Eric Ratcliffe in *Ithell Colquhoun: Pioneer Surrealist Artist, Occultist, Writer, and Poet* (Oxford: Mandrake, 2007), 125–26.

26. Though it made a foundational distinction between animate and inanimate nature, the not unrelated modern concept of vitalism was seriously entertained by mainstream scientists from the seventeenth to the nineteenth centuries. Only after the first quarter of the twentieth century was it finally consistently abandoned by most scientists.

27. Her comments concerning the relationship between the organic and the inorganic world must owe something to Roger Caillois. See his "Mimicry and Legendary Psychasthenia," trans. John Shepley, *October* 31 (Winter 1984): 16–32. First published in French, 1935.

28. Brian J. Gibbons, *Gender in Mystical and Occult Thought: Behmenism and Its Development in England* (Cambridge: Cambridge University Press, 1996). There is a vast scholarly literature on gender in esotericism and mysticism, but Alex Owen's work on occultism in the Victorian occult revival and in the modernist period helps set the stage for some of the gender issues that informed Colquhoun's early work and were developed more fully in her later occult and literary practices. See Alex Owen, *The Place of Enchantment: British Occultism and the Culture of the Modern* (Chicago: University of Chicago Press, 2004).

29. A full discussion of these beliefs appears in Shillitoe, *Ithell Colquhoun*, chap. 7. Some aspects are discussed by Victoria Ferentinou in "Ithell Colquhoun, Surrealism, and the Occult," *Papers of Surrealism* 9 (Summer 2011), http://www.surrealismcentre.ac.uk/papersofsurrealism/journal9.

30. See "The Myth of Santa Warna," *The Glass* 1 (1948): [21–22].

31. There was no such thing as waste matter in the prelapsarian Garden of Eden, so Adam had no need for bowels. For eye-watering details of how Adam actually delivered his progeny, see Milad Doueihi, *Earthly Paradise: Myths and Philosophies* (Cambridge: Harvard University Press, 2009), 21–22.

32. J. Donald Hughes, "Dream Interpretation in Ancient Civilizations," *Dreaming* 10, no. 1 (2000): 7–18.

33. As, for example, Francis Barrett argued in chapter 8 of *The Magus, or Celestial Intelligencer* (Leicester, U.K.: Lackington, Allen, 1970). This was a comprehensive work on ceremonial magic by a self-proclaimed practitioner that, after its initial publication in 1801, exerted influence on occultism across the nineteenth and twentieth centuries. It remains in print today.

34. Roger Luckhurst, *The Invention of Telepathy* (Oxford: Oxford University Press, 2002); Janet Oppenheim, *The Other World: Spiritualism and Psychical Research in England, 1850–1914* (Cambridge: Cambridge University Press, 1985), chap. 4.

35. H. P. Blavatsky, for example, in her seminal theosophical works *Isis Unveiled* (1877) and *The Secret Doctrine* (1888), portrayed theosophy as ancient *science*. She grappled intermittently with Victorian evolutionary science, chemistry, and physics. Theosophical luminaries Annie Besant and Charles W. Leadbeater attempted to explain the theosophical cosmos on the basis of clairvoyant explorations of a subatomic world in the decades of experiments they detailed in *Occult Chemistry* (based on an article originally published in *Lucifer* in 1895 and expanded in book form across three editions in 1908, 1919, and 1951). The occult revival of the period fostered a dynamic relationship between occult perspectives and the nascence of modern chemistry and particle physics. See Mark S. Morrisson, *Modern Alchemy: Occultism and the Emergence of Atomic Theory* (Oxford: Oxford University Press, 2007).

36. Colquhoun, *Sword of Wisdom*, 158.

37. Tate Archive, Tate Britain, London, TGA 929/5/21/2/39. The untitled manuscript is in note form. We have adjusted the grammar slightly in the interest of clarity.

38. Hughes, "Dream Interpretation."

39. See Colquhoun's unpublished essay, datable to 1979 based on internal evidence, in TGA 929/2/1/43.

40. Sigmund Freud, *The Interpretation of Dreams* (London: Hogarth Press, 1991). First published in German, 1899; first English translation, 1913.

41. Sigmund Freud, "The Occult Meaning of Dreams," in *New Introductory Lectures on Psychoanalysis* (London: Hogarth Press, 1967). First published in German, 1925; first English translation, 1933.

42. Alice E. Buck and F. Claude Palmer, *The Clothes of God: A Treatise on Neo-analytic Psychology* (London: Peter Owen, 1956).

43. André Breton, *Communicating Vessels*, trans. Mary Ann Caws and Geoffrey T. Harris (Lincoln: University of Nebraska Press, 1990). First published in French, 1932.

44. Buck and Palmer, *Clothes of God*, chap. 8. For a detailed discussion of how artists have responded to physicists' understanding of time, see Linda Dalrymple Henderson, *The Fourth Dimension and Non-Euclidean Geometry in Modern Art*, rev. ed. (Cambridge: MIT Press, 2013).

45. André Breton, *Mad Love*, trans. Mary Ann Caws (Lincoln: University of Nebraska Press, 1987), 84. First published in French, 1937.

46. Breton, *Mad Love*, 64ff.

47. Breton, *Manifestos of Surrealism*, 26.

48. Warlick, *Max Ernst and Alchemy*, 134.

49. Ithell Colquhoun, "Notes on Automatism," *Melmoth* 2 (1980): 31–32.

50. Max Ernst, "Inspiration to Order," in *Beyond Painting* (New York: Wittenborn Schultz, 1948).

51. See Gavin Parkinson, *Surrealism, Art, and Modern Science* (New Haven: Yale University Press, 2008).

52. Nicolas Calas, "The Light of Words," *Arson: An Ardent Review*, March 1942, 13–20.

53. Colquhoun, "Notes on Automatism."

54. The authorship of occult automatic writing is always a complex problem. Colquhoun once wrote an essay about perhaps the most well-known example of her lifetime: William Butler Yeats's *A Vision* (London: Macmillan, 1925; 2nd ed., 1937). *A Vision* was a collaboration involving W. B. Yeats, his wife George Yeats, and the source of George Yeats's automatic writings—whether one understands it as the spirits of the dead communicating through her, George's imagination, or something else entirely.

55. Martica Sawin, *Surrealism in Exile and the Beginning of the New York School* (Cambridge: MIT Press, 1995). See especially chapters 1 and 2.

56. Gordon Onslow Ford, *Yves Tanguy and Automatism* (Inverness, Calif.: Bishop Pine Press, 1983), 9.

57. Breton, *Manifestos of Surrealism*, 293.

58. Ithell Colquhoun, responses to a questionnaire, *The Glass* 9 (1953): [24–25].

59. Quoted in Philip G. Davis, *Goddess Unmasked: The Rise of Neopagan Feminist Spirituality* (Dallas: Spence, 1998), 250.

60. Whitney Chadwick, *Women Artists and the Surrealist Movement* (London: Thames and Hudson, 1985), 190.

61. Janet Kaplan, *Unexpected Journeys: The Art and Life of Remedios Varo* (New York: Abbeville Press, 1988), 164.

62. This description is based on one by Ben Fernee, the specialist occult bookseller who handled the sale of the mirror in 2011.

63. The source of Colquhoun's information on correspondences was Aleister Crowley's *Liber 777* (1909), available online at http://www.hermetic.com/crowley/libers/liber777.pdf. It contains the most comprehensive tables of attributions yet published. Crowley gathered his

material from the writings of MacGregor Mathers, who, in turn, assembled his from a variety of nineteenth-century and earlier sources.

64. Untitled manuscript in TGA 929/5/21/2/104–107.

65. In many medieval and early modern alchemical texts, the philosopher's stone is described as a fine, heavy powder the color of rubies.

66. Antoine-Joseph Pernety, *Treatise on the Great Art* (Boston: Occult Publishing, 1898). First published posthumously. Available online at http://www.hermetics.org/pdf/alchemy/The_Great_Art.pdf.

67. Although the essay was not published until 1970, there is documentary evidence that shows it to be contemporary with the painting.

68. Available online at http://www.hermetics.org/pdf/Mathers_Kabbalah_Unveiled.pdf.

69. The coloring of the body may appear curious but corresponds with Golden Dawn teachings that link each body part with a specific color.

70. For the nonspecialist reader, Dion Fortune's *The Mystical Qabalah* (San Francisco: Weiser Books, 2000) is a helpful explanatory text. It was first published in 1935.

71. In her writings, Colquhoun always employed the more unusual spelling of Taro without the final "t," believing it to be more in keeping with the pack's supposed Egyptian origin, and referred to the Suit of Disks rather than using its more usual name, Pentacles. She used the esoteric titles of the individual cards in preference to the everyday ones.

72. Colquhoun, *Sword of Wisdom*, 250.

I SAW WATER

A NOVEL

———+———

VIDI AQUAM EGREDIENTEM DE TEMPLO A LATERE SINISTRA

ITHELL COLQUHOUN

CONTENTS

AUTHOR'S PREFACE

I Saw Water explores in imagination the after death state of earth bound spirits. The characters continue, as in material existence, to be activated by fantasy and desire—whether mania or phobia—and to build round themselves the illusion of time and space. Most of them see themselves as still participating in physical life, so near is their consciousness to that of this planet; but the narrator becomes progressively more distant as the story unfolds.

Ménec is that Island of the Dead which is to be found in the mythologies under various names; it has many geographical locations. The characters who appear there are all discarnate, though a few of them may be so only temporarily, projected there in states of profound unconsciousness, however caused. As they arrive, they are received at the Ianua Vitae Convent where they remain until thirst for experience draws them away.

Only in the penultimate chapter, which explains the forgoing narrative, do living characters appear in an earth-life setting: while in the final chapter the narrator, having undergone the "second-death"* approaches impersonality and so achieves a measure of calm.

Ithell Colquhoun

1

PALE

It was my turn to herd our cows and goats, so I was eating a mid-day meal in the open air. But when I say it was my turn, that's not strictly true because I wangled it by getting round our Novice-Mistress, Sister Mary Paracelsus.* Not that I was still a Novice, but I often helped her in the still-room,* so had opportunities for tactful suggestion.

In our Order stress is laid on outdoor life: we have a *mystique* of nature-appreciation, you might say. (This, perhaps, is to counter-balance the miraculous character of our central theme). But as idle dreams are not encouraged, nor even Wordsworthian wanderings lonely as a cloud,* the love of nature is usually given the form of land-work. Some of our city-bred Novices don't care about it, and many a Postulant* has forfeited all chance of a Novitiate even, by not being able to take the bull by the horns. Yes, we do have bulls; our cattle are not the dispirited, de-horned, artificially-inseminated creatures that brood now, I've heard, in many an English field. And why not? Cows have a dull enough existence in any case, so it's a shame to deprive them of their one diversion. Our bulls are seldom savage because we don't keep them chained up but let them run with the herd.

It's an act of charity for someone like myself, who enjoys it, to undertake a timid Novice's turn with the cattle—when that can be discreetly managed.

It was the day of St. Januarius and so in some sense a doorway; perhaps, together with our festival of St. Mazhe* two days later, it is the Church's way of marking the Equinox.* Mazhe is more than a Saint, standing as he does at the opening of one of the year's quarters. The weather was fine with a haze that silvered the sunlight as I kept an eye on our beasts munching the grass-verges and strips of common-land on the outskirts of the town. I don't know if we are within our rights in letting them so graze; but few people like to fight with nuns, so no one has yet queried the custom. And then we may be doing the neighbouring farmers a service by letting our herd crop the rank weeds before seeding.

I must admit that I find it a relief to have an occasional meal away from the refectory. Not that it isn't very pleasant there: you don't have to make conversation, because one of the Sisters always reads aloud to us while we eat. This Lection is another thing we take in turns: usually an incident from the life of one of the Saints is chosen, or one from Church-history. Whatever it is, you needn't listen if you'd rather pursue your own thoughts, because no one questions on it. Still it's a treat to have solitary contact with nature once in a while; luckily this is in the spirit of the Order, or I should have a thin time.

Thank God I'm not a Cistercian,* with no let-up from the common-life! Not even a cell of your own, and having to sleep in a dormitory as if you were still at a child's boarding school. One writer has remarked that this unmitigated proximity to one's fellows is the most severe mortification that can be imposed on a religious of our time. Sartre said much the same thing in other words, if I remember: 'L'enfer, c'est les autres'.* (I haven't read an author of this type for some while so I won't be sure of the exact phrase. At the Ianua Vitae,* no ephemeral reading-matter is allowed; but if, as occasionally happens, a newspaper is smuggled into the precincts, it is left in one of the lavatories. An unwritten law forbids its use for wiping one's bottom and decrees that one leaves it for subsequent visitors to read. A queue tends to form outside the cubicle containing this link with a former life, while other compartments are left vacant.)

It's not so bad if les autres are quiet, and they have to be, in our Order. If you don't move quietly by nature you soon have to learn: no doors must be slammed or implements roughly handled; there is no chattering, scuffling or stamping. No noisy machinery is allowed in labour-saving devices because labour saving isn't one of our aims; and no radio because we are supposed to be able to do without mental and emotional drugs. Not that it's a stuffy Order at all—it's easier than most. Hidden in the tall herbage, I can often slip in a sun-bathe on my herding days, and sometimes even a bathe in the sea. But this latter we're not supposed to do unless a party of us is going to one of the deserted strands— in case we get into deep water. I'm not complaining; in general I like the life. All decisions on trivial matters, which use up your energy while you are in the world, are taken from you; in return for obedience, you are relieved of a good many boring things—like buying a suspender-belt for instance. Few of us wear stockings, usually just strong sandals on bare feet. In cold weather (or all the year round for some of the elderly Sisters) we are allowed a sort of wool sock which needs no support; worn under a habit no one outside can tell the difference.

Well, as I was saying, there was I seated on a low wall that divides the lane from somebody's field, eating my dinner from a tin plate. I'd taken off my headdress, the black and white veil that I always find troublesome. In some of our convents it has been replaced by a kerchief like the Postulants' which ties under the chin and which you can wear or not, as you choose. But Reverend Mother is a bit traditional in some ways and hasn't got around to that one yet. I really must drop these colloquial phrases—it's lucky my Superiors can't hear me think or I'd be on the carpet. There I go again! They're right, of course: nothing is dingier than outdated slang, and you can't expect a nun to keep up to the minute—except in the matter of gossip, and that a convent always seems to do, however strict its enclosure.

The Parthenogenesist Order* is directed to the contemplative life and most of its Houses are enclosed, but here at the Ianua Vitae, which is a pilgrimage-centre, complete enclosure is not practicable.

I was wearing the habit of the Order, which is made of a material something like loden-cloth* but lighter, the sage-green being protective colouration for the odd hayseed or splash of mud. I suppose it originated in the Black Forest,* for our Foundress was a native of that region and the Mother-House of our Order is still there. Even at our remote Ianua Vitae we have representatives from many nations.

Once when I was ill as a Postulant and had to spend some time in our infirmary, I was looked after by a student-nurse from Australia, who belonged to another Order. For special occasions, such as the presenting of a diploma, she used to wear a pill-box hat of white velvet trimmed with pearls, a filmy veil depending from the back of it and a long white satin dress off-the-shoulder. The effect was bridal, like the dress we wear during the first part of our ceremony of 'Clothing'—the last worldly gear we put on before assuming the final Habit.

I may have been delirious at the time, but I seem to remember that there was also some turquoise-blue velvet in her regalia, some copper-red with yellow and green brocade as well. She was young, fair and innocent-looking, with very white teeth which were perhaps not her own. She told me that when she went out at Ménec dressed thus, people in the roads would stare at her—no wonder, since they were accustomed only to nuns in our sober garb. A young fellow once called out to her, 'You should be going to the love-market!' Though she thought he meant a beat-session* much advertised at the time, I suspected a reference to Mme. Lacoste's establishment by the harbour.

Suddenly along the last alleyway leading from the town there shuffled a sorry figure. Her hair hung on her shoulders in rats' tails, her coat was torn and stained with sea-water, her nylons were laddered and her shoes caked with filth. She sidled towards me and, before I could divine her intention, had seized a slice of veal from my convent-platter with a ravenous gesture and hurried on, devouring it, towards the open country.

"Hi, you dirty thief!" I bawled, jumping up from the granite wall to follow her. "How dare you? This may be the back of beyond but there's law and order here, you'll soon find!"

The moment the words were out of my mouth* I realised that I was not behaving like a religious. Shouting, first of all; shouting insults and threats, at that. Then, why should I set such store by my dinner? Didn't this beggar-woman need it more than I? And interfering? It wasn't my job to do the work of the local police. Examination of conscience is part of our training and I saw at once that I had crammed a number of sins, at least three of them mortal, into the last few seconds. I made a hurried Act of Contrition, intending to repair what damage I could without delay; such Acts were given different names by Ste. Ermengilde, our Foundress, in her Manual *The Peerless Guidance:* instead of The Act of Contrition, she spoke of "The Breaking of Bonds"; for the Act of Hope, "The Stretching of Wings"; of Faith, "The Soaring"; and of Charity, "The Song at the Point of Day."

My tone had intimidated the waif, though she may not have understood my words, for I had spoken in the island-dialect which I had picked up since being sent here to Ménec. She came limping back towards me with a scared look and muttered, in English, a few words of explanation: she hadn't eaten for three days.

"Look," I answered in the same language, "I'm sorry I was hasty. If you're really starving they'll give you some food from our kitchen. Just go round to the side-door."

She looked at me vaguely, asking "Kitchen?"

"Yes, the convent-kitchen; the Ianua Vitae Convent."

"I don't know where it is; I've only just arrived."

"Come along then, I'll show you."

I judged the cattle could be left to themselves for a while, so I began to lead the stranger along the sea-wall in the direction of our buildings.

"Are you a nun?" she asked presently, her wild eyes flicking over me.

"Yes," I answered; then I felt embarrassed, for I had left my veil on the wall and without it I could have been mistaken for some local farmerette, since our habit is not unlike the regional costume. We don't shave our heads, just cut the hair short in a simple style. "I'll have to go back for my veil," I added.

As I retraced my steps I could not stop wondering where I had met this woman before. Not many people have eyes of that peculiar colour—yellow with dark dots like flies in amber. In fact the only person I could remember was Charlotte, a distant cousin of mine from Canada. "But it can't be her," I thought. "She's quite prosperous." It was true I hadn't been in touch with her for some time, even before my reception as a Postulant: was it possible that the years had reduced a glossy 'younger married' to this piece of human wreckage? The chestnut gleams had vanished from her hair, to be replaced by streaks of grey; lines furrowed her forehead, her cheeks were sunk into hollows, and her eye-sockets had that perpetually-darkened look—not the result of a hangover—which is one of the surest signs of middle age. Her modishly-lissom figure had become skeletal and the small breasts were now drained flat.

And where was the famous Charlottean poise? The assured tones, derived from an up-and-coming transatlantic background, which had held their own through the clamour of many a cocktail party, had become the 'scrannel-pipe'* of the unhinged. Yet the more I thought about it the more certain I became of the identification: the bedraggled clothing still bore vestiges of style and the awkward movements a trace of dignity.

I hurried back to the stranger, adjusting my veil. She was standing as I had left her, gazing into vacancy. I had to know at once who she was.

"I say, is your name Charlotte Mortimore?" I demanded.

Her answer was a look of terror.

"Why do you ask me that?" she choked.

"Well, if it is, I'm your cousin. Don't you remember, Ella de Maine I used to be; now I'm Sister Brigid."*

"De Maine," she murmured, and again her gaze turned to the middle distance.

"Come along and don't worry about anything till you've eaten," I suggested.

We walked together along the cliff-path where, on our left, walls of pinkish rock fell steeply to the sea. Presently the path widened into a dusty track and we approached the hamlet of Kervin-Brigitte* that has grown up, through the years, around the convent. On our right rose some buildings of Mediterranean character, such as one finds in this southern part of Brittany; among them was a sea-green hotel with the proprietor's name painted in semi-Gothic letters on the façade. Just beyond, a double flight of steps led up to a lofty white chapel; the west door was open and through it we could see that the dome was supported by twelve pillars in four clusters, oriented to the cardinal points.

"That's the Healing Chapel, dedicated to Our Lady of the Trees,"* I told my charge, pausing to glance inside. "You see, each pillar has the name of a tree and the disease it cures written at the base."

"I can see Willow for Diarrhoea,"* she replied.

"The story is that the chapel was built where a wonder-working tree used to grow long ago."

"Was it a Willow?"

"I don't know; no, a palm, I think—these are just stories handed down in our Order, not articles of faith," I assured her. "But I don't need to tell you that."

Charlotte winced, but I didn't think this was the moment for probing, so continued in my assumed rôle of guide.

"Some say that the columns are petrified trees—palm, cedar, olive and cypress;* others that all twelve varieties grew miraculously from the one original root."

The site has always commanded some repute, though its fame has waxed and waned like that of any similar shrine. In the arch between and below the double flight of steps is a kind of grotto, where a stream pours from rock with a tufa-like* surface made slippery by the moisture.

Charlotte stood gazing at this stream, apparently entranced by the sight and sound of the cascade, though indifferent to the traditions I was passing on. The water ran down from the small eminence where the chapel stood and flowed into a series of stone troughs. These were frequented by cattle that churned up the mud around them; but at Festival-time pilgrims would wash and even drink here like the beasts.

I led Charlotte forward to the main convent-buildings and left her in a small room, flag-stoned like the kitchen and opening off it. I explained to Sister Mary Cornely,* who was then in charge of preparing food, that there was someone in need of a meal; and finally left my cousin, once an exponent of 'gracious living,' seated at a scrubbed table and gobbling bread-soup and elder-flower-fritters* from a tin plate and bowl.

Meanwhile, I went in search of our Novice-Mistress, who was, as I surmised, busy in the still-room. Herbal remedies are the pride of our Order,* and Sister Mary Paracelsus is so knowledgeable on the subject of their preparation that she is known even beyond the confines of Ménec as *La Druidesse*. Nuns are supposed to be orderly, but no one dared to criticise this room with its creative chaos. It was like an alchemist's den, full of furnaces, presses and strange vessels that Sister Mary Paracelsus had collected from all parts. Apparatus of many kinds, ancient and modern, littered the tables or stood about the floor, while bundles of herbs were hanging to dry from the rafters above.

I suppose it's not surprising that, if you enter it with sympathy, the vegetable-kingdom should yield up to you its healing secrets. After all, God uses the products of two plants, wheat and the vine, when He wants to show Himself to us in the present age. He might have chosen animals, say the dove and the serpent; or minerals, rock crystal and topaz perhaps; but as far as we know He didn't.

Nothing astonishes Sister Mary Paracelsus—she is as patient as the plants—though people are often astonished at her. They wonder, for instance, how it is that she was allowed to adopt Paracelsus as her name in religion, instead of that of a Saint, as is the custom. I don't know the answer to this myself; of course it happened before my time and I've never liked to question her about it. I can only surmise that the Church was following her usual practice of making an exception for an exceptional person, while keeping the rules strict for the average. There is something to be said for this attitude, in contrast to its opposite, which allows a general vagueness and laxity in the hope of accommodating all types. When I had explained the situation to her she straightened her tall figure, which had been bent above a glass jar shaped like an egg, and looked at me with eyes clear as water. She only said:

"I will confide your cousin to your care, Sister Brigid. Give her the smaller guest-room and when she has rested, take her back to the fields with you. I am sure you will want to have a talk."

"Thank you, Sister," I curtsied, as is our manner when taking leave of a Superior.

I had to return to the cattle, which by this time might have been straying or damaging property: so I left Charlotte sprawled across her narrow bed. I told her to come and find me if she felt like it, but she looked so exhausted that I hardly expected her to do so. However, after an hour or two I caught sight of her picking her way along the path above the sea-wall, and ran to meet her.

2

SORROW

It was Charlotte this time, unmistakeably: a wash and a rest had restored something of her former elegance and she had even applied a lipstick which had been hidden, perhaps—her dearest possession—in some inner pocket. She carried no handbag, I noticed.

She still had a wild look in her eye as I made her sit beside me on the low stones of the wall.

"How is it that you are here in Ménec?" I asked. "And where is Ossian?"* I realised that this latter was the key-question, but I thought I had better put it without delay.

"He's with Beatrice;* we were all having a holiday together in Morbihan—"* Charlotte's voice, once confident, now often trailed away into silence, in the same way as her eyes would lose their focus and gaze into the depths of space.

"Rather an awkward triangle," I commented.

Beatrice was Ossian's mother; named after the heroine of *The Divine Comedy* by prosperous parents who desired for her a career in the arts, she had in fact achieved, as Beatrice Raymond, distinction as a violinist. Though now retired, she had been something of a *diva* in her day; something of a beauty too, if that is the type you admire: a long face with the bold features that show up well on stage or platform. Sometimes the hair is raven, sometimes golden-blond, but the eyes are nearly always grey and there is a high colour on the cheek-bones.

Beatrice's hair had been golden and was now gilded; she was ample but well-corseted. Her dark eyebrows nearly met above the root of her nose, giving her a truculent air which belied the habitually-honeyed tones of her voice. Altogether a formidable mother-in-law.

"It was worse than a triangle," went on Charlotte. "Daphnis Burge* was there too—that's Ossian's latest friend."

"You mean—?"

"Yes, most of our friends now are on the mauve list.* Ossian only told me at the last minute that he had invited Daphnis. We had a scene; I implored him to make some excuse and put him off. But he told me that if I didn't like the arrangement I needn't come with them. I wish I hadn't."

"Did Beatrice like Daphnis joining the party?"

"Like it! She was delighted. 'A charming boy,' she always calls him. And, 'What an *amusing* quartet we shall play,' she said. Well, they can play without me; maybe it won't sound so funny as a trio," Charlotte ended with a show of spirit.

"Does Beatrice understand what Daphnis is?" "I don't know, she pretends not to, but she's always had a liking for queers: 'so sensitive, my dear.' Perhaps she's never faced the facts of what they actually do. She connives, by not asking questions. But she'd favour anything that might separate me from Ossian: a tootsie would do, only another woman might be a rival. With friends like Daphnis, both 'boys' are rivals for Beatrice."

I recalled that Beatrice had always been opposed to Ossian's marriage, sensing neurosis beneath Charlotte's façade.

"I can't remember where you were married."

"In a registry-office—dreary enough, but not as bad as a cold church, warm champagne and—relatives."

"That was before your conversion."

"Before Ossian's conversion."

"How did you get away from the mainland?"

"I just left. I took a bus to the port and boarded the first boat leaving, I didn't care where it was bound. We had a bad crossing and I was very sick."

"The *Ile de Ménec* is a ghastly old tub at the best of times; she always knocks about if there's the slightest bit of swell."

"Just as we were getting into harbour, I was attacked by the captain's dog, a huge animal with a vicious temper. In the scuffle my handbag fell into the sea, so I had no money when we landed. I felt so confused, I didn't even grasp the name of the island."

"What about the children?"

A buffet from the sea-wind made Charlotte shiver.

"They're hardly children now. Jerome is doing well at Sandhurst* and Hilary is in her last year at school."

I felt that Charlotte had lost all contact with her children; they had existed for her primarily as part of the fabric of her marriage and now that this was crumbling, her link with them had become tenuous. The fact of their growing up also tended to isolate her from them.

"After all I've been through," she moaned. "How I hated the times before they were born; and what's the point of it now?"

"You found pregnancy an unpleasant experience?" I prompted.

"It's a constipation of the blood!" she burst out. "There's no longer a way through the body. One has no sense of participating in a new creation, only one of being poisoned. There's an interior exhaustion like no other tiredness, one's vitality drained at its source.

"Each morning when I woke up and before I was fully conscious, I felt a black cloud hanging over me, though I couldn't remember what caused it. Then I would remember, and the cloud sank lower and engulfed me."

"Were you physically sick?"

"Yes, but it's like no other nausea—you can't finish with it. All day I'd feel sea-sick, as though I'd just stepped off a boat after a stormy passage. If I smelled anything, no matter what, it would make me heave. It's nausea plus strangulation: it grips you first by the shoulders and neck, then spreads to the whole body and mind."

"I expect you didn't feel much like love-making then."

"No, pregnancy spoils one as an erotic being, temporarily at least. Nausea makes any pressure on the abdomen painful; then there are stabbing pains in the breasts and appallingly sensitive nipples—that doesn't encourage love-play. When the breasts begin to swell they become like lead, the nipples no longer point to the sky's horizon but to the ground, as though pulled downward by a malign force."

I was aware that Charlotte had never before spoken to anyone with such candour.

"Then what they tell you in women's magazines isn't true, about it improving the health and so on?"

"Don't believe a word of it. A few people may look and feel their best during pregnancy, but, believe me, they are the lucky few. When you hear someone who's 'expecting' say she feels well, she means 'well for a pregnant woman,' not well in comparison with normal health."

"In fact, the radiant-motherhood-health-and-beauty racket is a phoney?"

"Use your commonsense and observation. Child-bearing either coarsens or hardens one's looks, sometimes both; and as to health, I don't believe one ever has the same energy after it."

"I wonder if Ossian's attitude has something to do with your miseries?"

"Call yourself a nun! You don't miss much. Yes, Ossian didn't fail to quote Baron Corvo* at me, 'A pregnant woman is the most disgusting sight in nature.'"

I must admit that I agree with Corvo in this, though I see that it isn't a tactful thing to say to one's wife.

There was a long pause. Charlotte had something worse to tell me but she could not bring it out. I said it for her:

"I suppose Ossian has lost his faith?"

She nodded.

"You never had any," I persisted.

"No, he dragged me into the Church against my better judgment. Deep down, I never believed. But I felt that if we split on this subject it would finish our marriage, so I stifled my doubts. I even called it mortifying the intellect and a silly bloody sanctimonious bitch I was." She added without disguise, "I may also have favoured our conversion because Beatrice was against it."

"She saw in the Church a rival mother," I suggested.

"Yes, and so did I, in a sense. I thought I had weaned Ossian from Beatrice; but if I had made him a fully adult human being he wouldn't have needed to be reborn. As it was, he had to look around for a new mother and the Church was the obvious choice—preferable to Beatrice at least."

"Well, he seems to be back in the primordial womb again now," I said. "He must have found the Church inadequate too."

"But how much had Beatrice to do with his dissatisfaction? She never left him alone. And what about me?" she suddenly wailed. "I have nothing; no husband, no children, no mother, no Church, no profession, no health. They are gone, all gone."

"Have you any money?" I asked.

I knew that the Mortimore household had not been supported by Ossian, who had never earned a useful salary: though he enjoyed playing with children, he had never liked the idea of working for them. The most he could bring himself to do was a little interior-decoration. This entailed many visits to the Continent to pick up ideas, usually impracticable when it came to the point; and week-ends to discuss furnishing-schemes with friends who, though they only sometimes paid him for his advice, were all supposed to be useful contacts. Charlotte could not often accompany him on these excursions, being tied to house and children; and this suited Ossian admirably. He managed to make the best of at least two worlds.* In the main, it was Charlotte's means as well as Charlotte's presence which supported their home, with Beatrice making herself indispensable when a particularly stupendous bill had to be met.

"If you have, you can pull out and start again," I told her. "After all, you could keep a household going, so you should have ample for your own needs."

"But I have no heart, no heart for anything. I don't know how to go on alone."

It would have done Charlotte good to weep but she could not. Instead she added, with a sudden change of mood, "It all seems a long time ago." Her tone was less one of resignation than of wonder.

I've often thought that the Church is too tough on the idea of trial-marriage. You can't join a religious Order without a period of probation, and even after you are accepted as a Novice, you don't take final vows for years. But in marriage, which must be at least as strenuous a 'way,' you take final vows at the beginning, and with a chap whom perhaps you hardly know. An engagement is no equivalent to a Novitiate. Again, if you really can't make the grade as a religious, you can get a rescript of your vows, it may be after years even. No community wants to keep a dissatisfied member: vocational *malaise* is more infectious than smallpox. But there's no rescript for a marriage-vow; only sometimes an annulment, which is to say that the vow was never valid. Yet it may have been taken in good faith by both parties; and I must admit that to me such an annulment often has the air of a legal-fiction.

These are not my problems, I know, so I dare say I could be better employed than in considering them. But here was Charlotte whose problems they were—only that is putting it too mildly. Rather, such problems possessed her as a victim, since she had failed utterly to solve them in the working-out of her own life. She had put all she possessed into her marriage, only to find her effort of dedication useless. Ossian had scarcely suffered; but what happens to the partner who loses out?

Sister Mary Paracelsus had confided her to me but what was I to do with her? It was a responsibility; I began to improvise:

"Why don't you stay here for a few weeks? It's not long now till the date of our yearly Festival; why not stay for that? Our ceremonies might make you feel better."

"I told you, I've lost my faith—such as it ever was."

"You don't need any, as I understand it. Springs, trees and rocks have a self-acting power: they're not interested in your faith. Just follow the rites, and the virtue will come through."

"If one's fortunate."

"Anyway, give it a chance; and if you stay here till then, you'll at least have time to collect your wits. It's funny, your appearing just now," I went on. "I was thinking about you a day or two ago."

At this Charlotte became agitated.

"You must not, you must not," she cried. "Never think of me, it will bring you bad luck."

"Why should it?"

"My mind is always overflowing now; it will swamp you. It is infected: it will bring contagion."*

She sprang up and stood glaring at me from her mad yellow eyes. Though I was sorry for her, I felt her woes were in some way her own fault, or at least her own choice. The phrase 'Death by drowning'* rang in my ears: she had been drowned in her sorrows and the tears they evoked. Some gulf of misery within herself must have called down this tale of victimage upon her, as the ocean might reflect a tragic procession passing along the sea-wall. Only with her, the image had disturbed the water to its depths.

The sun of summer's end was already sinking, and it was time for me to call the cattle. As I drove them up the cliff-path toward the convent, Charlotte dawdled disconsolately after me, disregarding the beauty of the evening. The sea was not quite smooth, so that each ripple showed a blue-green upper side and a wine-dark one below, leading directly to the ocean's heart. Thus the surface was a silken purple-blue, fringed at the cliff-base with a lacey foam whose whiteness was lit by a glow that might have passed through the red of amber.

3

A WOMAN YOUNG

All next day and the day after I couldn't stop wondering why Charlotte had appeared, as if by chance, at this moment when it seemed that I was at last on the way to making my soul. Long before this, I had begun to desire a second birth* and had made several attempts at regeneration: now I felt that I had chosen the right mother,* just as Ossian had, though from different motives.

Charlotte had been linked to me in this quest for I remembered how, in the early days of her marriage, we together visited a group of people who claimed esoteric advancement.* From the first, Ossian had made it clear that he did not always wish to share his trips abroad with Charlotte, so it happened that she was free to accompany me. We had heard that the founder of the group was a man who worked with a 'hermetic wife':* together they led the Snake Dance* which brought down the Light to their neophytes—in so far as these could follow the intricate steps of the adepts. Anyone could participate or attempt to do so—anyone, that is, who found the way to the dancing-floor.

This arena was a circular plain of flattened ground about half-way up the side of a hill where the local peasantry had once been used to thresh their corn: hence the pallid earth was beaten almost to the consistency of stone. On two-thirds of the circumference it was surrounded by rocks, the dry stems of scrub and herbage, which would give off an aroma of mastic in the air of summer's end; on the remaining third, the hillside fell steeply away seaward. The evening when Charlotte and I arrived there the August moon illuminated a landscape, itself harshly lunar, with a frigid intensity. A score or so of aspirants were waiting for their Shiva Nataraja and his Shakti* to arrive; but it was difficult to judge their number, still less their character, since all were seated and the stony underbrush that bordered the threshing-floor gave them cover. Charlotte and I took our place unobtrusively amongst them.

We waited five minutes, ten minutes, a quarter of an hour; still nothing happened. No one spoke, no one moved, all sat huddled in a chained expectancy, broken occasionally by a sigh of frustration. One could sense rather than see that eyes had begun to burn, cheeks to grow flushed; but none took the initiative. In the silence one could hear the lapping of waves on the shore far below.

I could endure the tension no longer; I rose, followed by Charlotte, and stepped out to the centre of the floor. I don't know how, but the movements of the Snake Dance came to me as from the memory of a distant past; once I had begun to sway there was no hesitation—I was incapable of making a mistake in the figures as I was of breaking off before completion. The spectators sprang up and pressed forward to the edge of the floor; a circle of stamping feet and clapping hands was soon marking the rhythm for me. Charlotte, inspired by my confidence, followed well enough; and at the climax we both obtained the Light. This irradiation was not interior only; still less was it merely symbolic, for all those present were witness to the splendour that, as we danced, descended upon us, and reached out to the edge of the circle to touch all with its further rays. So dazzling was its golden glow that it outshone the beams of moonlight which, before its advent, had seemed brilliant.

As it faded* and we retired to our seats, a tall man with a fresh complexion, dressed like a fisherman in blue dungarees, emerged from the wilderness.* Our tardy hierophant seemed disconcerted to find that we were already self-initiated and therefore, as of right, members of his inner conclave. Seeing his perturbation, I said:

"If you feel it will be difficult to work with us, we'll stand down."

But he knew that this was impossible, so gave us a grudging welcome. There was no sign of his partner, and I guessed that her absence and his late arrival were connected. He was careful to assure us that we had only made a beginning; our subsequent test would be much harder, a battle rather than a dance—the trial of the cage of holly-stems,* through which the candidate must fight his way up in stages.

He then showed us a diagram* of a branching tree which grew diagonally across the page and ended in a small head or bud wearing a crown and surrounded with stars. The main trunk of this tree indicated the path of attainment favoured by his particular praxis; the life of the ordinary human being was shown to the left of it, at the bottom; while on the lower part of the diagram to the right was marked the way of lonely self-knowledge. I felt that I had gone some little distance along this latter path also; but I must later have been daunted by the holly-stem cage since I was unable to implement my first success and to achieve completely in the Fisherman's method of development. In that of solitary introspection, also, I found I could not go on.

All this was a long time ago, and seems longer than it was. Everything that happened before I came to Ménec as a Postulant is seen as through torn clouds, which half-disclose a distant panorama. The people who know us best call our Order the Convents of the Secret Room. Essentially, we pursue the same course as the Fisherman but more gradually, and I suppose for this reason it is better suited to some natures.

When I look back, I see that it was through Charlotte that I was led eventually to our Order. She had at that time been married for some years and the children were already at school, when Ossian announced his desire for reception into the Church. Whatever his motives—and he certainly graced a circle whose interests were boy-sopranos and ecclesiastical millinery—this was no mere whim, and he showed perseverance in bringing about his objective. Charlotte, as she had reminded me only yesterday, had felt obliged to follow him; she attended his 'instructions' and together they met priests, visited monks, talked and read voluminously about their prospective spiritual home. It was a long time before they were brought to a decision, chiefly because Charlotte asked all the awkward questions that reluctant converts do ask, and was never more than partly satisfied by the answers she received. Nor was Ossian, to do him justice, a facile catechumen; but though he did not look forward to his conversion, neither did he, once it was an accomplished fact, look back from it to his unfettered years. If, while still only a possibility on the horizon it had seemed to him as doom-laden as a storm-cloud, when past, it was accepted with a cheerful fatalism. In time he came to take his religion for granted as a necessary adjunct to his life but scarcely more disturbing than a table or bath.

I watched the Mortimores' progress, if such it was, at a slight remove since, having been born into the Church myself though far from always content in it, their soul-wrestling appeared to me as antic contortion. Nor was I impressed by the directors who proposed themselves, or whom the couple proposed, as their spiritual guides—these often reminded me of the Blind leading the Blind in Brueghel's picture.* Yet there was one who stood apart from the rest, a Brother of the Ultramontane Order* which is devoted to the restoration of temporal power to the Papacy. I always wondered how a character of such simplicity, which would have been at ease in Franciscan* meagreness and merriment, had gravitated to an Order with comparatively mundane aims. Brother Constantine Jaquasse* possessed so little social front as to seem naïf; he was so completely without pretension that this in itself gave one a feeling of goodness. His spontaneity was disarming and if it was sometimes unconventional, I never heard of anyone who misinterpreted it. He gave no thought to appearances and was not afraid to hug people if he felt inclined; he hugged me when we first met amid the modish bric-a-brac of Charlotte's living-room. Charlotte had already given me engaging reports of him; she was touched by his natural holiness though herself still holding aloof from his creed. As she told me, he spent all his allowance on other people so never had any money for himself. He did not preach at people but supplied their needs as far as he was able.

In the town near where he lived were three low dives—a restaurant, a cafe and a night-club—situated in different localities though not far distant from one another; all had an unsavoury reputation. Brother Jaquasse visited the night-club in the early hours of one morning and found, amid the smoke of reefers and the jazzy din of a radiogram,* several young men who had drunk too much but not eaten enough. He gave them four boxes of cornflakes and other groceries which he had bought for himself.

Ultramontanes don't always live in community; some at least are encouraged to mix in the world, presumably in pursuance of the Order's main objective. (Though they have been accused in some quarters of political intrigue, in others their aims are considered too fantastic to be taken seriously and their influence written off as unlikely to sway the course of international events). Thus it was that Brother Jaquasse was not, at this time, sharing in the common life of his Order but was staying with three sisters, well-to-do maiden ladies of uncertain age. All rode like Valkyries,* and spent most of their time hunting and attending race-meetings. He seemed happy with them in the country, their house being situated outside the town which was the usual scene of his duties: and was amused at their eccentricities which often amounted to mania. All were large-bodied and of striking appearance: one was dark, one fair and the third, who looked like an ageing tart, dyed her hair red and oiled it in order to make it darker. He confided to me that, if he were not a religious, he too would have preferred some calling connected with horses. He was small of build with brilliant blue eyes.

"I expect it is because you really love people that you are able to help them," I remarked.

Brother Jaquasse returned a disclaimer that I felt to be genuinely modest.

"But the Gospels say that you should love everyone, and you must believe that," I teased.

Brother Jaquasse produced a telescope from beneath his soutane and through it looked into my eyes: he often used such whimsical devices to impress his words on those he was trying to assist. I felt that he could see into my inmost being, knew everything about me and accepted all, liking me despite my imperfections. Here, I thought, was someone who could help me.

"You have a good heart but too avid an intelligence," he said. "Do you know the Parthenogenesists? If you could follow their rule you might find peace."

"I'm not suited to a religious life; I've no vocation."

"I am not so sure about that; the Parthenogenesists are very tolerant," he added with a twinkle.

"They wouldn't tolerate Ella!" snapped Charlotte, jealous that her priest-of-the-moment was taking an interest in me.

Nevertheless it must have been through his good offices that, some while later, I was conditionally accepted into this Order and sent to the Ianua Vitae Convent on the Island of Ménec to begin my Postulancy. I stayed at first for a few days at a lodging-house in the hamlet of Kervin-Brigitte while one or two legal questions regarding the disposal of my property were straightened out. Though I had told my friends that I should be making only a short retreat and would not be away longer than a week, I had already decided that I would not return to the world.

It was a lovely morning, my first on the island, and I emerged from my lodging in a light summer dress. I set out to cross the channel which divided me from the convent buildings. The surface of the earth was strewn with granite boulders—black traversed by seams of glinting quartz, the monstrous contrast of nightmare—and with pebbles ground smooth by the action of numberless tides. Workmen were busy making a path from these rocks, and since the previous evening they had so much altered the course of the channel that it was now too wide for me to jump. The well-built foreman in charge of them, seeing my predicament, deputed one of his men to show me the way round: and two of them, both handsome in the blue-eyed island-type, immediately offered to do so. Once they had indicated the way to me, the crossing of the water-course was easy.

I was admitted to the building by the Porteress and shown into a waiting room—aptly named, since I was there left to myself for the statutory twenty minutes* which elapses before an interview with any inmate of a religious house. The décor also conformed to type, the style being that of a bourgeois parlour towards the end of last century—plush table-cloth with chenille fringes, holy oleographs,* lace curtains and artificial flowers. When the Porteress returned, it was to conduct me to a small room adjoining; and to give me instructions to change into the uniform of a Postulant which I should find there. In our Order, Postulants are provided with a simple dress of charcoal-grey wool with a thin black kerchief for the head, but no veil or wimple. These latter are conferred, with our characteristic green habit, at the Novice 'Clothing.'

I was now led up a well-carpeted stairway, passing a small chapel on the mezzanine-floor where a nun's obsequies were about to take place. Round the bier candles shone, incense burned and bunches of rue for *aspergilla** lay beside bowls of consecrated water. From a side-corridor two blond nuns in white, members perhaps of some Order other than that of the Parthenogenesis, led out a procession of Sisters walking in couples, most of whom were wearing black.

"They are special habits for the Requiem," Sister Porteress whispered.

The line swayed as though in a moving train though this sign of grief, if it were such, was the only one visible. A pimply theological-student trying to marshal the nuns took hold of the shoulder of one immediately following the leaders in white, steadying it for a moment back and front between his two hands. As she passed me, this nun's face wore a withdrawn expression, as though she were enduring the contact for the sake of the procession's good order. It was my first sight of Sister Mary Paracelsus.

"He doesn't know about her vow to let no one at all touch her," explained my mentor.

"They are the equivalent of professional mourners,"* was the thought that crossed my mind.

I would have liked to accompany them, but my guide hurried me forward, up another short flight of stairs and along a corridor. Here at a wide window she bade me pause and look out. The view of the island-shore at this point was not rocky but level to the water's edge and lightly wooded; the coastline curved round to make a lagoon on the opposite margin on which stood a row of small towers, each in its garden-plot and backed by a spinney of larches. Each tower, like the main building of the convent itself, consisted of three storeys but here the top one was partly open to the air and partly covered by an acorn-shaped dome. Below this was a single large room, and then a darkish room on the ground floor which I took to be a kitchen and store-house. The whole structure, I was told, was in fact the "cell" of a nun, who lived there as a self-supporting anchoress.*

"We call them *Les Tourettes,*"* the Sister Porteress informed me.

"That is where I belong," I decided. Each of these Sisters had her own "ivory tower"; and I remembered that this phrase had not always carried its modern sense of condescension—implying that introversion is less than respectable—but that it derived from the adulations of

Turris eburnea
Domus aurea
Foederis arca
*Ianua Coeli**

"They are much further advanced in spirituality than the rest of us," warned my guide. "They are very ascetic; they sit for hours in the loggia at the top, whatever the weather."

This was often wet, as I had already noticed; indeed a light drizzle was falling at the moment.

"I don't see how one can meditate better by sitting in a pool of water," I objected.

"A kind of basin-seat is provided, that can swivel round," explained the Porteress, and in fact it seemed that I could see something of the kind in one or two top-storeys. I accepted for the moment that the contraption might improve matters but later, when I tried to think it out, I could not see that it did so.

Nor could I guess what was engaging the minds of those few silent figures as they sat gazing out upon the grey incoming waters which at high tide almost lapped the base of their turrets. At low tide instead of water, stretches of sand offered themselves to their contemplation. My first glimpse of the turrets had made me feel that I had come home, but now I began to have doubts.

Further down the corridor hung a large photograph of several Sisters walking up a forest-path: they were wearing dark hoods and cloaks, different from our present-day habit. Their faces seemed to glow with a superhuman beauty: traces of an aureole even were to be seen round one or two of the heads.

"That is Ste. Ermengilde, our Foundress, with some of the earliest members of our Order," declared the Porteress.

"But it can't be!" I exclaimed. "Ste. Ermengilde lived long before the days of photography. It's intriguing but it's obviously a fake. Those branches now, they've been 'interpreted' to look like the heads of youths; and the whole thing has a Pre-Raphaelite air."*

Sister Porteress did not argue; she merely stated, "Ste. Ermengilde is for ever," and carried me on to my ordained appointment.

On the first floor we arrived at a large room with many windows which I took to be the refectory, though it was much less austere than I expected. Indeed, all this wing of the building had rather the air of a country hotel than of a convent. My guide bade me enter: I saw nuns grouped round a table, waiting. From among them Mother Ste. Barbe,* Superior of the Ianua Vitae, rose at once to welcome me. She looked small in her habit, and her face wore a sweet expression as she greeted me like an old and valued friend.

Involuntarily I cried, "Do you know me?"

"You have such a noble face," she responded, "that I feel sure you will one day be head of a community."

"But do you know who I am?" I persisted.

She seemed baffled as she replied, "I've lectured to you."

"Where?"

One of the other nuns, a younger, large-boned woman in close attendance on Mother Ste. Barbe, whom I soon came to recognise as the Mother Vicaress,* interposed to save her Superior embarrassment, saying it must have been at Oxford or Cambridge. I formed the opinion that she had made herself indispensable to Reverend Mother by relieving her of all practical details.

"I'm only asking," I told her, "because I thought Reverend Mother might be confusing me with a cousin who is rather like me."

"There is too much 'I' and 'me' in your conversation," Mother Vicaress rebuked me.

"What else can I use? The Papal 'we' is hardly appropriate, and the impersonal 'one' sounds a bit precious."

"It will be some little while before you grow accustomed to our ways."

During this exchange Mother Ste. Barbe, seemingly deaf to our words and bemused by prevision, reiterated what she had said about my noble appearance.

There followed a simple luncheon at one of the long tables; I was directed to a place of honour between Reverend Mother and Mother Vicaress. I realised that I should not occupy so exalted a position again for many a long day. Already Mother Vicaress seemed concerned to find fault with me on minor points—for instance, on my putting a finger through a slit in the embroidery of the large table-mat, evidently an antique, which had been laid under my plate. I felt it was unfair of her to pick on me, when this fidgeting on my part was due to nervousness at the impending crisis in my life. Her criticisms were usually followed by a mirthless chuckle.

"You and I will never agree," I thought; but aloud I merely made some general remark about its being better to look at the large intent rather than to concern oneself with trifles. She did not seem put out, nor in any way affected by this.

After the meal, I made my excuses and went over to another table where the lawyer was waiting to talk to me. I suggested that we could discuss our problems more easily if we returned to my lodging, and he agreed. Outside, the foreman was still standing about and looked surprised when he noticed my change of attire. I drew from his presence a subtle current of vitality. I realised that in my new life I was going to miss male companionship more than I had thought for. Within the walls of the Ianua Vitae brooded a rarefied air that already I began to find suffocating: outside I breathed more freely, and I made the most of my brief respite.

Some boys who were trundling ancient bicycles from a shed, paused in their chatter to look at what the workmen had been doing.

"Is there a school here?" I called out, and one replied:

"There are four—we go to the one for Public School rejects!"*

I gathered from their talk that there was also an elementary school, a grammar-school, and another for handicapped or backward children, and I supposed that there must be some men teachers, as well as the nuns.

As the lawyer and I mounted the stairs to my musty room, there was a sound of wailing and moaning; a child passed us crying 'Aha!' many times. This I understood to be a secret signal or pass-word, AH-HA; or perhaps even an omen. On the table in my room lay some letters, all opened except one, which was from the lawyer himself. I now drew it from the envelope and found it was a greeting-card of elaborate design with cut-out frames, depicting a drinking-scene in a mediaeval tavern, and containing a scribbled message of good wishes for my new life.

At the Ianua Vitae, though far removed from the heady triumphs of the Snake Dance, our life is not without its moments of perturbation; that, for instance, when we were in choir for the visit of the Bishop of Orascoule, who had come over from the mainland to celebrate Mass in our convent-church. This is a larger building than the healing-chapel which I had pointed out to Charlotte on her arrival: and on certain feast-days it is thronged with the island-workers in their traditional costume. This occasion was the feast of carpenters and bakers, so wood-work and bread-making formed part of the ceremonies. On Ménec more than in most regions there linger echoes of that golden age when the practice of a craft was itself a way of initiation,* before modern industry crushed even the possibility of this.

The Bishop was beginning to speak.

"Hatred and creation are linked," he was declaring, when a huge bubble-like form produced itself from the top of a cupboard near the vestry-door. It extruded a narrow pipe of ectoplasmic* material, and remained there until he finished his address. I don't know what else he said, for I was too fascinated by the sight of this phenomenon to listen; but to judge from his opening remark, the rest of the homily may have been stimulating. Being still only a Novice at the time, I kept a tactful silence about what I had seen.

On another occasion when I was herding, I must have let the cattle stray further than usual, and had crossed the boundary into the island's most remote parish. I came to a granite church on a hillock above a hamlet of low grey-and-white houses. It was an autumn day, and the scent of burning wood issued from their chimneys in a lichen-tinted plume which bent before the western breeze. The breath of the dead, hanging about the pale shadows of the church's interior, seeped outward to the tree-girt vicinity, where the living too were caught up in a trance of suspended animation.

I had never seen a Gothick interior with so many corbel-heads;* and in all their faces a family likeness could be traced. It was as if the unknown sculptor had taken as model the features of the minor nobility whose dead lay in these vaults. Men, women or monsters, these carvings all wore an expression of serene expectancy, their blank eyes looking outwards to the infinite. The head, whether crowned, coiffed, bearded or horrifically lolling-tongued, stretched forward on a neck half-turned—still at peace, but waiting. For what did they watch and listen? The last day, the resurrection of their bones and flesh; they waited unappeased by their life of shades with its too-subtle senses: they starved upon the bouquet of wines and of blood, the perfume of honey and incense, deprived too by the like attentions of touch and sound which were their lot. They longed for their bodies, yet with a calm that was almost resignation, their ears are strained for the first flourish of Gabriel's trumpet.*

Wanting to know more of the place's history, I approached a cottage-gate where a man was working in the garden. His dog barked boisterously, and he dropped the sack he was carrying—as I thought, to come and speak to me. But instead he disappeared into the house and did not return, while a woman drew a curtain further across the window.

I tried another cottage, which seemed to be also the Post Office: here too the ground-floor windows were closely curtained, and there was no reply. Next, I rang the bell of a larger house where some windows were open—it might have been the Presbytery—and a door leading from the front garden through a wall to the southern lawn. Again a dog barked, this time from the depths of the house, but no one answered my summons.

The west door of the church suddenly opened and a procession emerged headed by three priests whom I recognised as frequent celebrants at our own convent-church, though now they were wearing black out-door clothes and hats. The one in the centre was carrying on high a dead chicken by the legs, which he was supposed to have slaughtered as a climax to the ritual. I wondered whether he had actually done this, since the bird looked as though it had already been plucked at a poulterer's, having only a feather boa left around the neck.

At a casual encounter on the road returning, I asked what name was on the place, telling how I could make no one hear, but not mentioning the procession. The answer was, "Ah, that is Michael Penmarch,"*—which means

'Horse-Head'—as though the name explained everything. Yet the site, in spite of its elevation, did not remind me of others sacred to St. Michael, most of which are windy and open to the sun.* Rather was it Western Gabriel* who reigned there; from the coolness of water in a sea-creek hidden by the vegetation, and from the tall enclosing trees, Gabriel was gathering his as-yet unspoken message.

I must have missed the path, for I found myself urging the cattle through a small fair, with booths along the lane. One of the side-shows consisted in aiming three elongated triangles of silver-like metal at a coloured design set up on a board as target. This represented a geometrical star-shape: it was not necessary to throw the triangular darts at it—indeed, they also were fixed at the base of the board. By means of some obscure magnetism jetting out from their apices to the target was the diagram traced.

I realised, as I made my way back to the Ianua Vitae, that the fair must be connected with the sacrifice of the chicken, both being relics of a festival of the Autumn Equinox which the Church had done her best to incorporate.

Our convent-church is of cathedral-like proportions and contains many works of art and curios from different epochs. When I had any time to spare I would make my way there and wander round the interior, looking at its treasures. Sometimes I would encounter the Chaplain who came regularly to the convent to hear our confessions; on these visits he would wear ordinary clerical garb though he was, I knew, a religious from one of the island's communities. He was a man of about sixty years of age with the face of a scholar, lined and pallid, and with thinning hair that had once been black. At first his manner to me was distant if not disapproving; but gradually he became more friendly.

One day I lingered in the adjoining graveyard to pick some flowers—late primroses that were turning puce-coloured—and I had gathered a bunch before noticing the watchful gaze of the Chaplain upon me. He did not reprove me directly but remarked that boys sometimes came out from the town of Ménec to steal the flowers. At this I felt bound to apologise, though I added in mitigation that they were wild and in any case their roots had not been disturbed.

I then entered the building and sought my favourite among the larger side-chapels which housed, behind its altar, certain objects of beaten metal.* These were traditional images, rather less than a metre in height, of the sun and moon—the sun of gold and the moon of silver, a crescent with a face in profile. Near them hung a portrait of a Church-dignitary connected with our Order in former times who had invented a portable appliance to bring the luminaries into conjunction, no matter where on earth one happened to be. This was only achieved if the instrument was correctly calibrated, a process not easy to understand or to regulate. I seated myself on a throne facing the back of the altar so that I could contemplate the heavenly representations.

Later, when examining the altar-stone itself I saw that it was moveable and could be made to reveal a tank of water below: the altar was in fact a cistern. Having an impulse to relieve myself, brought on no doubt by excitement and a sense of expectancy, I used it as a lavatory. Needing paper with which to wipe myself, I found one or two old letters forgotten in an inner pocket and tore them into scraps, each about the size of a franc-piece, and pressed a handful against my bottom. I then threw them into the water and replaced the flat stone; there was a sound of flushing.

People were now moving about in the church, Sisters of our community and villagers from the neighbouring regions; but no one seemed to hear the sound of the rushing water or to have noticed what I had done. I wondered whether the handwriting of the letters, a Victorian copper-plate in fading sepia ink, might not serve as a clue to trace my sacrilegious action? I did not know where the fragments might be carried.

The Chaplain now reappeared, but his uncensorious attitude suggested that he had not witnessed my behaviour, or if he had, was not scandalised by it. Indeed, his manner held more than his wonted affability as he inquired if there were any period of the church's antiquities which I wanted especially to study? I replied, The Medieval, indicating the sun-and-moon appliance; and he promised to arrange for it to be explained to me.

He then asked whether I had any perplexity or question regarding Catholic doctrine? I answered No, the only question worth asking was how to become enlightened and no one could tell one that. He nodded his head in sombre agreement.

Other incidents which occurred in the first days of my Postulancy I well remember. I regret to say that my motives for entering conventual life were not of the highest: I wanted to spy, it seems to me now, to find out—what was it?—about something or someone. But perhaps I am not now doing myself justice, for what I experienced was in fact a desire for knowledge of the fundamentals of life, the unconscious, dreams and the soul's intercarnate phases,* presented to myself under these crude symbols.

When I first arrived at the Ianua Vitae, I was met by Sister Mary Paracelsus who was in charge of Novices and Postulants. She took me up to the attics which were rather dark, having dormer windows and ceilings that sloped, and told me that I might choose among several of these the one I preferred for my cell. There was little enough to choose between them, all being equally austere in their furnishings: they did, however, contain beds with sheets and covers, at which I felt relief, having half-expected what some Orders give one, namely, a sack of straw and a few grubby rugs. I quickly selected a cell where the bed did not face the window since the curtaining of all was inadequate.

It seemed that this room was a favourite, however, for two Novices at once entered, demanding to share it with me. One of them, whom I was afterwards to know as Sister Mary Fursey,* even wished to share the bed. I protested, and the Novice-Mistress agreed with me; so the two intruders were obliged to ensconce themselves elsewhere. As I was bestowing the very few possessions I had been allowed to bring with me, scarcely more than a toothbrush and a bowl for consecrated water, the future Sister Fursey and her companion re-entered the room. They told me to hurry as we had, in company with other Postulants, Novices and their relatives, to attend a meeting in the main hall; and they had been deputed to show me the way. Their tone was one of subdued gaiety, without any resentment at my victory in the matter of the cell.

The convent-buildings rambled over a considerable area of ground; they seemed scarcely to have been planned, but to have grown together by chance. My guides told me that the main hall was somewhere at the centre of these structures, but even they didn't seem too sure of the way. Sister Fursey took the lead, making us scramble through byeways and over all sorts of hazards, finally telling us to climb a wall. This seemed an unreasonable demand, encumbered as we were by our habits; and I refused to attempt it. She insisted, so I lost patience entirely and struck her face. This assault she took in such good part that she might have been expecting it, our previous divagations having been, perhaps, some kind of test. But a test of what? Obedience, or commonsense? If the former I had certainly failed: if the latter, I was successful.

However this was, Sister Fursey agreed to take us another way round; she was possibly influenced by the re-appearance of the Novice-Mistress who, though she supported my refusal, engaged afterwards in an amicable discussion with Sister Fursey about her studies, telling her that she was on the contemplative line. Sister Mary Paracelsus was pre-occupied also about a sea-bathe which she had intended to take that evening; but she thought it might be too late for this after the assembly. The atmosphere of these conversations seemed to me like that of a girls' boarding school; no doubt I was judging hastily.

We scurried up a grassy lane and across a road; by this time it was growing dusk. Suddenly we came upon a group of what I took at first to be dwarfs, or even Korrigans,* dancing in couples on the grass-verge. They were all much of a height, but on looking more closely I saw that they were not dwarfs but children, the little girls having padded their bosoms to look adult.

"They come from our orphanage," Sister Mary Paracelsus explained.

"Isn't it long after their bed-time?" inquired Sister Fursey.

"It must be, but it's not my duty to nag them. Too often as it is we break the childhood-dream," the Novice-Mistress added with a sigh.

We stood watching their capers until it was almost dark. I asked Sister Mary Paracelsus to give us a light, and she produced several electric torches from beneath her robes, shining them in various directions. The children scattered with bird-like cries, and we were enabled to pick out the main building just ahead of us, which was circular in shape and constructed of dark red brick. In the centre of this was the hall where Postulants and Novices were to meet for prayers and a lecture. Not all of them were devout for I had heard, before leaving our quarters, one or two of them groaning at the imposition upon them of this devotion beyond the prescribed Office.

We entered the hall, which was furnished with long benches like a class-room, and sat down to wait. Not until then did I notice the beauty of the other Novice (not Sister Fursey) who had come with us. She was sitting a row in front of me and a little to one side; her skin was of that clear colour which often goes with auburn hair—though of course no hair was to be seen—and her eyes too were of a deep red-brown.

Though I knew that this assembly-hall was not the Secret Room, I realised in a flash the inner truth towards which the Rule of the community was directed. This was no less than the mystery of Parthenogenesis,* wherein the lunar soul that perceives and feels is fertilised—a long eclipse over—by rays from its own hidden sun, to bring forth at last the radiant Child. All our members were aspiring to this, though none had the clue that might enable them to achieve it.

4

CONJUNCTION

Despite the shortening of the days, our evenings seemed to extend themselves into a twilit reverie more prolonged even than in summer. The sun-light permeating the haze that hung over everything cast a silver spell: space lost some of its definition, time slowed down, voices were hushed in the unmoving air. The seventh of October, feast of the Holy Rosary—*Rozero,* as we call it—had come with scarcely a chill in the dew; benign weather promised a blessing on our yearly Festival. Symbol of this halcyon interlude was, not the kingfisher but the redbreast, his autumnal southward-flitting delayed by the warmth, who followed one with his poignant trill from cloister to barn, from meadow to orchard, his plumage resuming in itself the tints of leaf and berry.

Ménec has never been developed as a resort for the average tourist: nevertheless, among the pilgrims who cultivate our healing shrine there are always a few who combine with their devotions a St. Martin's summer holiday.

Charlotte had followed my suggestion and was remaining with us until the Festival at least. She had become more tranquil of late, perhaps influenced by the still weather and our simple routine. She had no financial worries, since hospitality is one of our traditions and we offered her board and lodging, such as they were, without payment. No one asked her whether she had written to her Bank; in any case, a reply might be some time in arriving at this remote retreat. I had the impression that she wished to lie hidden and so was less than anxious to communicate with the outside world.

My programme was full, what with the Office, study and chores in and around the convent; so apart from my herding-times there was little opportunity to speak to her. She would wander about the island, sometimes taking with her a mid-day snack, and return only in time for the evening meal. She never bestirred herself to attend an early Mass, but sometimes she would be seen sitting near the back of the church at Compline or Vespers,* a strand of black gauze draped over her head. Mother Vicaress was troubled, and perhaps annoyed, by Charlotte's lack of occupation.

"I think she should be assigned some task," I overheard her say to Reverend Mother.

"Pressure of any kind would not be helpful, in her state," was the reply. "Still less, compulsion. But I will suggest that she design a new under-garment for the Sisters. I have felt for some time that we should have something less bulky than what we have worn hitherto."

So during the next few days Charlotte busied herself with scribbling sketches, and cutting and sewing scraps of cloth provided by the linen-room. She finally evolved a forerunner of the body-stocking which she showed me with pride.

"D'you think it's altogether practical?" I demurred. "It looks to me like the converse of the dinner-gown Ossian once designed for easy love-making."

"O, I knew you'd tell me it would be awkward—but in most religious houses one only drinks at fixed hours and it must be the same here."

"Yes, at breakfast and in the evening, with a sup of water in between if necessary."

"Well, then! And some nature-cure adherents recommend a liquid-free diet. All the fluid one needs can be absorbed from salads and fresh fruit."

"But we don't get enough of those here. You can't combine the two systems."

Charlotte ripped up her model in an access of fury; and that was the end of work-therapy for her.

I daresay she was lonely; she was certainly delighted when she met some acquaintances among the first pilgrim-arrivals.

She peered round the still-room door one evening when I was trying to sweep and tidy after one of Sister Mary Paracelsus' busy days with the herbs.

"Dr. Wiseacre is here!" she exclaimed.

"Who is he?" I asked. I didn't know many of Charlotte's friends, not having been in touch with her since before my reception into the Order of the Parthenogenesis.

"Why, you know that terrible migraine I used to have? He made it so much better; I went to the hospital where he works—I was there several months as an outpatient. But that was a couple of years ago."

"And now he's not too well himself?"

"That's it: he has come mainly for the cure."

This news didn't surprise me, because members of the medical profession sometimes resort to us when other treatments have failed—though they usually come incognito, fearing the ridicule of sceptical colleagues.

"You recognised him at once?"

"Oh yes, but I've promised not to tell anyone he's a doctor—except you, of course," she added hastily.

I felt that Dr. Wiseacre's secret was by no means safe, but said nothing.

"Poor man!" Charlotte sighed. "He always overworked, and now he's suffering from anaemia and nervous exhaustion. He has terrible nightmares too, he was telling me; really, I almost felt as if I were the doctor, or at least psychologist, and he the patient!"

Charlotte was beginning to sound like her old self; however ill her doctor-friend was, he could still, apparently, do her good.

"My brother went to the same hospital for his ulcer," she chattered on. "Quite natural, like two members of a family going to the same university! Keith used to give me news of Dr. Wiseacre; there's no place like a hospital for gossip, except, of course, a convent!—everyone there knew he believed in 'water cures' and had visited a sacred spring in Cyprus the year before."

"What, the Bath of Venus?"*

"Yes, I think so; other wells too. He had been taking 'baptismal waters,' Keith was told; though whether he drank them or bathed in them I don't know."

"Either way, they don't seem to have done the trick."

It's a nice point, the correct attitude for us to adopt towards miraculous happenings in the Eastern Churches: Lourdes and Fatima are one thing, but the Black Madonna of Tenos,* which is supposed to talk, and the well of 'Ste. Salomoné' are another. It's not for me to decide on their relative merits but, being what I am, I have to avoid sailing near the wind of heresy.

"Perhaps our ceremonies will be more effective," I suggested guardedly. "We may see your friends when we are next out herding," I added, but without enthusiasm. I was bored with Charlotte's talk of the Doctor, though I did not want to wet-blanket an interest which had put new life into her. Not noticing my ennui, or else indifferent to it, she went on describing him.

To Charlotte, Dr. Wiseacre looked younger than when she had last seen him, if not healthier: his skin, though less crêpey, was polished to a waxen smoothness that disquieted her. She had remarked also for the first time that one of his upper front teeth was a false one—when he smiled, the edge where it joined the gum was visibly discoloured. Despite this, she relished his brief kiss and the tweedy whiff of his suit which proximity brought her. He had spoken to her eagerly yet hesitantly: she could tell, she said, that he wanted to become better acquainted.

"Where is he staying?" I inquired, less out of curiosity than courtesy.

"He's taken one of those villas beyond the hotel and brought his family: I suppose they don't bother too much about schooling; anyway the younger boy isn't quite—"

Before she could finish the sentence there was a knock on the door and Dr. Wiseacre himself entered, clad in a white gown; but this was the one we provide for ritual immersion, not his accustomed hospital-coat. He was a well-built man in the late forties who must have seemed handsome, especially to women who admire a woodenly-masculine type. Beneath an all-but impermeable mask lurked the sore soul of the refugee; it had cost him an effort to anglicise Weitzäke to Wiseacre for, while he realised the advantages of a Teutonic name in the medical world, he yet chose the symbol of a more complete social assimilation. The set of his eyebrows made him look Mongolian rather than Semitic; he remained attractive, though the blondish hair had faded and there was a darkness under the skin that was almost green. Charlotte's cheek-bones flushed as she introduced him.

"I would much like you to take us on the Little Pilgrimage,"* she said diffidently.

"I also," said the Doctor.

This was a round of the smaller springs usually patronised by people for their private devotions as a preliminary to the communal celebrations, which culminate with a special Vespers held at Our Lady of the Trees.

It was plain that the Doctor was anxious to set off at once; impatient gestures broke through his assumed stolidity of manner. As it happened, I could spare half-an-hour to accompany them, though I was doubtful whether he had reckoned on my presence. But as neither had made the pilgrimage before, both may have felt self-conscious and glad of a guide.

There are several wells possessing curative properties in different parts of the convent precincts; Charlotte and I led the Doctor to a sloping field below the knoll known as the Mont Ste. Anne. Here a spring bubbles up to make a sandy pool where devotees can bathe, while to the right of it an iron panel covers another small well. Unlike the waters in the Chapel of Trees, these have no specific healing virtues, but are beneficial in a general way, an exception being the one with a heap of rubble to the left of it at the top of the incline. A faintly sinister atmosphere hung about this well and no one would say what good it was supposed to do; but from the fact of its dedication to St. Méen* I guessed that its chief use was in cases of psychological distress, and on this account I had specially recommended it to Charlotte—without giving her my reason.

Even Ménec is not immune from the interference of conservancy authorities; recently they sent some technicians to incorporate our wells into a new development-scheme. I found their men, black with grease, excavating the well-meadow without leave; and I saw to it that the news reached Mother Vicaress, who quickly banished them. In fact there is no need for their activities, since, where necessary, the wells are covered with a metal lid which is only raised on ceremonial occasions; and so the water is kept clean.

During the Festival one of us, usually a Novice or Postulant, is chosen to act as attendant; her duties are to raise the panel and see that a kneeler is in position as each pilgrim approaches to contemplate the water, to wash and to drink. It has to be someone strong, as these lids are heavy; and since our Novices were rather frail this year, Sister Mary Fursey was selected for her peasant stockiness of figure. She succeeded to the unofficial title of 'Sister Well-Meadow' for the duration of the week stretching from the Festival to its octave.

It was sunset by the time our little group reached her; as we trailed, shades among the shadows, toward the sandy pool, a tapestry of sound on a background of distant surf wove itself into our consciousness: furthest away, the exultant screaming of gulls* on an unseen skerry* and the strange laughter of a yaffle* from the narrow valley sloping down to the sea. Nearer, the alarm call of a blackbird sounded along the hedge that bordered the meadow, while titmice twittered up and down the sparse twigs. A linnet chirped from a conifer perpetually bowed to the east by the prevailing wind, now at rest; and across the meadow itself, where a rank growth still bore tufts of plumey seed, goldfinches tinkled their glass-bell cries.

I was about to immerse myself when Sister Fursey reminded me with a restraining touch that I had already done so that morning, and I remembered that more than one bathe a day was not allowed. I retired tactfully as Dr. Wiseacre plunged in: Charlotte shivered, but would have wished to do likewise only that, having been taken by surprise at the still-room door, she had not robed herself appropriately. Instead she followed me as I made my way to the centre of the Meadow, where a minute chapel had been built over a triple well dedicated to Our Lady, Ste. Catherine and Ste. Anne.

On the main wall of the interior, dimly lit by votive candles, a fresco of this feminine trinity* had been painted long ago. In the centre of it reclines the mother, blue-draped and serene as a full moon, nursing the child about whose conception she wrote a poem; on her right kneels Ste. Catherine,* freshly nubile and robed in the pastel tints of spring, holding out a jewel-like heart in exchange for the proffered ring of the child; while to the left stands Ste. Anne, hawk-faced and darkly-cloaked, at once a dignified Mediterranean peasant and Mother-Time. Though stained with smoke and damp, the colour of this painting still held a suggestion of the warm south, and I always looked upon it with pleasure. Yet today it perversely recalled to me that other trinity which, as I knew, was still

74

placated in the peasant-homes of the island—Ankou, the god of death* and his children, Anken and Ankoun, sorrow and oblivion.

The Mont Ste. Anne which loomed above us, looking higher in the dusk than it does in daylight, is still the scene of a midnight bonfire lit by the islanders when the last of our ceremonies have taken place. On Ste. Catherine's day, blazing wheels are still rolled down it from the top, with emulation between the parishes as to whose wheel shall go furthest. Antiquaries have declared* that it's not Ste. Anne's Hill at all, the name being but a monkish corruption of the Hill of Tan, a Gallic fire-divinity. For myself, I can't see that it matters: the main point is to mark the knoll as a holy spot by keeping up the fiery customs associated with it. No doubt its immemorial guardians are gratified, even if their titles change with the passing centuries. Still, I suppose such notions would be officially unacceptable, and for the sake of orthodoxy I don't express them.

Beneath some hawthorn-bushes was a half-hidden spring which did not seem to be included in the prescribed round. Perhaps it yielded insufficient water and so, being shallow, too easily grew muddy. I could not decide whether it was very new or very old—whether it had only just begun to percolate to the surface and had still to attain its full virtue, or whether it was in process of drying up, its underground sources having wandered elsewhere. However this may have been, I saw, one morning early as I was traversing the Meadow, a group of three figures standing beside it. Their green robes and mantles were so light that the air seemed to permeate them: and whether they spoke or not they conveyed to me a message that this was water to heal every ill.

Afterwards I made a point of visiting this spring whenever I could manage to do so, but I did not tell my Superiors anything about it. Thinking over what I had seen, I came to the conclusion that these guardian spirits could not be identified with the figures of the fresco in the Shrine of The Triple Well, for they were all of the same age, young maturity, and all dressed alike. What could Mother Ste. Barbe have made of them? Mother Vicaress would have denounced them in no uncertain terms. Sister Mary Paracelsus perhaps would have understood them; but would she have allowed herself to give in to it?

Presently the Doctor joined us; Sister Fursey, new to her duties, struggled to raise the metal cover for him to kneel. It was a particularly weighty lid, since it covered three wells in one, and even her muscles were unequal to lifting it. We all helped her, pulling and tugging; but it had somehow become jammed in its socket and refused to move. When our efforts proved useless the Doctor hurried away—relieved, perhaps, that he could the sooner change his dripping gown.

Sister Well-Meadow then drew from a niche a sheaf of flowers wrapped in tissue-paper which he had left with her earlier, telling her that he was a market-gardener, a heraldic device adopted to justify the nature of the gift. (What cover-stories medical men invent when they come to us!) He had asked her to present this tribute to Charlotte, who was delighted. The sprays bore clusters of small bells,* and were assorted into shades of acid yellow, shocking-pink and deep red.

"I shall write him an exquisite note of thanks," she cried, "and compliment him on his choice of colours."

Those flowers spoke more clearly than words, even though The Doctor had been, apparently, too self-conscious to present them in person. Charlotte could almost hear him thinking aloud, tentatively suggesting marriage yet still uncertain as to whether she would be suitable. Though she knew his wife was living with him—was, indeed, here with him on Ménec, Charlotte had no doubt that he was planning a divorce of which she, in her present state of mind, would not scruple to take advantage. Even I wondered whether his petitions to Heaven's Queen* had been wholly concerned with his state of health, or whether they had not taken on a more romantic tone. Further, it occurred to me that his ailments and his flirtation with Charlotte were connected, and that by the simple fact of his age: he had reached a time of life when his psycho-physical being was in a state of flux, and when perhaps failing virility needed the stimulus and assurance of fresh conquests. Strange maladies, too, might be expected to accompany unusual emotions. Even so, I wondered how an experienced physician could fail to take Charlotte's neurotic condition as a danger-signal and hesitate before paying court to her. I could only suppose that he found her attraction so intense as to efface all preoccupations, medical or moral, which might counsel caution.

A pilgrimage may bring unlooked-for results.

FIGURE 1   Man Ray, *Ithell Colquhoun*, ca. 1932. Collection
du Centre Pompidou, Mnam / Cci, Paris, AM 1994-394
(3461). © Man Ray Trust / Artists Rights Society
(ARS), N.Y. / ADAGP, Paris

Carnac — Alignements du Ménec

CARNAC. — Dolmen de Cruz-Moquen.

Coll. Z. Le Rouzic

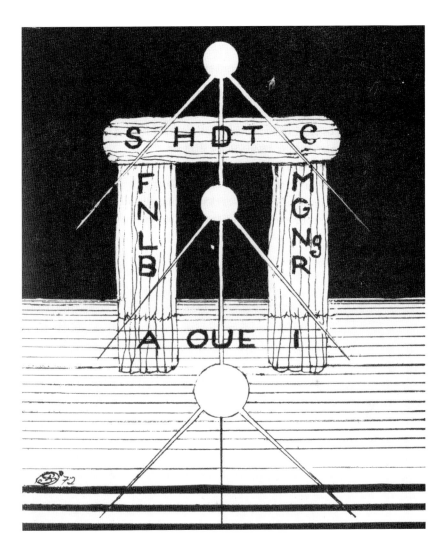

FIGURE 2 (*opposite*) The Neolithic stone rows at Ménec, Brittany. © Collections du Musée de Préhistoire de Carnac. Photo: Z. Le Rouzic, 1920–25

FIGURE 3 (*opposite*) The Neolithic dolmen at Cruz-Moquen, Ménec, Brittany, Christianized by the addition of a stone cross. Before restoration. © Collections du Musée de Préhistoire de Carnac. Photo: Z. Le Rouzic, 1920–25

FIGURE 4 Ithell Colquhoun, *Beth-Luis-Nion on Trilithon*, 1972. Ink on paper. Reproduced in *Grimoire of the Entangled Thicket* (Stevenage: Ore, 1973). Courtesy of the National Trust, U.K.

FIGURE 5 (*opposite*) Ithell Colquhoun, *Dance of the Nine Opals,* 1942. Oil on canvas, 22½ × 28 in. (51 × 69 cm). Courtesy of the National Trust, U.K. Photo: The Sherwin Collection, Leeds, U.K. / The Bridgeman Art Library

FIGURE 6 (*opposite*) Ithell Colquhoun, *Linked Islands II,* 1947. Watercolor and ink on paper, 12¼ × 17½ in. (31.1 × 44.5 cm). Private collection. Courtesy of the National Trust, U.K.

FIGURE 7 Ithell Colquhoun, *Second Adam,* ca. 1942. Watercolor and pencil on paper, 17¾ × 12½ in. (45.7 × 32.4 cm). Tate Archive, Tate Britain, London, TGA 929/4/17/8. © Tate, London 2013. Courtesy of the National Trust, U.K.

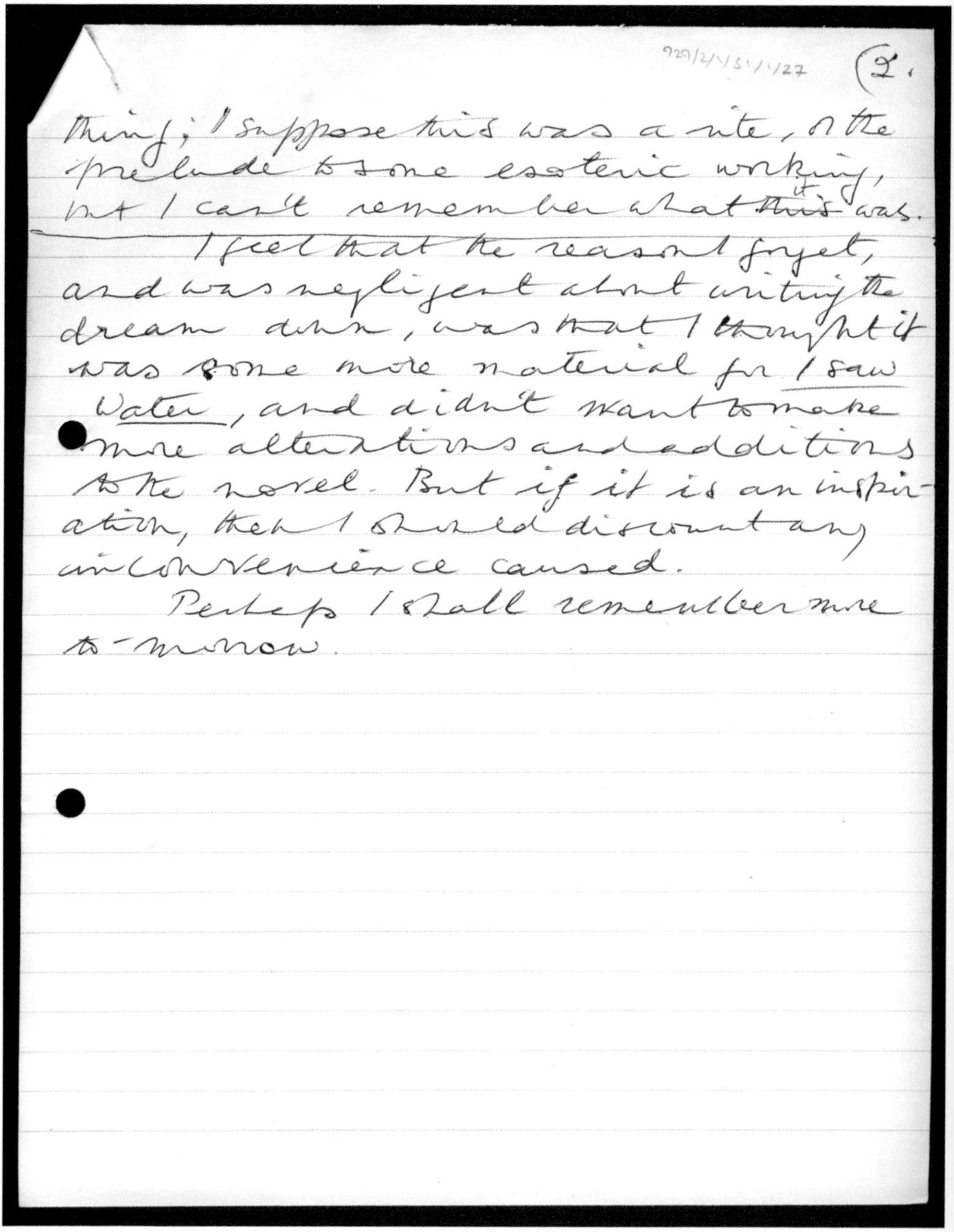

thing; I suppose this was a rite, or the prelude to some esoteric working, but I can't remember what this was.

I feel that the reason I forget, and was negligent about writing the dream down, was that I thought it was some more material for I saw Water, and didn't want to make more alterations and additions to the novel. But if it is an inspiration, then I should discount any inconvenience caused.

Perhaps I shall remember more tomorrow.

FIGURE 8   Ithell Colquhoun, extract from a dream diary, dated June 21, 1964. Tate Archive, Tate Britain, London, TGA 929/2/1/31/1/26. © Tate, London 2013

FIGURE 9   (*opposite*) Ithell Colquhoun, *Un grand invisible*, ca. 1943. Gouache on paper, 9½ × 6½ in. (24.1 × 16.5 cm). National Trust Collection. Courtesy of the National Trust, U.K.

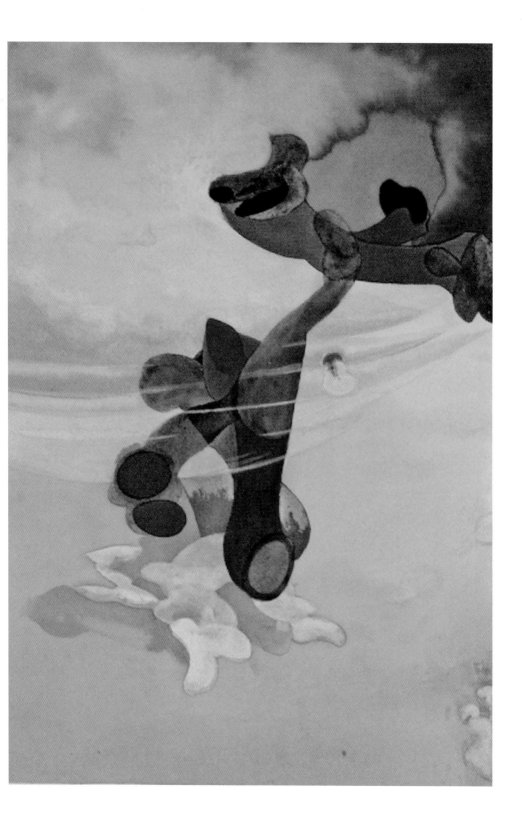

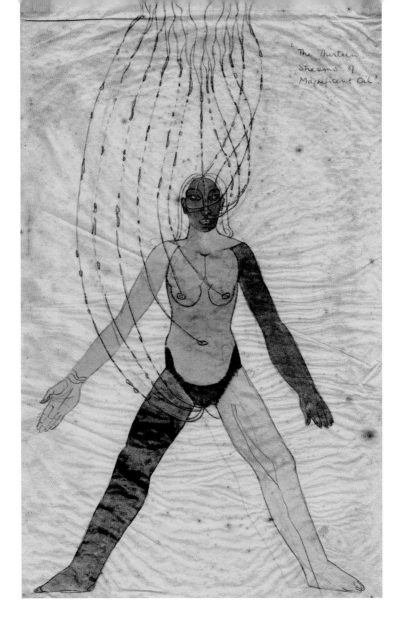

The Thirteen
Streams of
Magnificent Oil

FIGURE 10   (*opposite*) Ithell Colquhoun's scrying mirror.
Convex mirror in beaten copper frame, total diameter 19 in.
(48.3 cm), with umbilical cord. Courtesy of Ben Fernee

FIGURE 11   (*opposite*) Ithell Colquhoun, *Torso*, 1981.
Enamel on board, 10½ × 9¾ in. (26.7 × 25.3 cm). National
Trust Collection. Courtesy of the National Trust, U.K.

FIGURE 12   Ithell Colquhoun, *The Thirteen Streams of
Magnificent Oil*, ca. 1940. Watercolor and pencil on paper,
12¾ × 8 in. (32.7 × 20.7 cm). Tate Archive, Tate Britain,
London, TGA 929/4/17/15. © Tate, London 2013. Courtesy of
the National Trust, U.K.

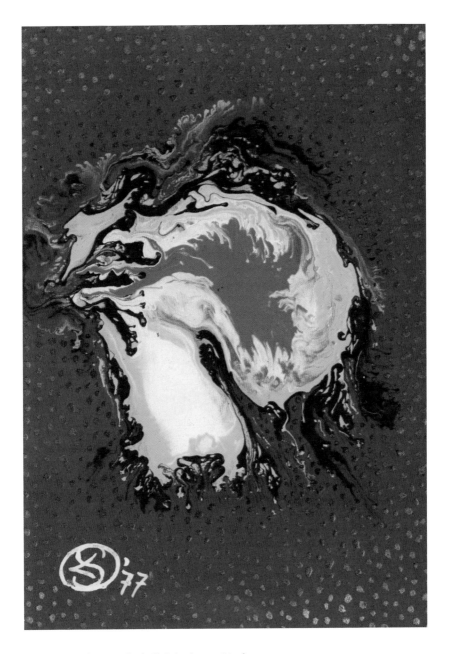

FIGURE 13   (*opposite*) Ithell Colquhoun, *Binah*, 1979.
Enamel on paper, 10 × 6¼ in. (26 × 16.4 cm). National Trust
Collection. Courtesy of the National Trust, U.K.

FIGURE 14   Ithell Colquhoun, *The Lord of the Winds
and the Breezes, the King of the Spirits of Air* [The Prince
of Swords], 1977. Taro card. Enamel on paper, 9 × 6¼ in.
(23 × 16.2 cm). National Trust Collection. Courtesy of the
National Trust, U.K.

5

BOUND

Next evening, the day of my patron, Ste. Brigid, brought me the realisation that the Doctor himself was not the only member of his family to be ailing. I was hurrying towards the Well-Meadow in the dusk to give Sister Mary Fursey a message, when I heard some strange cries. All young children make odd noises, but these had an undirected quality that gave them a sound less than human. They proceeded from the Shrine of the Triple Well, and I could not forbear to glance within, though it was not strictly in the line of my duty.

The mother was sitting on the stone bench opposite to the fresco, the child on her lap—conceived apparently, towards the end of her fertility-cycle*—lying backward so completely relaxed as to seem unable to support himself upright. Though he must have been three years old at least, he could not even sit up. Close to her stood a boy of about seven, while behind them in the shadows the tall figure of the Doctor and Charlotte's slight form could be discerned. The attention of all was focussed upon Mother and Child in the fresco, but the inarticulate cries of this other child from time to time distracted them from their devotions. Lit by the wind-blown candles of the tiny sanctuary, his face showed full and smooth, the skin without a trace of colour in the cheeks, and the eye-lids folded at their corners like those of a Chinese. It was plain that having no control over his limbs he could neither speak nor move effectively: unable to help himself, he was dependant on those about him. Yet in the expression of his face there was something better than intelligence—the appeal of a serenity which could only continue in the absence of ordinary development. I am no sentimentalist as regards children; but looking at this one I could understand his parents' affection for him, understand even that they preferred him to Stefan, their normal-witted first-born, who in his turn gazed without resentment at his supine brother.

Forgetful of my duties, I continued to observe this strange and pathetic family without their suspecting my presence. It did not seem to have occurred to the parents that, should their petition be granted and the child cured, their love for him must change, since he would be transformed from the afflicted one who had called forth their devotion into a boy as unremarkable as their elder son.

My first impression of Mrs. Wiseacre was that she was much older than her husband but as I watched, the years seemed to drop away from her. The greenish eyes, which had been filmed (as I supposed) by middle-age, widened—perhaps they had been dimmed with tears; and the wisps of faded hair fell into place so as to look well-groomed merely through her occasional gesture of pushing them back from her face. She seemed to develop herself backward into the neatly attractive matron which some years before she must have been.

Presently Charlotte caught sight of me and, detaching herself from the group, glided round toward the entrance of the shrine.

"That's Roli," she whispered as she joined me outside, "the younger boy. They hope so much that he will recover here, or at least improve."

I could see that in some way Charlotte had identified herself with this child; that she felt the warmth of the father's affection enveloping her equally with the younger son, and that this warmth brought her a sense of calm. The Doctor's eyes followed her as she left the shrine, his wife accepting these roving glances without rancour. Though not as old as I had at first thought, she was still his senior by several years, and may have expected him to be attracted, temporarily at least, to younger and better-looking women.

"Roli isn't his real name," went on Charlotte. "It's the nearest he has ever come to pronouncing Rudolph. But they quite like it because it might be Rowley—so English!"

I could wait no longer, having already dallied in the Well-Meadow which I should only have traversed on the way to more pressing employment. For the remaining history of Charlotte's friendship with the Doctor, which continued to bloom, I had to piece together the scraps of news which she gave me from time to time.

The next evening celebrated for her the feast of Saint Denez* with an invitation to dinner at the Wiseacres' villa. Her place was laid at one side of a long table, the Doctor at the end on her left and his wife at the opposite end. He handed Charlotte a wine-glass of hot water saying:

"This is for human junkets!"

The Doctor's sense of humour was peculiar, and frequently his tongue had a tang.

After dinner, while Mrs. Wiseacre was clearing away the dishes (in which her husband did not offer his help) Charlotte found the weather still mild enough for her to recline on the terrace above the garden. Here Dr. Wiseacre joined her, drawing his chair close to her *chaise longue,* and confided to her that his wife had recently had a long illness but was now quite recovered. He did not say what the malady was, but Charlotte gathered from his manner that it was cancer. Perhaps it had entailed amputation of a breast, a fact which might prove unaphrodisiac to the most uxorious. Having at times tried to telephone his home when he was unlikely to be there, out of curiosity, to hear how his wife sounded—of course, before she had met her—and receiving no reply, Charlotte now accepted that this illness provided the explanation of the empty house, and for some reason this eased her anxiety.

Unable to tear herself away from her hosts by the time the doors of the Ianua Vitae were locked for the night, Charlotte returned very late and had some difficulty in effecting an entrance. The hot water offered by the Doctor had been no more than a teasing preliminary, and had been followed by such a variety of stronger drinks that next morning she was in need of help from St. Biniané,* patron of those suffering from a hangover—or *katzenjammer,* as the Doctor would no doubt call it.

Next day, Charlotte found herself in a state of extreme nervous tension; obscurely realising its cause, she set off to consult the Doctor, if only professionally. As she approached his villa, she noticed how the end of the garden merged with the open spaces stretching beyond.

On arriving, she was shown into a semi-basement room with a barred window. Presently, the Doctor, who seemed to be in a hurry, glanced in through the aperture, and passed her a tablet and some powder: without listening to any recital of her symptoms, he simply gave her directions for taking these specifics, muttering something about other patients to be seen—though why he should have any others during his holiday, Charlotte could not imagine—he departed. She swallowed the tablet with a drink of water.

The children then came in, Stefan carrying Roli. He gently deposited the dead weight of his brother on the floor, and tried to devise a game to amuse him. In the course of this he pretended to cry, but instead burst out laughing.

The room, which was long and low, was not arranged as a waiting-room or surgery; it was perhaps mainly used by the children as a play-room. At the far end, the floor was raised to form a wide dais, so that the windows were further above ground-level than the barred one. Gertrud, looking almost handsome in a yellow dress and pearl choker, entered by a door at this end, and crossed the room towards the sill of the barred window, where she mixed with water the green powder which her husband had left. She gave the resultant paste to Charlotte, who obediently began to eat it; but the more she ate the more there seemed to be.

"What is this?" she demanded in exasperation.

"Dried fish,"* replied Gertrud curtly.

Charlotte went on eating, as she felt she must try to finish it.

"I hope you don't mind being in this cellar?" Gertrud presently inquired.

"I'd hardly call it a cellar; but if it were, I should mind very much."

"There's no need to be rude."

The tablet began to take perceptible effect on Charlotte: it was a combination of pep-pill and tranquiliser. She had no idea what the effect of the paste might be: it tasted peculiar, though not fishy or otherwise unpleasant. Surfeited with it at last, she gave up trying to finish it.

A portrait of Gertrud, drawn in charcoal with washes of colour, hung on the wall; it was an unflattering likeness. Gertrud handed her several envelopes addressed to her, and as she did so, Charlotte suddenly saw the pulled-aside look on the other woman's face which the artist had caught, but which she had never noticed before.

"Your letters were sent to this address by mistake," Gertrud remarked pointedly.

Charlotte surmised that they concerned the various healing springs in the convent precincts, and saw that there was an enclosure in one of them which was written in red ink on yellowish paper, the rest being in blue on white.* The dates showed they were years old—they seemed so stale that she could not summon up sufficient interest to read them. She wondered if this ennui was produced as a side-effect of the medicines she had taken. Her gaze wandered to the window and to the steep green slope beyond, to the white walls and box hedges of that part of the Ianua Vitae demesne which was in view. A spring trickled down the slope to a well in the garden which had been made into a fountain with basin and sculptured lead figures—a pilgrim kneeling at the brink was from this distance indistinguishable from one of these. Half-formed suspicions drifted into Charlotte's mind—the Doctor might have administered an aphrodisiac to her, either now or on a former occasion; or his wife might be attempting to poison her; or both might wish to incarcerate her or at least curtail her liberty? But she discovered that she was free to return to the Convent; and the curious effect of the drugs, if such it was, wore off after a few hours.

She soon found it impossible to accommodate her affair to convent-routine; and it was a relief to Sister Mary Gildas,* who was on duty as Guest Mistress, when she announced that the Wiseacres had invited her to stay at their villa until after our Festival. Beyond that date they seemed to have made no plans; Charlotte herself may have formed part of their attraction to Ménec—at least for Gerhardt Wiseacre, though both he and Gertrud had confidence in the efficacy of our springs and so were willing to remain in the vicinity for an indefinite period.

It was now already the twenty-fourth of October, the day sacred to St. Raphael,* archangel of healing.

On her side, Charlotte had promised to help them in looking after Roli—no light task, for he was so constant a responsibility as to become a burden even to the most adoring parents. Gertrud, thus freed from some of her domestic problems, was even able to undertake a little work outside the family circle in the cataloguing of our library. This was, to tell the truth, in rather a muddle, never before having been arranged by anyone with professional experience. Then the stimulus, not to say rivalry, of Charlotte's presence caused Gertrud to give more attention to her looks: I noticed that she began to brighten her hair with a henna rinse. Having occasion to refer to a book in the library while she was at work there, I was struck by her sleek appearance. Nor was she by any means an intellectually limited *hausfrau* with no thought beyond the three K's:* her perspicacity soon discovered some autograph letters, in the hand of our Foundress, of whose existence even Mother Vicaress had been unaware. I found her easy to talk to, and I remember that we had a discussion about swimming-pools before I left the library.

One day she presented herself at the still-room with Roli in her arms and begged Sister Mary Paracelsus to prescribe some herbal remedy to ease him. Our Novice-Mistress was sympathetic but frank, saying that she could suggest nothing that would alter his basic condition, and all that could be done was to pray and hope for a miracle at the Festival. Meantime she offered a decoction of poppy-seeds which would calm his more restless moods and quieten his disturbing cries. Gertrud accepted this eagerly.

It seemed natural to Charlotte to find herself installed in the Wiseacres' household, though this did not preclude in her a feeling of vindictive triumph.

"Like being in love itself," she caught herself thinking, "Natural, inevitable even; yet exciting too, an achievement."

Gertrud's efforts at glamour, which Charlotte had noticed before I did, merely amused her, secure as she was in her own charms. Nevertheless, these latter were enhanced by Gertrud's generosity in lending her a filmy nightdress and housecoat such as our convent-wardrobe certainly could not supply. Gertrud assigned her a room with two beds, and it was here that Charlotte, arrayed in her borrowed frills and engaged in her evening toilet—since she had intended to retire early—was interrupted by the Doctor, who looked in for a little relaxation.

The evening round of the wells had tired him; his leave from the hospital was by no means a complete rest, for he still kept up his spare-time employment in the editorship of two magazines, one of them called *Hobbies** devoted to the pastimes of small boys. Charlotte wondered how he found time for these activities in addition to his ordinary work. He sat down on one of the beds.

Charlotte rose from the other, on which she had been reclining while she varnished her finger-nails, as she wanted to urinate; but as she was leaving the room, Gertrud called to her from the passage that the lavatories would not flush until later in the evening. Domestic water-supplies on Ménec were inclined to be unreliable. Charlotte thought perhaps she could make the lavatories work; but not being successful in this, she threw on a coat and wandered out of the villa.

The garden which extended at the back of it had in the evening light no defined boundaries, and was full of late roses which climbed the walls of the house and covered the roof. The sunset air was heavy with their scent, enveloping the scene in a magical ambiance. The far end of the garden seemed to merge with a small public park which bordered the fire-station. Here people were resting on the seats to enjoy the last of the sunshine, while firemen off-duty and sailors from the port sauntered to and fro.

Having relieved herself among the wildgrown bushes, Charlotte re-entered the villa and mounted to her room, where Gerhardt was still seated on the second bed. She lay down on hers and though she did not undress, felt that this was the moment to bare her soul.

"I've come to your house," she said, gazing earnestly at him, "feeling that you are my teacher. I have absolute confidence in you as a master and will do as you tell me, whatever it may be."

The poor man was overwhelmed by this declaration: a holiday *flirte* was one thing, demanding doormatry another.

"Do not rely too much upon me," he begged. "I am an ailing man with many responsibilities. It is pleasant, this time together on Ménec. But you have your life and I have mine."

At this Charlotte must have shown signs of a return to her manic phase.

"Don't think you can escape me,"* she cried. "My mind is overflowing and will flow towards you wherever you are."

Her raised voice brought a discreet tapping at the door and Gertrud entered with a tray of coffee-cups. If she noticed the perturbation of her husband and Charlotte's distress, it did not appear in her manner; she poured out the coffee, which was strong and well-made, and they all sipped it. Charlotte calmed down, Gerhardt relaxed; and soon he was bidding her a kindly goodnight as he left the room in company with his wife.

But this was no solution to the problem, as all three recognised. The following afternoon, while Gertrud was out with the children, Gerhardt came again to

Charlotte during her hour of siesta. Without a word he kicked off his slippers and lay down beside her, his hands parting the sheer material of her housecoat to caress her sunken breasts. As the nipples began to stand out Charlotte gave a moan of pleasure and flexed her knees. Her hands pulled blindly at his clothes as their mouths met in an embrace. Panting, they fell apart and Gerhardt pulled off his sport-shirt while Charlotte fondled the bulb-like form which tautened the front of his trousers. His fingers fumbled with the fly-buttons, and finally skinned off his slacks.

He plunged into her with energy behind his thrusts; her pelvis, seemingly fragile, bucked under him adroitly, interchanging force with force. Clasping his phallus with the strength almost of a hand, she stripped it as one might milk a cow. At their mutual climax both were shrieking in ecstasy: and as the viscous warmth poured into her, a vision flashed across Charlotte's inward sight. She saw their sex-organs marked each with a diagram resembling the hexagrams of the Yi-King.* Those most like them were, for him, number twenty-seven, earth of fire, meaning 'nourishment': for her, number six, air of moon, meaning 'inmost sincerity.'

Sleep slid over them, brief but profound; and when Charlotte opened her eyes her lover, mindful of his wife's imminent return, had departed. He had left a sketch beside Charlotte's bed, a kind of *mandala** consisting of three concentric oblongs with an upright line in the middle and three short horizontal lines on either side of it. This she interpreted as a message of love, and knew by it that he too had seen the diagrams.

It was a few days before they had an opportunity to renew their love-making. The autumnal sun, never rising to the zenith, dazzled her by its near-horizontal beams as, wandering restlessly about the little town of Ménec, she came upon a church that recalled a temple of classical times. Priests were descending its steps, two at each level, in black-and-white robes while they chanted a prayer. Some goats were tethered in the forecourt; and had the temple been as Pagan in fact as it was in appearance they might have been destined for sacrifice. Three dogs floated drowned in a tank below the level of the road, oil scumming the surface of the water.

Charlotte had arranged to meet Gerhardt on the deserted strand of Kerlud,* so had been obliged to take her precautions before she set out. She was preoccupied, thinking she would have, for security, to put in more paste immediately before their love-making. In spite of Gerhardt's medical knowledge, he neither took any care nor assured himself that his partner did so; and this negligence puzzled Charlotte. An unwanted pregnancy would be almost as awkward for him as for her—socially, legally and financially at least, even though in health and self-development he could never be touched so nearly as she. For these two latter reasons she was resigned to taking all contraceptive responsibilities upon herself, since she could thus be certain of safety. At the same time she experienced a feeling, none the less painful for being recognised as a delusion, that despite her care she had become pregnant.

One of her mind's 'overflowings' was that she had actually had a baby by Gerhardt—a very small one, who sucked a little milk from her left breast one morning. She went out for the day, and when she returned at evening she wiped his bottom. He sucked a little more milk, smiled, said he had had enough and thereafter dwindled away. He became a toy, with limbs flat as if made of tin, cardboard or plastic; then somehow he seemed to be mislaid altogether, and Charlotte assumed that he had died. She was now worried lest she should be legally blamed for neglect, and thought of consulting the Doctor about it. But she never did so, and ultimately the nightmare faded from her days.

Next morning Charlotte put on a print dress which Gerhardt had bought for her; its greenish colour and leafy pattern suited her well. She found herself on all-fours upon the floor of the room which opened upon the terrace, reading a note which he had just handed to her. Though written in his rich calligraphy, it was not addressed to her but to his younger brother, an antique-dealer of about her own age. In the first line it explained that he loved Charlotte and wanted to marry her—some phrase like 'love and marriage' swam before her eyes, and she read no further. She looked up at him questioningly, indicating these words as if to ask whether he were serious? He nodded emphatically, and in his turn gave her a questioning glance as though to seek her agreement. She consented, either by a nod or by some such phrase as 'With all my heart.'

Then it seemed to her that they were joined together* by a shaft of etheric light,* the particles in it moving from him to her and her to him with a kind of circulation. One might even compare it to the angels ascending and descending the ladder in Jacob's vision,* except that here the movement was horizontal instead of vertical, since the lovers' two spheres of being were on the same level. A sense of complete happiness at this wordless betrothal enveloped her.

Gertrud stepped in from the garden, talking more volubly than was her wont. She darted a look at Charlotte from her yellowish-green eyes, which today were neurotically pale and staring. For the first time Charlotte sensed the strength of the wife's hidden jealousy and feared she might attack her; yet nothing could deeply disturb her serenity, nor did she feel the slightest jealousy of Gertrud.

Piecing together Charlotte's fragmentary narrative, confided to me at odd moments, I guessed that what appeared to her as sheer animal possessiveness was rather a manifestation of forethought on Gertrud's part, however much mingled with resentment. After all, Gerhardt ran a professional risk and so jeopardised his family, in taking as lover a married woman who had lately been his patient. Gertrud no doubt wished to prevent him causing too great a scandal, though she was uncertain how this was to be done. At first she tried toleration and even connivance, then a show of temper and finally more drastic means to achieve her end.

One night when Gerhardt had slipped into her bed and they were on the brink of ecstasy, Charlotte felt the touch of a cold hand* on her left thigh. She cried out, telling Gerhardt what she felt.

"It is Gertrud," he said.

"But she doesn't know?"

"She has not been told," he answered enigmatically.

Charlotte seized the hand, which was small and white, and rubbed it, thinking that this would disperse it if it were made of ectoplasm. Gerhardt handled it also but it did not go, and it succeeded in casting a chill over their embraces.

Charlotte wanted to give her lover a present but could not decide what form it should take. On the subject of a suitable gift she wished she could consult her brother Keith, who seemed to her a model of tact and worldly wisdom. She considered a pig-skin suit-case, a pair of royal-blue swimming trunks or a wooden object, made partly of cotton-reels, which she sometimes wore as a sanitary-towel. If she chose the suit-case, it might look as though she wished him to travel; and even the bathing-trunks would be as useful in his swimming-pool at home as they were on Ménec. She even wondered whether there were not a pun hidden in these two things, namely the word 'trunk,' which could also apply to his own body; and by its material the suit-case would call him a pig, which she did not wish to do.

"What is the use of giving him what he already has?" she demurred. "Unless perhaps I want to give him the bodily health which he does not possess at the moment. But on the whole I think the wooden object is best, as something more personal to me."

Charlotte may have been swayed in her choice by the fact that the two former alternatives would have been difficult to acquire in the small shops of Ménec— apart from the fact that she had no money to buy anything. But Gerhardt had not penetrated deeply enough into the underworld of emotion to appreciate her gift; or perhaps he received as a warning the incident of the cold hand; or again, perhaps he felt that his irregular relationship with her was tempting the Providence whose help he daily implored on behalf of his child. In any case, their affair deteriorated after she gave him the present; and though Charlotte continued to live at the villa, she never again saw him alone. Gertrud manoeuvred to keep them apart and Gerhardt allowed these tactics to succeed. It may have been strategy rather than tactics, if she had reckoned on letting the affair go a certain distance and then clamping down on it. She even bought a police-trained Alsatian to roam the house at night and give the alarm if anyone tried to play creepy-creepy.

Charlotte, much hurt by Gerhardt's evasion, herself retired behind a façade. In exchange for a bunch of roses which she plucked in the garden, she obtained two pieces of cast-off finery from a stall-holder at the market. One of these was a length of filmy black material glittering with spangles, in which she tried to imagine herself as Queen of the Night;* but lacking her consort, this was but poor consolation. The other, which was blue, had a circular wet patch above the sternum when I happened to see Charlotte veiled in it one day—for either stole was worn over her head, reaching to her waist like a blouse. But whether this dampness was caused by tears or sweat I could not determine.

The situation was becoming intolerable, from whichever side of the triangle you looked at it—as, indeed, might have been foretold. Charlotte conveyed to me that she had made arrangements to leave the neighbourhood as soon as our Festival was over, which was almost at once. I did not inquire, but I supposed that Gerhardt was supplying the necessary means. She did not wish, for some reason, to tell me where she was going and I did not press her to do so. We at the Ianua Vitae had done what we could to help her; but she had to continue her own life and whatever direction this might take, we saw that she could not remain long within our sphere of influence.

6

LOSS

During the last few days of October, the *Ile de Ménec* made the voyage to and from the mainland every twenty-four hours instead of twice a week only, arriving each day with a load of pilgrims. We still have no air service, or aircraft would no doubt have been landing equally full. The private villas were all let, the two hotels by the harbour overflowing with guests and many island-families who had rooms to spare were accommodating relatives or more distant connections. Visitors who had no such foothold and could not afford to pay for rooms were camping, despite the lateness of the season, among the sand-dunes or in sheltered corners of the farmsteads. Fortunately for them, the weather still held, seeming inclined to prolong its warmth and silvery hazes until the coming of Sant Marzhin.*

Our guest-house at the Ianua Vitae was full also, for to us each year falls the main responsibility for housing the Church dignitaries who conduct our ceremonies, and any other visiting clergy or religious who wish to take part in them. Though there are one or two other religious houses on Ménec which help us in this, we are always very busy during the week preceding the Festival, and this year was no exception. Those Sisters who were not preparing food or rooms were rehearsing special music or taking instructions in how to marshal the pilgrims and assist the more seriously ill among them. Others were decorating the convent with lights, sprays of autumnal foliage and festoons of fruit or late flowers. Yet others were looping lengths of brightly coloured cloth to form arches over door and window, or fastening them so as to cascade in curtains over a blank wall-space. Most important were the decorations of the convent-church and of Our Lady of the Trees where the Vespers of Healing were to be sung; and it was here that I was chiefly engaged.

It is difficult for anyone without experience of life in a religious community to understand how satisfying such work can be; and this, not only when the buoyancy of a feast-day bears one up, but in the day-to-day routine of the liturgical year. Even the most tiresome or repulsive task may take on, in convent life at its best, an aura of play, to be accomplished with a deftness and gaiety unknown in the world. When everything is done with goodwill, everything seems innocently amusing: I suppose this lightness of heart has its source in the charity which may inform all action while itself remaining hidden.

Our 'obedience in detail,' though carried to what seems an obsessive length (precluding as it does even a visit to the lavatory without a Superior's leave) lifts from us by our very dependence those trivial decisions which in the world become the focus of an exhausting emotional tension. The narrowing of choice, the fixing of a life-pattern bring a cradled consolation to the torn soul.

This year the Bishop of Orascoule, whom we already knew well, was to be our officiant; he was something of a *gourmet* and in general, fond of his creature-comforts. He always wanted a hot-water bottle in his bed and an egg-nog brought to him the last thing at night; and he would certainly demand one of Sister Mary Paracelsus' best liqueurs after meals. When one gazed at his hieratic figure arrayed in a chasuble* as he raised on high the chalice of precious wine, one could with difficulty connect it with the elderly man in a nightshirt from whose chamber-pot one had that morning emptied a load of amber urine. Yet such anomalies are the condition of human life, and to declare too strong an opposition between different aspects of existence is to be guilty of dualism*— that, one must avoid at any cost.

We found many small matters needing attention at the last minute. Sister Fursey was crossing the Well-Meadow laden with a vicious-looking iron hook of several prongs fastened to a coil of rope—in appearance, a veritable instrument of torture but in fact an aid to the rescue of a vessel which she had let fall into one of the deeper wells. Sister Gildas walked beside her carrying a sheaf of still-leafy branches which she had plucked from a hedgerow to decorate our chapel for the morrow. I followed them, my arms full of those late-flowering pink lilies that grace the cottage-gardens, and other autumn flowers pressed on me by pious islanders for the same purpose. Even Mother Ste. Barbe, who seldom concerned herself with practical details, was hovering here and there with the feeling that she must make sure all the arrangements were well in hand. Catching sight of us, she called out:

"Here come three great days—*Pasion, Ar Bleuniou* and *Ar Sakramant!*"* (Our names for *Passion, Rameaux* and *Fête Dieu*).

She smiled on us benignly yet penetratingly, as if she beheld in our chance-assumed burdens a symbolic indication of our future. I was thankful that my Day was not that of the body doomed or fleetingly triumphant, but of the body transformed.

The first of November, *Hollsent*,* dawned forlornly bright as the wisps of mist that had lain all night in the hollows were drawn upward to the empyrean.* I know, for by this time of year our rising-bell rings before the rising of the sun and today Sister Fursey and I were up especially early to put final touches to the fruit and flowers with which we had decked the Chapel of the Trees. Their colour glowed against the white-washed shed walls as lanceolate rays pierced the east window and the cooler zenith-light diffused itself through the crystal ring below the dome.

There was no time to shiver at the dawn-chill as we hurried back to Mass in the convent-church, and then served breakfast to our guests before eating our own. Soon afterwards we began to form into procession for the round of the Well-Meadow. First came children from our orphanage dressed in golden-yellow and singing like finches; then a *posse* of visiting clergy, their vestments contrasting with the simple habits of such religious as were also escorting the Bishop. Though he was not the focal point of the procession, since he was saving his strength to officiate in the more arduous ceremony later in the day, yet his authority demanded an important place in it. Then followed crucifer and thurifer,* with a few moppets specially chosen from among the orphans to walk backwards as they cast petals from their baskets before the feet of our chaplain and his canopied burden. Next came Mother Ste. Barbe, Mother Vicaress and the choir, of which I was one; and following us, the invalids who were making a last round for a healing intention, among whom were the Doctor and his family. The more feeble of the sick were helped along by some Sisters of the Partheno-genesis, while others surrounded the Black Banner, which needed two of us at either side to support it, so heavy were its staves. On this relic of our past the embroidery is so dark with age that Our Lady's features can only with difficulty be discerned. Tradition tells us that it was worked by Ste. Anne* herself to a speaking likeness of her daughter, and that she left it here when she first visited our shores. Crowding behind it came representatives from the island-parishes wearing their regional costumes and displaying their own banners, the women of each characterised by a differently-starched head-dress. Finally a crowd of the less devout pilgrims and sightseers followed our lead and our plain-chant as well as they could.

We entered the Well-Meadow at the upper end and made for the centre where stands the Shrine of the Triple Well. The order of the round was arranged so that the sandy pool should come last, thus allowing those pilgrims who were to take the plunge to return immediately afterwards to the convent: and this, most of them were glad to do. Mother Ste. Barbe held the commonsense view that to linger in a wet bathing-gown in weather that could not be relied upon for clemency was unlikely to cure whatever complaint one had, and might make it worse. She did not adhere to the more fanatical school of thought which declares that no colds or other ill-effects ever result from participation in a pilgrimage. The sun though bright, had not yet gained strength to disperse the morning dew, so that footsteps and the sweep of gowns left a snake of darker green where the procession wound along, brushing aside the drops that made the herbage look pale. To our left rose the Mont Ste. Anne, islanded by a mist that still clung about its lower slopes.

The Festival-rites are held chiefly for the benefit of our guests so, as Sisters of the Parthenogenesis, we don't claim their virtues for ourselves unless we are seriously ill. We (and the islanders also) have the advantage of the healing waters all the year. So now we remained outside the diminutive shrine, grouping ourselves about the Bishop, the chaplain and others of the clergy while the pilgrims filed through, entering by one doorway and leaving by the other on the opposite side. Within, two Sisters were on duty, one dipping a bowl in the well and offering it to each pilgrim to drink and bathe brow and hands, the other filling any vessel they might have brought so that some of the sacred water could be taken home.

While the last were passing through, the main procession began to join up again on the far side of the shrine and move away to the left where, on a slope of the Mont Ste. Anne and half-hidden by a heap of rubble, the spring of St. Méen is situated. Other Sisters were in attendance here to conduct those who had need of its soothing drops and return them to their places. Gerhardt stood aside; but Charlotte approached, followed by Gertrud carrying Roli in her arms. The child lay with his usual passive serenity, his peculiar cries but occasionally piercing our music. Flat stones had been arranged in a pathway encircling the well; the custom is to make the circuit three times, the more pious extending this to three times three; and some will even make it on their knees, murmuring invocations the while. Whether the Bishop disapproved of this practice as stemming from a cult more ancient than his own I cannot say; but it seemed to me that he showed signs of impatience as we in the main body of the procession stood apart waiting for the crawling and shuffling devotees to conclude it.

Again we re-formed and moved down the Meadow. There was no pause at 'my' spring, the marshy puddle below the thorn-trees, but I saluted it inwardly before we made our way to the little well beside the sandy pool. Here nearly all the pilgrims circumambulated the spring and those who could face immersion then plunged, clad in their white gowns, into the wider water, to emerge trembling with cold and ecstasy. They tried not to hurry too obviously over the last hundred yards or so of the route but most of them, including the Doctor, were thankful to take shelter in the changing-rooms where hot towels and their dry clothes were laid out to await them.

The mid-day meal followed at noon, after which the pilgrims were free for rest or meditation. But for us there was no time for either, since we had not only the domestic responsibility for our guests but also preparations for the special Vespers in the early evening.

The last of the sunshine* gleamed on the petrified columns supporting the dome of Our Lady of the Trees and glinted at an angle through the windows of the nave as we soundlessly assembled in choir. Here the immortal tree and the fountain (whether springing or still) enclose, equally with the water and wine, our worshipped Soul and Divinity.

In spite of the bustle of our many duties, great recollection is enjoined upon us, for this hour is the climax of the Festival and also in a sense of our conventual year, and is always infused with a feeling of expectation. I believe that we Sisters of the Parthenogenesis contribute as much to this as do the visiting clergy and religious, and the most devout of the pilgrims—although it might be supposed that having laboured behind the scenes and stage-managed the affair, we had become a little disillusioned. In fact, though dramatic incidents are the exception, they do sometimes occur; and in the course of our history a few of them have, after the usual exhaustive inquiries, been pronounced miraculous. Many more than these count as miracles in the popular mind, having convinced those who were present when they happened. Mother Ste. Barbe has record of hundreds who have written to tell us that their improvement or recovery has been maintained, so their cures cannot be dismissed as due solely to suggestion or the excitement of the moment. The votive offerings that hang round the interior of the Chapel recount the same story.

We had threaded our way through figures kneeling on the grass or clustering around the stone troughs and grotto, for the environs of the Chapel were crowded by those who had pressed unsuccessfully for an entry. First place in the miniature nave is always accorded to pilgrims and their relatives who have asked for healing, and this year a number had presented themselves. The west door is always left open so that those outside can see and hear something of the ceremony; and such as can look in at the windows are not discouraged from doing so.

The Vespers continued its accustomed way through psalms, prayers and ancient hymns, and then came the special responsories which we chant while the pilgrims line up in the centre aisle and approach the Bishop in turn. Last of these and immediately following Charlotte, stood Gerhardt, now waiting in the chancel with his younger son supported in his arms. Gertrud and Stefan were kneeling in one of the more forward ranks.

Though Roli lay for the most part inert, his head would sometimes loll from side to side, his buttocks wriggle slightly or a hand or foot shoot out in some meaningless gesture. Lacking as he did both reason and emotion as commonly understood, his nerves and muscles obeyed impulses which could not be foreseen and were perhaps dictated by some force other than his own.

Women's voices alone always sound to me a little thin, but today our choir was augmented for the occasion by members of other religious houses, so had at its disposition the male voices to which we were unaccustomed. This made more effective our antiphonal chant* in praise of Her who was carried up to heaven in a chariot of water.

> *Quasi cedrus exaltata sum in Libano,* sang the sopranos.
> *Et quasi cupressus in monte Zion,* the tenors responded.
> *Quasi palma exaltata sum in Cades,*
> *Et quasi plantatio rosae in Iericho**

The plain-chant continued, drowning the rush of the waters above which the chapel stood, and wandering through many sustained *melismata.* * I have seen it stated by our apologists that this kind of music brings out the sense of the words, but I cannot agree that it does so. When a syllable may be stretched out to the length of a sentence, intellectual content is distorted beyond recognition. But this, as I see it, is the very point; the discursive mind is to be lulled or entranced while 'the high dream'* takes over. Here, as elsewhere, it seems to me that we do the right things for the wrong reasons—or at least, the right reasons are not given out. (I must stop or I shall be divagating into heresy).

The paean proceeded, glorifying the plants sacred to Our Lady—cedar, cypress, olive, palm, rose, terebinth, mastic, plane—trees famous for strength or beauty, fragrance or food. Water from the fountains below the petrified tree-roots whose trunks now served as pillars for the dome, and also from the springs of the Well-Meadow, had been set aside, each in its silver flash of characteristic design. Where possible, we provide a sprig of the appropriate plant as aspergillum; but for the Well-Meadow waters, which issue direct from the ground, we use boxwood twigs.

The chant had reached the point where the Rivers of Eden* are invoked for their beneficent flow:

'*Qui implet quasi Phison sapientiam,*
Et sicut Tigris in diebus novorum
Qui adimplet quasi Euphrates sensum'*

It was Roli's turn, and Sister Fursey lifted the flask containing water from that sombre well whose reputation was to cure the mentally afflicted and handed it to the Bishop with an obeisance. As he drew out the twig glistening with potent drops and shook it over the child, the chant ceased and a hush fell, only the voice of the twelve springs in confluence being audible. After sprinkling him from head to foot, the Bishop dipped his hand in the flask and made the sign of the Cross on Roli's brow, lips and breast.

The child uttered a cry different in tone from any we had yet heard from him and struggled out of his father's arms. His feet touched the tessellated floor, actually supporting his weight; then he spun round to face the nave, his arms outstretched as if to embrace the crowd. For an instant his strangeness dropped away from him, his face was lit up by a look of lively intelligence and he stood before us as the child he might have been. He took one step forward, then collapsed and lay unmoving, his eyes fixed on the dome alone.

A gasp went up from the congregation and Gertrud dashed forward with a scream, seizing Roli before Gerhardt could do so. Both parents saw that their child's expression was again one of sublime idiocy, now intensified in death;* and they carried him out of the Chapel, Stefan sobbing at their heels. Charlotte continued to kneel upright in her place as though numb, her face empty of expression.

It was as though a current, dammed up so that it merely trickled in the earlier part of the ceremony, had burst forth and swept away the involuntary pilgrim whose hold on life was already insecure. Powerful enough to transform him, it was not steady enough to maintain the change. We did not break up in confusion, though everyone knew that Roli would never move again. Little more than the final thanksgiving remained and the ceremony closed in due course; but the Bishop's usually rubicund face was pale, and his thick hands trembled.

x x x x x

When Roli's obsequies were over, Charlotte had no longer an excuse for remaining in the Doctor's household. Strangely enough, all its members seemed to have benefited from our cure, even Gerhardt; in spite of the shock of his younger son's death, he became calmer and more vigorous, as though renewed by the vitality of the departed child. Gertrud too, after looking pale and sad for several days, regained her poise; no doubt the strain of caring for Roli, however devotedly undertaken, had aged her, and now that the burden was eased she could relax. Stefan came fully into his own. Charlotte had grown more tranquil, and even achieved some independence. I gathered that the family would soon be on its way: and the last time I saw any of them was on the occasion of Charlotte's departure.

Near by their villa a rustic station was served by the island-railway; and into one of its trains Charlotte disappeared. My last glimpse was of a figure waving a hand from one of the quaint open coaches while Gerhardt waited on the platform to see her off. As the train receded, he raised and extended his right arm several times in salute, a tribute which brought a look of rapture to Charlotte's face, pallid between the curtains of her bronze-lit hair.

7

THE DRAGON'S TAIL

In the course of my work as herdswoman in our community, I often passed over a stretch of park-like country through which ran a right-of-way used from time immemorial by the Ianua Vitae. What was my amazement and indignation to find, one damp and gusty day in autumn—for the unusual summer weather had continued only until the end of our Festival-octave*—that the entrance to it had been barred. The iron fence defining the boundary of the park-land had been extended to cross the driveway; and a stream, swelled by recent rains, which ran just within the confines of the demesne, had been dammed up to form a stagnant mere stretching across the road. A number of young trees, too, had been felled and heaped up to block this further—wood, water and metal enlisted to assert someone's claims and intentions.

Who would it be? I asked myself. Then I remembered a snatch of gossip heard passing between two of our Lay Sisters, to the effect that the management of the island *Manoir* of Kerlescan was changing. It seemed that the present owner, being incapacitated through age or illness, was handing over his responsibilities to his Heir, a nephew.

"But he has no right!" I fumed, hastening up to the barricade. I peered over it and descried a small car approaching from the direction of the manorial buildings, which were hidden from sight. I was wearing what might be described as my best clothes—actually, the newer of the two habits I used, donned in anticipation of the special Benediction due that evening in honour of Sant Marzhin. (Yet I should not have used the prefix 'my' for, as individuals, we own nothing; we are allowed to make temporary use of the Order's property). The other habit, which I usually wore for herding, was more worn than this. Disregarding the fact that I should take care of the cleaner one, I scrambled up the extended and reinforced fence to get a clear view, not only of the disagreeable changes, but of the oncoming vehicle. I felt sure that the new owner of the *Manoir* was drawing near.

It was a sports-car, so I could see its occupants distinctly—a man with his girl-friend beside him. At the sight of my figure the driver braked, sprang up and stood on the seat to confront me. He was fine-boned and pallid, with black hair blowing to his shoulders.

"How dare you!" I was gesticulating in fury as I shouted against the wind.

"Smug little fool!"* he jeered. "You think you're founded on a rock." (This was galling in view of my unsteady perch). "That the gates of Hell will not prevail against you. But they have already prevailed!" he exulted. "They began to prevail centuries ago; and now those gates are opening; soon they will be gaping wide, letting loose the hordes within!"

A current of agonising recognition shot between us: precariously balanced as we both were, our faces were contorted in a mutual ecstatic spasm. Meanwhile the girl-friend became (what she always was) a nonentity, and faded from our consciousness. I continued to arraign him on the subject of the enclosure, his injustice to the Order of the Parthenogenesis and so on; but both he and I knew that compared with our own doom, these were trifles.

On regaining the Ianua Vitae I informed Mother Vicaress of the obstructions; and at her dictation Mother Ste. Barbe, in her delicately-beautiful script, wrote to de Kerlescan.* She pointed out, with great politeness, that our Order had enjoyed grazing-rights on the confines of the manorial grounds for centuries, and she trusted he would raise no objection to the continuance of the custom. He replied without delay that the disputed park-land was now his property, to dispose of as he thought fit: and that he required it for purposes of his own. This was the beginning of a lengthy correspondence which, I regret to say, became more acrimonious with every letter exchanged.

How the case would have been decided if it had reached a court of law is an open question: on Ménec the *Code Napoléon** has never entirely superseded ancient Celtic usages,* particularly in respect of land-tenure. The result would have depended on whether the earlier system, which favoured the Parthenogen-esists, or the later, which supported the Heir, predominated at the hearing.

I did not see him again till over a week later, on the day of Sant Vran;* the weather was sunny, and in the afternoon Sister Mary Fursey and I were driving the cattle towards the village of Kerlescan, which is situated some little way from the convent. Suddenly a gay procession came out of the church, which was dedicated to Sant Vran: some of the participants walking sedately, others dancing round on the one spot at each step with elaborate gestures. Though the movements of these people were much quicker than those of the ones who walked, they yet progressed no faster. The best dancer was a young boy fantas-tically dressed who whirled around before the canopy.

The procession grew more secular in character towards its tail, and was brought up by the Heir on horseback, dressed as a cavalier. Catching sight of us, he broke away from the rest and approached. A cellar-man pushed through our herd and handed him two glasses, a large one holding ale and a smaller one with a pale drink like mead. The Heir offered the smaller one to me, but when I stretched out my hand to take it, he tried to pull the glass away in order to tantalise me. However, I held on persistently and he then gave it up.

From that moment I forgot Sister Fursey as completely as he had forgotten his girl-friend on the occasion of our first meeting. He invited me into the *Manoir* and when I accepted, led me into his study. He told me his name was Nikolaz; and saying he wished to change his fancy costume for more conventional attire, he went into an adjoining room, having given me some dresses from which to choose. Whether these had been left behind by his *petite amie,** who may have departed, in a hurry, I don't know; but they seemed quite new so I lost no time in exchanging the sage-green habit of our Order for a creation of turquoise-blue which fitted me perfectly.

When he returned I inquired how he used to spend his time before he inherited the *Manoir,* and gathered that he worked at something connected with buildings and estates that had once been Royal property. Time passed quickly in small-talk about art and architecture; yet I was uneasy, and at last I burst out with,

"What did you mean when you told me that the gates of Hell had already prevailed?"*

"History is edited for you, no doubt," he replied. "But if you were free to investigate, you would find that in earlier centuries the Church knew more than she does today. She has gradually separated herself from her own illumination; and since the fourteenth century that separation has become almost complete."

"But the religious Orders—" I began.

"Once, knowledge was taught within them," he cut in. "Now even there, the light is obscured by platitudes fit only for the stupider sections of the laity— which itself is growing less perceptive year by year."

"The Parthenogenesists still have secrets," I declared, feeling that I must defend the faith.

"Your Order may have retained a fragment," he conceded. "But make no mistake, my little nun: you are left unmolested only so long as you remain unaware of the treasure you guard. If you recognised what you possess and used it, authority would soon intervene."

Since this theory confirmed some of my own private impressions, I could find no convincing retort.

"Today, the laval floods are moving swiftly," he continued, his dark eyes glittering. "The Church, a second Eve,* has yielded to the powers of confusion, deceived by their promise to disseminate more widely the one true faith. A second Faust,* she has made a compact with infernal forces; and the day of reckoning is near."

"What do you mean?"

"I can best show you by taking as instance the vitiation of ritual—though this is but the superficial evidence of a profound emptiness or consternation. How can the Holy Father bless the City and the World from a balcony crowded with television cameras? Priests have become film-stars and their rites a charade."

> *The blood-dimmed tide is loosed, and everywhere*
> *The ceremony of innocence is drowned**

I quoted.

"I see that you understand me. In broadcasting, there is now scarcely a station which allows even the Mass to speak for itself, but fades it out at intervals in favour of a commentary by some garrulous cleric. If the intention were to dissipate its virtue, a more effective method could hardly be devised."

"At the Ianua Vitae we don't listen to such things."

"Not yet; but it is only a matter of time before you too will be engulfed in the tide of vulgarisation which passes for progress."

He left the room again for a few minutes; remembering Sister Fursey outside, and frightened by his prophecies, I decided to cover myself with a robe of concealment and vanish before he came back.

I slipped out of the study carrying some clothes, though not my habit; then, taking sudden alarm, I hid in a passage-cupboard. I found that there was just enough space for me to change my clothes inside it; and the cracks and crannies of the woodwork let in a certain amount of light. On a high shelf at the back of it reposed a massive leather casket such as usually contains jewellery. Letting myself out, I fled down some corridors and through a lounge or hall, passing two elderly ladies walking arm in arm, who regarded me curiously but said nothing. They might have been relatives who were staying with Nikolaz; or part of the house may have been open to the public on the occasion of the patronal feast.* In either case, I must have seemed to them a strange-mannered intruder with my long white dress flowing out as I ran, and a white scarf catching on valuable objects as it floated from my hat.

When I reached the front-entrance, I found it surrounded by a circle of Sisters from the Ianua Vitae demanding charity to help our orphanage, which was situated opposite, in the village of Kerlescan. It was impossible for me to avoid them; and I could only hope that I should go unrecognised by reason of my change of attire, and of the fact that most of them were Novices, with whom I had little to do. When one accosted me, offering me two sprigs of rosemary* as a token, I found that I could give her no coin, having left my handbag in the *Manoir,* where such accessories as this had been provided to accord with my new outfit.

There was nothing to do but go back for it; and on regaining Nikolaz' room, to which he had still not returned, I discovered there several more articles which seemed to belong to me—papers, gloves, an embroidered veil—which I collected together in a suit-case. Laden with it, and dressed now entirely in black, I tried once more to return. I reached the corridor outside, and had not gone down it more than a little way, when I heard Nikolaz' footsteps. Not wishing to meet him again, I dashed into the cupboard a second time and shut the door. I crouched down beneath the shelf on which the treasure had rested. But this time it was missing from its place.

I saw in a flash what a difficult situation I was in, especially if the treasure could be proved to have vanished between my two visits to the cupboard. I put on my convent-clothes again and packed the other things into the suit-case. Before I could think what to do next, I heard the sound of steps which I recognised as those of the cellar-man, and a key was turned, imprisoning me. But it did not take me long to see that the lock was placed so high in the door that a determined assault on the lower panels would release me. I attacked them, battering them with all my weight. The wood quickly split and I was out again.

This time I did not make for the front door but tried to pass through the servants' quarters. In a large hall a banquet was in progress, and I sat down among the assembled retainers and their friends, hoping to pass unnoticed. But the cellar-man soon caught sight of me and began to accuse me. I challenged him to search my belongings, assuring him that he would not find what he sought.

Suddenly there was a hush. At the far end of the hall stood the Heir-apparent, bearing the family-treasure aloft.

"Where is my guest?" he cried. "On this day of days I wish to make her a gift."

I advanced and took the casket from his hands, and he turned upon the cellar-man.

"Why did you cover our Heirloom in your underground lair?"

"Sir," replied the cellar-man with servility, "I was about to replenish it."

"Then you knew this lady had not touched it; you blamed her so that you could gain time to conceal it for yourself."

"What was she doing in the cupboard?" grumbled the cellar-man, finally beaten.

"That is her affair," answered the Heir.

All this while I had left Sister Fursey to mind the cattle; but now I explained to Nikolaz that it was time for me to attend to my duties. Though he expressed regret, he did not try to detain me, and I left with him the suit-case of clothes which now also contained the Heirloom.

We found Sister Fursey and her charges on a patch of waste-land outside the manorial grounds. I must say that she took my dereliction well, making no comment but a mild suggestion that our return to the Ianua Vitae was overdue. We made our farewells and I helped her to collect our beasts together.

As we trudged along the muddy lanes, my heart was in a ferment. True to my vows, I had tried to banish the demonic image of the Heir from my thoughts after my first encounter with him, but now it became clear to me that I could do no such thing. Why did I not seek advice in this deadlock, either from my Superiors in the Order or from its spiritual director, the Chaplain who for some time past had shown me at least a distant kindliness? Though the parallels between confession and psycho-analysis are usually drawn by people with no experience of either, he must have felt that something beyond the sacrament of Penance was needed to deal with one's difficulties, for it was his custom, after hearing a confession, to ask if one had any queries. Many of the Sisters would avail themselves of this opportunity and open their problems to him. I had never done so; perhaps on account of spiritual pride, for I certainly did not think he could answer the profounder questions; while the more trivial, it seemed to me, would solve themselves in the course of time. If he had resembled Brother Constantine Jaquasse I would not have hesitated to confide in him, knowing that I should receive more than a text-book reply. Alas, I had long ago lost touch with Brother Constantine, and our well-meaning Chaplain was no substitute. I already knew what my Superiors at the Ianua Vitae would say.

Not being entrenched in the religious life with sufficient firmness to withstand the erotic suggestions of her narrative, as I now saw, I should not have allowed Charlotte to describe to me her love-affair in detail. Yet my Superiors did not discourage our confidential talks and so presumably did not disapprove of them; though Mother Vicaress, if not Reverend Mother herself, must have known of

Charlotte's irregular life. Or could they have been so guileless as to suppose that, at the Wiseacres', she was no more than a 'friend of the family', or 'mother's help'? Again, were they testing me? If so I had, by their standards, failed.

Their standards? What, then were mine? Was I already separated so far from our Order as to set up in myself a standard of value different from that which it inculcated or rather, assumed?

Unable as yet to face this question and give it an answer, I let my mind stray again to Charlotte. I felt a twinge of pity as I compared her sad marriage, and now her faded affair, with the girlhood dreams which we had shared when we were both, I suppose, searching for Adonis. If Ossian had represented to her something of this image of youth and beauty, with his stream-lined good-looks, how dearly she had paid for her attempt to realise fable! As for Gerhardt Wiseacre, he could not be said to approach such an ideal, though in more promising circumstances he might have offered her a valuable relationship in terms of greater maturity.

During their married life, Ossian had cheated Charlotte of much, including the full expression of her motherly instinct. Though he had contrived to divert something of this upon himself, Charlotte had always felt as a perversion this jockeying of her affections into a falsely maternal rôle. (Why had she chosen to marry him? Partly because her background was peripheral to traditional culture, and she saw in him the epitome of a ripened civilization. That in some respects it was more than ripe must at first have escaped her fascinated view). She had to be the provider, the getter-out-of-scrapes, the maker of sacrifices, while he played the naughty child, using his childishness to re-ingratiate himself after each escapade. His behaviour put a serious strain on Charlotte, forcing her into the unwanted positions of nanny, governess, mental-nurse, doctor, lawyer, bank-manager and even policeman. She came to see that any partnership between them as mature human beings was out of the question. But it was children upon whom she had wished to lavish herself, not an emotionally retarded if physically adult male. It is true she had a son and daughter, but she felt that with mother-hood her life-work, her family was too small. If Ossian had played his part in providing the expenses of the household, this longing for more children need not have been thwarted. But whenever she expressed it to him, he insisted that it would be rash to increase their commitments before he was well established in his profession. And when she reluctantly agreed, his conscience became active on the subject of the Church's teaching about contraception. Not content with depriving her of children, he defrauded her, with the highest sanctions, of the centre of marriage itself; their sex-life had ceased after Hilary's birth. As he pointed out with unanswerable common-sense, the allowed 'safe-period' was not safe enough for their purpose. Marital abstinence suited Ossian since it left him free to pursue relationships less likely to become a responsibility; and this he did without consideration for Charlotte's feelings.

Sister Fursey may have wondered at my long silences; apart from an infrequent call to the cattle (but this was scarcely needed, so well did the beasts know their way home) I did not speak. Though our Rule allows us to talk on such occasions as this, it enjoins silent prayer whenever possible. The purpose of a monastic Rule, as I understand it, is to make the whole of life a ritual for those who follow it; and to a great extent it does so. But it can never be the full text of the ritual—rather is it the rubric only and for many of the day's eventualities one has to rely on improvisation. When our Foundress Ste. Ermengilde laid down our Rule in *The Peerless Guidances,** she provided nothing for circumstances such as those which now perplexed me. I remembered how she told us of the three states of being: first, a kind of Chaos beneath us, continually knitting-up and unravelling, which she called The Power to Destroy; then, that which she named The Holy Welcome, the here-and-now that accepts us as manifested entities with a promise in us of accepting, in our turn, divinity; and lastly, the sphere to which we aspire, The Scintillating Light, where apprehension of that divinity may be enjoyed to the full. But how could such revelations help me now?

One learns to keep up a kind of background prayer while doing most manual jobs, though any task requiring mental concentration tends to dissipate this. Perhaps Sister Fursey guessed that I was not so engaged, for when speech is restricted, telepathy soon develops between the members of a community: but she forbore to break in upon musings which she connected with the afternoon's visit.

Far from praying, I wandered back to the time, so distant as to hold for me a period-charm, when I used to stay with Charlotte in her parents' country-house for week-end parties.

Even then, a strain of melancholy was perceptible in Charlotte's temperament though she strove to hide this beneath buoyant chatter; and already she showed signs of a capacity for devotion, personal or impersonal, which had found no object worth its constancy. In contrast to her striking looks, her manner was withdrawn; she took little notice of her guests with the exception of myself, and I became her chosen companion. Indeed, we two were linked by a strange fate, whose influence we felt even before any untoward manifestation had taken place.

We both could see him, but he appeared only to one of us at a time. I was the first to be selected. One day I had left the garden to post a letter, and was crossing the green near the pond outside, when a car driven by a young man, his girl-friend sitting beside him, drew up nearby. Perhaps this incident was brought to my mind by the afternoon's happenings at the *Manoir*, which naturally recalled my previous meeting with Nikolaz. But the youth of former days was of a different type; at first I noticed nothing strange about him, thinking that the couple were dressed casually for a summer outing: but when he stepped from the car, I saw that he was completely naked. This did not surprise me as much as might be expected for his aspect was angelic—tall, bronzed, classically-muscled, with gold hair curling back from his face, and eyes that met mine sweetly. I looked down, expecting to see a penis below the tendrils of pubic hair, but he had none: nor could I see any testicles. He seemed neuter rather than hermaphrodite.

He put me in mind of a man I had met during a visit to Spain, whose good-looks had a touching quality that made me want to weep. Darker than the angelic youth who had stepped from the car, he could not be called dark, for his eyes were grey and his complexion fresh. He was tall, but I could see beneath his simple clothes hips rather too fleshy to look well in a matador's costume.

His character was friendly and intuitive, entirely without the conceit which barricades many handsome men. I understood that he was a martyr though I was not sure which one; I confused him with Garcia Lorca whose violent death might be considered a martyrdom. Or was he 'the Bull made for Death,' the *torero** celebrated by both Lorca and Alberti?

He was followed by a younger man with blond wavy hair; this one's looks also had a quality of innocence, though he was more narcissistic and therefore less sympathetic to me. The older man gave him a light caress by stroking his cheek and I realised with astonishment that they were father and son. There seemed scarcely enough difference in their ages for this to be possible; however, I suppose the elder may have been in his early thirties and the younger in his late 'teens. He also was a martyr: could they have been S.S. Protus and Hyacinth,* the progenitor and the flower sprung from a wound?

As we neared the walls of the Ianua Vitae, already rising dark against a glimmering sky, I returned also from these past scenes of *bourgeois* plenty and perturbation to the stark quietude of convent-life; and I recognised what a deeply-unsettling effect Charlotte's recital of her recent intrigue must have had upon me.

So much was this so, that I was not even astonished when a few days afterwards Sister Fursey, who had evidently constituted herself my accomplice, slipped a note into my hand on her return from herding alone in the neighbourhood of Kerlescan. The envelope bore the manorial crest, and I did not need to open it to know what it contained.

8

ON MY WAY

"Well, Sister? You wanted to see me?"

The voice of Sister Mary Paracelsus was calm, even reassuring; but I could not at once reply because of the constriction in my throat.

"Yes, Sister," I choked. There was another pause, while the familiar clutter of the stillroom was telling me to stay; each vessel begged me not to give words, irrevocable words, to my decision to leave; each instrument implored me to make no mention of Nikolaz.

"Sister, you are disturbed. You had better tell me your trouble at once. Try to speak."

I felt as though, if I tried to tell at that moment what was on my mind, I should only dissolve into tears. Should I bring up instead some triviality on which to ask her advice—the question of headcloth or veil, the delineation of the marches where our herd had the right to graze? Anything rather than come to the point! But procrastination was no use; I had to finish the interview now that it was begun.

"Sister, I must leave!" I burst out at last. "I can't continue in the religious life."

"Why is this, Sister?" The voice was still calm.

"I've never had a vocation, I see that now. I feel hemmed in; I can't stay here forever."

"We don't rule life by our feelings, as you know," was the reply. "But I am sure you have reached this decision only after much meditation. And it does not surprise me; I am more surprised that you should have remained with us so long."

I gasped.

"Yes, Sister Brigid, you have done your best, and we have appreciated your help in many matters. But you are primarily a poet, and we are aiming at something other than poetry."

"Thank you, Sister," was all I could find to say.

"Of course we must consult Reverend Mother about a rescript of your vows and she will be sorry, I know—as we all will be, all. It is not a light thing to lose one of our number. The formalities may take some months, but I don't think there will ultimately be any obstacle to your release. That is the right word for you, 'release,' isn't it?"

"I suppose so, Sister."

I was more completely crushed than if she had scolded, pleaded, or questioned me closely. Yet her manner covered no spite; she saw things as they were, and spoke as she saw.

"I will make only one suggestion," Sister Mary Paracelsus added. "When you leave us, try to find out where you are and where you are going. Perhaps I should not say even so much, but—"

A pulse in the Novice-Mistress's temple, just visible beneath her veil, told me that if the worst part of the interview had been for me at the beginning, the worst part for her was now, at the end. She was always pale but today much paler than usual. I curtsied, and vanished without another word.

That is how it should have happened, but it didn't. I could not summon the courage to face Sister Mary Paracelsus, so I left the Ianua Vitae swiftly and by stealth instead of withdrawing in a slower but more regular way.

I had it all arranged with Nikolaz; we had fixed the details on the occasions of our last meeting by the cromlech of Crucuno.* At the dark of the moon I was to slip out and make my way to the Strand of the Cormorants where he would pick me up in his yacht.

It was the fateful day, Nikolaz' own, December the sixth;* and Sister Mary Paracelsus was on my mind all morning. She had sent me out on some messages, so I found myself roaming through that quarter of the little town where open spaces were devoted to market-stalls. In one of these booths various kinds of shoes and sandals from the mainland were displayed, some of them strung together in bunches. I looked at the cheaper sandals, coloured dark red or tan, which I had been commissioned to buy for the Postulants. A tall nun had forestalled me and was already inquiring about them. In spite of the fawn-coloured habit she was wearing, I had to look twice at her before I could be sure that she was not our own Novice-Mistress. To my guilty conscience, it seemed that it was Sister Mary Paracelsus herself who had followed me, half-divining my intention of escape, to see whether I carried out her behests. As I was making an inquiry about the sandals, the strange nun gave me a sidelong look, as though doubtful of my good-faith.

Finding the price too high, and her glances too suspicious, I was moving away when she called after me, asking if I came from the North.

"No, from the South," I replied, meaning the South of Ireland.* But I understood that she was asking whether or not I was a Catholic; she fancied, perhaps, that our somewhat unusual habit might have been designed by some High Anglican group with a yen for conventual existence.

I tried to hurry away, but she pursued me with questions about what Order I belonged to, where our convent was situated and so on. Finally she said,

"Your name is Sister Brigid, isn't it?" But she pronounced the name strangely.

Near the markets was a quarter where houses clustered on either side of twisting byways: and as I set off along one of these in an attempt to elude the tall nun, I came upon a domed chapel approached by an alley-way. I did not remember noticing it before but it could be easily missed, being hidden behind other buildings. I entered, drawn by a sense of peace which emanated from the thickness of its ancient walls, hushing the noises of the market. The interior was still except for the bemused dance of motes in a sunbeam which slanted down from a high window.

Scarcely had I seated myself in an obscure corner when two figures, dressed in priestly robes of red and gold, glided into the sanctuary and began to celebrate Mass. With less surprise than the strangeness warranted,* I saw that their vestments had been discreetly tailored to the feminine figure. The celebrant, a woman of austere and commanding beauty, was attired as a Bishop, while her companion, who was darker and some years younger, acted as Server. With a wonted grace they moved through the ritual, no word of which could I catch, only a murmur as of subdued breezes. The priestesses seemed unaware of my presence: and having all at once the feeling that I should not be there, I withdrew in silence.

How long I had watched them I do not know; whether it was as one would expect, some thirty minutes, or whether beneath the shelter of this dome one's sense of duration varied, I cannot say. But by the time I left, the tall nun had had time to catch up on me. She now invited me, in most friendly fashion, to visit the convent where, she said, she was staying for a rest. When I made objection that I must return at once to the Ianua Vitae, she assured me that there was a short cut to it through her own convent-building. I could no longer refuse without churlishness, so I followed her in. As she passed on ahead, I was greeted by a young Lay-sister in a dark habit who was acting as Porteress.

"How did the tall nun know my name?" I asked her.

"O, we are quite accustomed to Sister Mara's seership," she answered gaily.

I then realised that this Sister Mara* was indeed Sister Mary Paracelsus, our Novice-Mistress; and that she possessed, among her other powers, that of bi-location.

Inside the building, I hurried through a number of rooms that made little impression on me. But the penultimate one looked out upon a street that had a more meridional air than most in Ménec; one of the windows was too high above ground for a jump, but opposite was one overlooking a courtyard. Large gates barred its access to the street and they were locked.

A sensation of claustrophobia overcame me. I was sure that the Novice-Mistress had been spying on me and was now tricking me—this place was no short cut but a more effective prison than the Ianua Vitae had ever been. Our convent was not in fact a difficult place from which to make one's escape: some of the cells were situated on the ground-floor where it would be easy to climb through a window. But now, even if I managed to return there by some devious route, I felt that I should certainly be watched and perhaps guarded. So my escape, planned for the evening, must be put into execution at once if it were to have any chance of success.

For the moment at least, I had the run of the building where I now found myself; no one was directly supervising my movements, so I hastened onwards to the last room, which was lit only through the slats of the shutters and contained nothing but a bed. Across this bed I knew I had to squeeze, face downwards with the wire springs beneath me and the mattress above. There was just enough space for me to do this, so I felt no panic but accepted the task as one of the ordeals which traditionally precede entry into a new life. Reaching the far side, I gave a final heave and freed myself from the lumpy flock mattress that overlapped the foundation. Once at the other side of the room I opened the interior shutters.

I looked down upon the same courtyard as I had seen from the previous room; but I found myself much nearer to the gates and had a wider view of the neighbourhood beyond them. This was a mews-quarter adapted now as a number of garages, in one of which I spied a fire-engine and its crew making ready for a practice-run. Three red engines, each with a golden or a silver bell, stood like lions ready to dash out of their hutches at the first call of flame.

Several of the men saw me at the window and smiled with good humour. Thus encouraged, I climbed on to the outer ledge and so to the top of the huge gates, the thickness of which provided a foothold; but I could descend no further, so I singled out one of the firemen and called to him to help me down. He seemed willing; but warned me that it was illegal for them to aid anyone in escaping from the convent, and that a *gendarme* was always lurking in one or other of the garages. However, after consultation with another fireman, he agreed to my request.

"After all," he remarked, "if I am questioned, I can be vague about the date."

But at that moment a *gendarme,* whom we could see was grey-headed because he was not wearing his uniform-cap, came out from some place of concealment and arrested him. The representative of the law marched off my would-be helper without so much as a glance at me; evidently he thought that such escapades could be dealt with by the Church, the State not interesting itself in them except in so far as they might affect the civil population.

By this time I had explored for a foothold some way down the gate, though my head and shoulders were still on a level with its top. The fireman with whom my vanished friend had parleyed now seemed eager to come to my rescue. Undeterred by the fate of his comrade, he suggested pushing some fire-fighting apparatus towards the gate, but warned me that I might get scorched in climbing down it as it had only just returned from the scene of a conflagration. The contraption was standing in the angle formed by one of the garages and the outside wall of the convent. Clinging even as precariously as I was, I regarded it with misgiving; it was some kind of steel ladder, perhaps extensible, but it did not attract me as an aid to descent.

Then the fireman picked up some young leaves of monstrous size and membranous texture which were lying on the ground. In shape they resembled the leaves of rhubarb or gunnera*—refuse, perhaps, of the markets and blown here by a gust of wind. The fireman threw several of these up towards me and I caught one of them: while the rest, wafted by favouring eddies, flew to different parts of the convent.

Suddenly Sister Mara emerged from a garage, rushed towards one of the leaves and seized it.* Together with the fireman she unfolded it and looked inside where a nude hermaphrodite* had been drawn. By craning forward, and downward I could see that the breasts were female but the genitals male. Though the head of the sketch was missing or at most but faintly indicated, I recognised that it represented Sister Mara herself.

She came close to the foot of the gate and looked up at me: then nodded in the direction of the fireman, who was still scrutinising the sketch.

"Can he guess from that how old I am?" she inquired of me anxiously.

I did not know how to answer her; but I now felt as secure on my perch as a statue in a niche. Though still poised between two worlds, it was as though I had already discarded the habit of a religious; and was glad when Sister Mara, by stretching to her full height, was able to help me to earth. I realised that my feeling of safety was an illusion, in no way justified by my position, and I would be better off with my two feet on the ground. I call her Sister Mara but perhaps now some other name would be more appropriate, seeing that she was no longer wearing a nun's habit. She had assumed instead a flannel skirt and gray jersey; I supposed that she had a confederate among the firemen or garage-hands, who provided her with an opportunity to change her clothes.

Having thanked her for easing my scramble down the gate, I told her that I was already late and had no time to talk to her. Though I still could not accept her as identical with Sister Mary Paracelsus, I did not wish to divulge my plan of escape to her further, and this in spite of her own seeming dereliction of duty. She replied that she was going abroad, and wrote my name against the address of the Ianua Vitae in a notebook. As I said goodbye I begged her, with some hypocrisy, to keep in touch with me.

9

ACQUISITION

Choosing its less-frequented lanes, I hastened through the little town of Ménec towards open country and the desolate seashore of Rosharho where I was to await Nikolaz. I knew the spot already, having grazed our herd some time ago on its southern borders, a country of sand-dunes and rough pasture. The only living creatures there today were the sea-gulls that with necks outstretched congregated on rocky islet and promontory or wheeled overhead, uttering the desperate cries that lure mankind to a watery doom. A sad-voiced rivulet wandered towards the shore, to spill itself finally in a delta over the sand. As I slipped off my sandals to wade across, a rhythmic thudding was wafted to me downstream—the sound of wet garments beaten against a stone. I caught my breath, not daring to glance inshore, for the sight of the *Laveuses de la Nuit** was an omen much dreaded by the islanders. To have heard the sound of their washing was terrible enough; and I knew that if I looked down at the water flowing past my ankles, I should see it stained with blood.

I gained the north-western end of the territory where formidable cliffs crumbled into the sea. The granite in this part of the island, unlike much of that near the port of Ménec and the villages of Kervin-Brigitte and Kerlescan, was of a reddish tinge. Cyclopean blocks,* their strata tilted vertiginously, were heaped together at hazard; struck by the declining sun, they glowed as though they had hardly begun to cool after the volcanic spasm which had long ago forced them outward from the centre of the earth. They were strangely bare of the lichens that grew on the other side of the island; sole vegetation here was the gigantic tangle. Sprawling over those rocks which had tumbled from the cliff and lay at the margin of the sea, it reached with stems sinewy as a man's arm into awesome depths, where its fronds floated and swayed like strips of dusky flesh.

Here I picked my way, according to the directions in Nikolaz' letter. No difficulty arose in following these, and only the roughness of the going hindered my finding the oval entrance at the foot of the cliff which they described.

Stooping, I slipped inside; before me a narrow tunnel slanted upwards. As I followed it, the pathway levelled until it was more or less horizontal and soon debouched into a cavern. The expanse of a subterranean lake formed the floor, the brink composed of shingle dual in colour—reddish-purple and dull-green— like a variety of limestone found in the County Kerry.* Through the vault above, a radiance from some source which was to me imperceptible, but which I imagined to be a hidden cleft down and across which the light ricocheted, was diffused over the scene below. Too tense with expectancy to feel any sense of oppression from the enclosed space, I made my way round the narrow shore, searching the anfractuosities of the rock for the ledge where I should discover the panoply of my new life.

I could not find it. I made the circuit of the sombre lake more than once while the crunch of my footsteps re-echoed from the soaring walls. The water was clear but too faintly illumined for me to look into its depths, and its unrippled surface gave back no sparkle at all. Though I could not see what I was searching for, I noticed in my circumambulations a fissure in the rocks which seemed to lead into another cave—a gully filled with water, though unconnected with the lake and so narrow as to be scarcely touched by the light filtering through the roof of the main cavern. I felt that my only chance of gaining what I sought was to plunge here.

I stripped off my clothes and slithered in, gasping at the icy shock of the water, which soon became too deep for wading and compelled me to swim. There was so little light that I could not see where I was going and my strokes frequently touched the gully's sides. Then the beginning of a phosphoric gleam, similar to that which I had left behind in the cavern, showed the way ahead; the water grew shallow again and I was able to draw myself out upon a miniature strand. The cave now arching above me was much smaller than the one I had left and its floor was dry, a continuation of the pebble beach where I had just landed.

I rose shivering* but prepared to search anew for the desired cranny, when I was confronted by a girl who stepped out from the shadows at the far end of the grotto. She wore a red sweater and black jeans and carried a book in her hand; she stared at me fixedly but without sharing my astonishment at our encounter. To break the silence I opened, crudely enough, with:

"What is the book you're reading?"

"It is called *Contes de Jeune,* Stories of Starvation."

"What is it about?"

"It concerns a monstrous people called the Guermes, somewhat like the Anthropophagi.* In one story the narrator describes how he made music by dancing on a puppy."

She began a macabre solo with trampling movements of the feet.

"Indeed," I remarked, trying to keep calm.

"In another tale the slim dark man is marked out for sacrifice."

I felt, if possible, colder than before.

"And in another there is a race of people like leaves or sepals, half-vegetable. Do you know anything about them?"

"One can't take all one reads, literally," I suggested.

At this the girl's face became distorted* into the semblance of a baboon's and was thrust snarling against mine. I crushed it with one blow of my left fist. Coupled with this muscular smartness, I had the mental celerity to recall that the left is the appropriate weapon with which to combat the dark forces, and congratulated myself on my resolution in dealing with an averse manifestation.

Before the baboon-girl could recover I plunged into the gully and swam back to the larger cavern. There I resumed my search for the hiding place described by Nikolaz; and this time without difficulty I came upon it, about half-way round the circumference of the lake. Resting upon a ledge in a rocky cavity and just out of view, was the suit-case which I had left at the *Manoir*. This I opened and unpacked, and found it to contain all I would immediately need for my escape; though, except for the little black dress, the formal clothes which I had wrapped around the Heirloom were no longer there; nor was the treasure itself.

Trembling with cold, I was glad to put on clothes of any kind; but the sophisticated lingerie, an almost-forgotten luxury, which my lover had provided, raised my spirits as much as the warmth of the outer garments.

"Well," I thought, as I pulled on the tailored trousers, the caressing sweater, the enveloping coat, even the socks and casual shoes, "if one is going to have a man, one may as well pick someone who knows his way around the world."

Everything in my secular outfit was simple but of excellent quality: even the scarf bore the design of a famous Paris house. Nikolaz had thought of all I might need, from a stream-lined make-up kit and perfume to a rug. There was a wrist-watch, handbag, torch, even a box of sanitary tampons. He had not forgotten a small flask of cognac and a light but delicious meal: the sight of these made me realise how hungry I was, and I ate and drank with avidity.

I scarcely wondered whether the baboon-girl would attempt to follow me, so sure did I feel that she would not. And when I glanced round at the place where I had emerged dripping from the gully, it eluded my sight as though it had sunk away into the shadows, or the rocks had closed together to efface it.

My convent-clothes lay where I had thrown them on entering the water—the worn habit and veil, the much-mended sandals, the unglamorous underwear, all now seemed pathetic encumbrances to be left behind me as soon as possible.

I recollected with what touching ceremonial I had received them—the outer garments at least—on the day of my Clothing as a Novice, when they were conferred upon me as emblems of an inner robe of glory. Underclothes were not (I suppose understandably) included in this symbolism; though it occurred to me that, our far-from-Phrynean* knickers might serve as well to remind us of chastity as the Girdle. I now discarded them all forever by stuffing them deep into the cranny from which I had drawn the suit-case; and then I had nothing to do but wait, listening for the sound of the yacht's engine.

I realised I should not hear it from within the cavern so, although I knew the hour to be too early yet to expect it, I found myself retracing the way down the tunnel to the strand. Keeping within the shadowed entrance, I peered out: my adventures in the cavern must have occupied some hours, for night was now well advanced. All was still and moonless, the sea visible only as a denser band of dark beyond the sand, and inaudible but for a susurration* as the waves died at its margin. If a strong wind had been blowing off-shore I might have noticed no sound until the beaching of the dinghy; but on such a night as this I was certain of hearing the engine from some distance away.

I heard nothing, then and for a long time. Hour after hour I waited in suspense, not daring to emerge from my hiding-place. What should I do if no one came? To be sure I had my new clothes, to which I had already become attached on account of their comfort and quality, to give me a sense of poise. But I had no money, contacts nor means of livelihood; and I wished at all costs to avoid altercation with Church authorities or with anyone at the Ianua Vitae. I could scarcely remain at large on Ménec—too many people knew me by sight. To return to the community and acknowledge myself in the wrong did not even occur to me as a possible course of action, so thoroughly had I sloughed off my conventual existence.

I was beginning to shiver again, for the air outside the cleft was taking on the cold of the small hours and that of the tunnel within was dank from the miasma of the sweating rocks. Wrapping myself in the rug, I lay down near the opening of the passage and remained perfectly still, hoping thus to avoid dissipating any bodily heat. I must have dozed, for it seemed I heard an intruder walking stealthily, first round the lake and then down the passage towards me. He said to me,

"Will you drink a draught of the ruby?"*

I realised that he was offering me poison, and woke up terrified. The next thing my conscious mind registered was the sound of footsteps on the sand outside. I was awake and up instantly, my heart pounding.

Someone slowly approached, not from the direction of the sea but along the foot of the cliffs; whoever it was had difficulty in locating the tunnel—the beam of a torch raked the cliff-face for a moment and was extinguished. Crouching to one side of the entrance, I waited. Nearer and nearer drew the hesitating steps: then the torch shone directly into my refuge. I replied by switching on my own, which showed me only that this man was not Nikolaz before a shaking voice queried:

"Mademoiselle Ella?"

"Yes?"

"Mademoiselle, let us not be seen." A figure pushed past me into the tunnel. "I have some shocking news for you:* M. de Kerlescan cannot fulfil his assignation."

He need not have continued: I was frozen with the certainty of disaster. I could not speak, only gaze blankly into the darkness.

"Where is he?" I managed to choke out, after a pause.

"We do not know. On his way out to the yacht, the dinghy capsized—a sudden wave took it, rising out of a flat calm. The coast is treacherous hereabouts, Mademoiselle; de Kerlescan was no swimmer and he sank immediately. They have not found his body. No one else was drowned."

As if I cared whether they were! But a wild hope invaded me: could this be some cruel ruse? Who was my informant? I shone my torch now full upon his face and recognised him as the cellar-man at the *Manoir,* a sallow rat of a man. Could he still bear me a grudge? But I saw that his message was genuine even if he had some hidden satisfaction in delivering it to me.

"Yes, Mademoiselle, I was servant to de Kerlescan," he continued, as though aware of my suspicion. "There is no hope," he added brokenly.

"What am I to do." It was less a question than a complaint.

"No one knows what will happen to any of us," he replied. "But for you, Mademoiselle, matters are more urgent. There is to be a Requiem to-morrow in the Abbey, you will wish to be there?"

"Yes."

"I can arrange it. Meantime, stay hidden; and afterwards I will help you to depart."

"I've nowhere to go."

"This is not the only island in the region. If you remain here, your community will feel in duty bound to pursue you; but they will scarcely do so beyond Ménec. Do you know where the yacht was bound for?"

"No."

"It was the island of Cruz-Moquen:* he intended that you should stay there until you grew accustomed to your new life. You could still go there."

"You're most kind."

"He would have wished it."

Indicating a basket in which he had brought me provisions, the cellar-man bade me farewell.

"Mademoiselle, I must leave you; I have much to do. Till tomorrow," and he shuffled away through the darkness.

I ate and drank, then slept again, this time profoundly and for some hours. When I awoke, the sun's position told me that it was past mid-day: I hurried back into the cave, and dashed some of the lake-water into my face; then by the light of the torch, applied the make-up which Nikolaz would not now appreciate. I changed my sea-going outfit for the black dress, and by the time I had finished I could not have looked much like the Sister Brigid whom the islanders were accustomed to see tending cattle. Nevertheless, on my way to the *Manoir* I was careful to take advantage of any cover which presented itself. I avoided the main gates of the demesne, through which Sister Fursey and I had left on the occasion of my only previous visit, and sought out a track leading through boscage toward the mansion.

The cellar-man must have divined my intention to take this route, for almost at once the thickets parted to reveal him, dressed entirely in black.

"The night-boat for Cruz-Moquen sails about half-past nine," he told me. "You had better take it, Mademoiselle; there will not be another for a week— longer, if the weather should turn stormy."

"I'll be there."

"You know the way to the harbour? Good. I shall not be free to accompany you, so must wish you a safe journey now."

He pressed a ticket and money into my hands; then produced a certain leather casket. I hesitated to accept this, but he insisted, declaring that the Heir had always intended it for me. While I was still protesting he hurried away.

I followed him through the coppices, which thinned out as we approached the ruined abbey adjacent to the *Manoir* itself, where the Requiem Mass was to be celebrated. Gothic pillars marked out the plan of the vast nave, roofless but floored with green turf. The scattered worshippers by no means filled it; I noticed three children dressed in scarlet near the front and a group of late-comers standing at the back near the remains of the west wall.

The cellar-man pushed through this group to a place further in, then knelt down and crossed himself in a matter-of-fact way. I did not follow him up the nave, not wishing to make myself conspicuous. I glanced round to see whether any members of our Order were present on behalf of the Ianua Vitae: but as far as I could judge they had boycotted the ceremony, probably on account of de Kerlescan's highhanded action in blocking the right-of-way. I also feared that my outfit would be considered by some of the congregation as too casual for such an occasion—even though, being held in the open air, a little informality was allowable—for, unlike them, I was bare-headed.

The east wall of the abbey had long since crumbled away, and the present *Manoir* had been built in such a way that its west gable-end rose above the foundations of the vanished apse. The altar had been set up within a balcony-window of this wall, overlooking the remains of the nave: and was heaped with such late blooms as might persist in sheltered corners out of doors, supplemented by more exotic plants from the conservatory. Their varied hues showed up delicately against the stonework in fitful sunshine; but I was too far off to distinguish their species. Three priests edged their way through the massed flowers to the front of the altar, accompanied by the sound of an organ issuing from the room beyond. A choir was already assembled in smaller balconies to right and left.

The Requiem began; the well-known rite, moulded by the custom of centuries to the exigencies of death, unfolded itself with accepted dignity. I felt happy and at peace, lulled by the balsamic chant which I would have wished to continue forever. Why do our proselytisers confront the would-be catechumen* with dogmas demanding intellectual assent? (though pertaining to matters beyond the intellect's domain). Would not converts be more numerous and more deeply convinced if they were simply asked to watch and listen, above all to listen? A ritual well-performed, especially with traditional music, should carry its own power, more effective than that of discursive statement or emotional appeal, to project its participants into a changed sphere of consciousness.

> *Tuba mirum spargens sonum*
> *Per sepulchra regionum*
> *Coget omnes ante thronum**

The clarion of the *Dies Irae* broke in upon my musings, and for a moment it seemed to me that the voice of the choir was indeed that of the last trumpet, which had summoned us assistants hither to the very region of the grave, and the altar suspended above us in its decorated balcony nothing less than the throne of judgment. Strangely, I felt no grief at the passing of one whom these ceremonies would speed on his way: I had been drawn to him not only by liking but by a current of passion that flowed between us so strongly as to disrupt my life. My future was uncertain and without promise, yet I felt no rancour, regret nor resentment. Fate is, I said to myself; it is the medium, like the ether,* in which I dwell.

Before the *Ite, missa est** I slipped away, to conceal myself once more in the nearby woods; I could not afford to take chances, and resolved to remain there until dusk. I now had the opportunity to open the casket and examine closely the jewel left me by the Heir. Though of a bracelet's shape and size, it was not quite a bracelet: it was of gold set with three large amber-coloured stones, each in a leafy-spray converging to the middle of the circle. Seen in profile, these fronds rose towards the centre like the heads of ravenous serpents, making the whole a piece of sculpture rather than a trinket to wear, since it was impossible to pass it over one's hand and along the arm.

I experienced a sense of recognition: Nikolaz had already given me this treasure before his death—on the occasion of my visit to the *Manoir,* when I had been accused of stealing it—for it was indeed the family Heirloom. I could not accept it while still living as a religious, but at one of our subsequent meetings he had confirmed his wish that I should have it.

10

RED

Lying hidden in the woods of the *Manoir,* I had little to do but speculate on the destination for which I was that evening to set out. I had never been to the neighbouring island of Cruz-Moquen, which was far enough away to be invisible from any point on Ménec: but I had heard something about it in the days of my Novitiate at Ianua Vitae. During the War, Mother Ste. Barbe had departed with most of our community for this island which (though we had not hitherto been molested in any way) was thought to be safer than our own.

Soon after the division of our community, however, the military authorities on Ménec took over a large part of the convent-buildings and here quartered their 'personnel.'

I was for some reason chosen as one of the few to remain, under Sister Mary Paracelsus, during the occupation by the armed forces.* No doubt it was hoped that our presence would check the proclivities of the soldiers by moral example if not by authority—dissuading them, among other things, from damage to the fabric of our House.

The remnant of us had retained a portion of the buildings for our own use; and though this was out of bounds for other ranks, we could not prevent their officers from straying about wherever they chose. I must say they did not abuse this commandeered privilege; but one day when I was helping in the still-room— the military had developed a taste for some of our recipes as a change from their own commissariat—a fair-haired Lieutenant passed one of the open windows. He tossed a note through it in my direction, and I seized this and concealed it inside the front of my habit.

An hour or so after this incident, orders were given for the bulk of the force to evacuate Ménec, and a dark Lieutenant was left in charge of the detachment which stayed to occupy the position as rearguard. I had as yet had no opportunity to examine my note, and the thought crossed my mind that with the increasing danger, my sweat would make the paper so limp that it would cease to crackle conspicuously. Sister Mary Paracelsus had detailed me to act as her special *aide,* but I did not think she had noticed anything. Before the final withdrawal, the dark Lieutenant and myself were summoned to a room on the ground-floor where the C.O. was seated with other officers behind a long table. Upon it in front of him reposed an ancient chest which he handed over to us, asking if I would dispose of it somewhere in Kervin-Brigitte, the hamlet in the neighbourhood of the convent. I suppose he thought I would know the locality and therefore be able to suggest a hiding-place for it. But I refused, saying it was a task for the Lieutenant. The senior officers and their forces then left.

The blond Lieutenant had also been directed to stay behind, but in some capacity junior to the dark one. I had no clear idea of the military hierarchy, and assumed that in an emergency such as this the more formal distinctions of duty tended to be ignored. It was in fact Sister Mary Paracelsus who took the lead, and suggested to the two young men that the remaining religious should join forces with the detachment still under their command for the defence of the buildings. To this they agreed, and decided to reconnoitre their position with a view to deploying the defenders to the best advantage. In the course of these manoeuvres, the blond Lieutenant made occasion to approach me and told me not to be afraid, as he would protect me.

Alas! His promise proved to be of no practical value since, on reaching the main stairway, we found that we had been surprised by an advance-party of the enemy who had made an entrance unperceived. We were severally overpowered and I was separated from my Lieutenant.

My captors began to hurry me along one of our endless corridors, making brief investigation of the structure as they went but following me closely so as to prevent my retreat. I heard the voices of schoolgirls coming from the rooms on either side of the corridor; it was a part of the convent which I scarcely knew, where some of our Sisters used to give classes to the village-girls. The voices cried out that one of these children, whom they called Mimi, had been cruelly beaten; she had been found bleeding and half-dead and who would be next?

As we reached the end of the corridor I glanced into a little room opening on the left. It was panelled with wood and had very small windows, one of them barred. The floor was covered with a mattress under a sheet; there were blood stains, but Mimi had disappeared.

There was a room on the right still smaller and seemingly empty: it must have been immediately above one of those occupied by the children, for I could hear their voices rising muffled through the floor-boards. Then an orderly emerged from the room on the left, saying that he had cleaned up the blood.

I was now pushed through the doorway facing me at the end of the corridor. An elderly woman whom I recognised as Madame Lacoste,* keeper of the

brothel by the harbour, was sitting in a double bed. I had occasionally encountered her as she bargained at the market-stalls. She was not a Bretonne, having
migrated to this lost region from the Mide; and she must have had good reason
for so doing, since for one of her profession it would have been less profitable
than more southerly and more frequented shores. She spoke with an accent so
guttural that she could hardly have been a woman of the South; I felt sure she
must hail from Central Europe, though from which country I could not tell.

Nor had I heard what, if anything, was the 'speciality' of her house; but
regarding her personal diversions, market-gossip credited her with a taste for
very young men of the epicene type.* It was rumoured that she had lately beaten
one of these to death for her pleasure.

Her appearance, indeed, disengaged a horrifying quality; harsh as to skin
and feature, she had so frizzed and gilded her cropped hair that one could no
longer guess its natural shade, and her eyes flickered like the small blue flames
of sulphur. Her favourite costume for marketing was a pair of tapered trousers
which, since her hips were not heavily fleshed, might have looked well enough
had she not topped it with a jersey through whose mesh the breasts, triced into
some formidable 'foundation-garment,' strained as they jutted from her ribs like
two enormous lemons. Now they were lolling loose under a flowered *négligée*.

It was evident that she had attached herself to the invading forces. She beck-
oned me to climb into the bed beside her; it seemed the only thing for me to do.
Her voice was smooth with welcome but it veiled a threat. I knew that I was to
be the next victim.

Madame Lacoste began by showing me a folded card elaborately printed
with colours in the style of an illuminated manuscript. Examining it I saw that it
recorded her numerous marriages, nine or ten of them, in pious and sentimental
phrases. Ironically I drew in my mind a contrast between the contents of this
card and her present situation; meanwhile, she continued to talk with her glib
friendly menace.

"It is the little herdswoman, is it not? Many times have I seen her bareheaded
in the lanes. Now perhaps she would like to take off—other things!"

The men who had brought me to her were still standing about the room—
each appeared to have his allotted space. Now they began to bring forward and
show off their instruments for beating, one of which was a long rod ending in a
kind of steel ladle; and there were others.

I became aware that while in the bed I had shed my convent-knickers; how,
I do not know—whether Madame Lacoste had adroitly hitched them down
while she was speaking or whether I had done so myself, under the influence of

her subliminal suggestion. But the upper part of my habit remained in position and I was thereby assured that the Lieutenant's note was safe. I had not read it, nor even unfolded it, but I felt convinced that it bore a message which must not fall into enemy hands.

"What do you want from me?" I asked Madame Lacoste in desperation.

"Just tell me what you and your Novice-Mistress did together!"

I knew what she was insinuating, and protested that my relationship with Sister Mary Paracelsus, though friendly, was sedate: so that I had nothing to tell. In vain; since I lacked the presence of mind to invent a story spicy enough to satisfy this harpy, the torture must proceed.

The men took up their implements. One of their number re-entering by the open door, attracted my eyes to this avenue of escape, and I saw that for the moment it was left unguarded. Could I dash out? I made a half-movement towards it, but the man who had just come in forestalled me. He took his stance in the doorway and, drawing a long-bow, shot an arrow outward and down the length of the corridor. Was this to show me how I should be transfixed were I to attempt to get away, or was it a signal for the torture to begin?

Merciful oblivion obscured what followed, nor could I recollect further details of this war-time episode in our annals. Liberation may have supervened not too long afterwards, followed by the re-uniting of our community. But looking back now upon these events, I saw that the dark Lieutenant must have been Nikolaz; I had failed to recognise him on the occasion of our first meeting because the intervening years had changed the correct young officer into an eccentric country-squire. No doubt the coffer which his C.O. had asked me to hide contained, even then, the Heirloom; and Nikolaz had guarded this himself until the day he first offered it to me.

Now, I determined always to carry the treasure with me as a safe-conduct wherever I might go; and this, not only on account of its material value, though that may have been considerable: but rather because of some talismanic virtue* which I sensed to reside in it and which, far from diminishing with the disappearance of its giver, was in some mysterious way enhanced.

11

SAFEGUARD GOING OUT

In the late afternoon I left the sheltering trees of the *Manoir* and made my way towards the port. It was a quarter of the town which I scarcely knew: indeed I could not recall that I ever had occasion to visit it since the day of my arrival. Usually my excursions beyond the convent-grounds took me to open country, in quest of pasturage for our beast: if I were sent into the town of Ménec it was to buy something needed by the community. The latitude which was allowed to us while herding did not extend to urban expeditions, and explorations beyond the market-square were not encouraged. If it seemed to our Superiors that any of us had been over-long on a message, we were asked to account for every minute spent. I blessed those rules which I had often in the past found irksome, since now the hazard of being recognised was thereby lessened. I had at least a fair idea of the way I should take, and already I was in sight of the coast.

The sun was setting in wintry splendour; below a moon waning in the zenith, cumulous sailed eastward, golden, full-blown. Southward along the sea-horizon a red wound gaped in a bank of cloud showing blue-green beyond. Due east, the expanse was striated by wind-spun cirrus, while to the north a rosy suffusion was fading. The eastern vault grew cooler, more leaden; beneath it the ocean surged slate-green, breaking white against the islets.

Just north of west, a two-fold nacreous gash rimmed with pallid fire appeared on the horizon; here the upper side of the drifting clouds was ink-blue, threatening; thunder scudded over the whole western sky. Southward the gashes widened, blown all the while from the north-west where masses of vapour careered like smoke, extinguishing the occidental glow.

A single cloud still capped with fire towered above the bank of haze to the south-east, its head rising against a sky darkly striated. Further east the cumulous, also fire-capped, still floated, though pushed all the time further away by the gale; in the north hung a cold pallor.

A band of blush-rose suddenly stretched itself from beyond the declivity westward of the town and increased, only to be over-powered by a canopy of greyness, bringing rain. Yet it managed to expand further south over the sea, becoming milk-pale as the water darkened. Again the incandescence lighted up, grew brighter, again subsided. Instead an elf-light flowed south while the zenith lowered; the sea lay almost brown, meeting the base of cumulus at the horizon; above, the clouds melted, seeming to run with ink.

A shallow arch of vapour now spanned the distance from west to east; the glow returned, silhouetting the headland beyond the town. Rain fell; the sea blackened, sucking in its foam. The western sky, a watery yellowish-grey, muffled the outlines of cliff and skerry.

"It'll be a dirty night," I thought.

So also thought the captain of the boat for Cruz-Moquen; when I descended the cobbled road to the jetty, I was told that he would not be sailing for a day or two owing to the threat of storm. There was nothing for it but to find a lodging; but this was not difficult, since the householders of the quarter were accustomed to the weather's vagaries and the human flotsam brought thereby to their doors. I took a room in an unpretentious house and deposited my case, feeling impatient at the delay; the sooner I could leave Ménec, the better; too restless to sleep, I decided to risk a stroll; the rain had stopped and there was even a lull in the wind.

The strains of some Celtic tune rendered on a *cornemuse** and the singing of seamen were borne up to me from the water-front as I wandered through the tiny fishing-port sheltered from the weather, the air of its byways warm with the suffocation of love. There were a few street-lamps of antiquated design and these I avoided, even though they served to intensify rather than mitigate the darkness.

Next morning I found the sailors and fishermen still shaking their heads over the outlook—no one would attempt the voyage to Cruz-Moquen for at least several days. It was a rough passage, I gathered, even in settled weather. The wind was gusty and at any moment might blow up into a gale; but there was no rain, so I decided to have a look at the Château of Brésil-Peulven,* home of Nikolaz' parents. This was situated a little way inland beside the lake of Locqueltas,* an artificial lake begun in 1924 and not completed until 1931. This work was put in hand by Nikolaz' father, who was looked on as a public benefactor since he thus supplied most of the island with water.

Leaving the port of Ménec behind me,* I set out along the coast and watched the recurling waves of Brittany dash themselves in spray upon the rocks. Soon my road turned inland, bringing me to the entrance of the Château. The gateway to the avenue was of baroque design, its escutcheoned stonework supported by the totem-beasts* of the lord and his silver-blue lady.

The gate was opened by a swart dumpy woman who accosted me in the local *patois,* asking if I were the new pupil they were expecting? On an impulse I replied that I was, and requested her to fetch the suit-case from my water-front lodging. This she promised to do, but first insisted on conducting me up the avenue. I gathered that the noble but impoverished pair held a kind of court or rather, a school of etiquette for their own daughters and those of their landed neighbours.

"Perhaps it is not too late for me also to achieve sophistication," I mused.

But soon I recognised that the instruction by them must be somehow faulty; their daughters, far from marrying well, had all three contracted doubtful alliances; and I had to admit that from their point of view, this must also be true of their son, whom they never mentioned.

The eldest and most beautiful daughter, a *rousse* after the style of Rossetti,* was conjoined with a young man named Sammy who favoured pearl-grey suits of too slick a cut. He was always moneyless and was engaged—when he worked at all—in shady pursuits.

The second daughter was black-haired and her marriage was no more satisfactory, for her husband was never with her. He had abandoned her, it seemed, for she did not even know whether he was still living.

The third, who consoled herself with a lover, had married a cripple; and in her own pale intense features there was a trace of the facial set and expression of the hunchback.

The two husbands who were present lived under the patriarchal roof—an arrangement which was not unhappy: no one was cramped, the Château extending ample accommodation to all. Yet a sense of futility hung over the household, making its activities seem without purpose.

One evening soon after my arrival the pupils, together with members of the family, assembled in the lighted hall. Though no one spoke of Nikolaz, I knew that the festivities were to be held in his memory. I was offered a dish of ritual food—a kind of salad, slivers of vegetables sauced with a thin cream which I ate with relish. Then the chief nurse-instructress, a blonde peasant-woman assisted by the dumpy girl who had led me in, appeared with some very holy food. This was an aromatic herb with leaves about the size of mint; but though some of these were green, others were fuchsia-red or purple-blue, in shape more like sorrel or shamrock.

I took the herb of grace* and added some to my salad, enjoying the variety of taste. When I had finished eating I scattered the remnant of this attenuated meal ceremonially about the hall. Immediately a cry of 'Sacrilege!' went up from the company.

Whereas before this incident I had been in a fair way to becoming a favourite with all, I was now an object of execration. Though I was older than most of the pupils, I now tried to make friends with some of the younger ones, two dark-haired girls who were always together. Their answer was vehemently to clasp my wrists and hands, digging in their fingernails which were varnished and filed to a point.

I realised that I should not have scattered, even with ceremony, the remains of the special herb: if I had instead taken care to consume every fragment with the rest of the salad, I should not have scandalised my hosts. Yet I did not regret this *gaffe* since I could now leave them without hindrance, and I had come to feel that their approval meant little to me.

Next day, though the weather had scarcely improved, I determined to return to the harbour, where I hoped to find some craft, whether of the regular line or another, with a captain intrepid enough to undertake the journey to Cruz-Moquen.

12

BEARDLESS

Beatrice did not like being alone: the boys had gone out for the day in Ossian's car to see a collection of expensive bric-à-brac which was on show in a town some distance away. Daphnis Burge had declared that they 'ought' to see it; to miss it would label them as not keeping in touch; and Ossian needed little persuasion. On the way back they would probably stop, between bursts of speeding, at bars patronised by their kind, and not return till mid-night at the earliest.

They were referred to as 'the boys' though Ossian was nearing forty and Daphnis only a few years younger. But youth, like gaiety, was a pose which they had to sustain if they were to remain socially acceptable in the circles they frequented. At a deeper level the Peter Pan *persona* was in fact connected with the irresponsibility of their natures, and with the fact that the laws prohibiting their favourite pastimes were unenforceable or at least unenforced.* Ossian's broad pinkish face with its mask-like smile was almost unlined, and his wavy hair was barely touched with grey above his elaborately-rimmed sun-glasses. (It was *chic* among his friends to adopt a fashion in accessories which had been popular with women a season or two before).

After lunch, Charlotte had retired to her room with a headache which was genuine enough, though produced by jealousy out of humiliation. To Beatrice, whose health had always been robust, her conduct seemed sulky. Charlotte was always *difficile,* as temperament without abounding talent usually is. Beatrice passed a barely-tolerable afternoon in the company of some hotel-acquaintance with whom she would not have associated in England; but she always had to hold court, and these naive tourists were impressed by the glamour of the concert-platform which still clung about her like some exotic scent.

At dinner Charlotte again did not appear: and after sipping her coffee and liqueur Beatrice, overcome by a mingling of ennui and curiosity, mounted the stairs, more stiffly than she cared to acknowledge, to her daughter-in-law's bed-room. Pinned to the door was the expected notice, "Please do not disturb," but below in the left-hand corner, written small, were the letters P.T.O. Beatrice knocked, tried the handle and then tore off the paper. On the reverse she read:

'Key in lock on inner side; push through and draw out below door.'*

How like Charlotte! Always trying to attract attention by some tiresome whim. But Beatrice felt uneasy as she prodded the key out with her nail-file and heard it clatter to the floor on the far side. There was a space between door and floor; by crouching down beside it and stretching inwards with the file, she managed to reach the key and coax it out.

When she opened the door she saw at once what had happened. Charlotte wrapped in a dressing-gown lay on the large bed; her skin, already the colour of earth, shone with a congealed sweat that glued strands of hair to her brow. A trickle of vomit had run from her open mouth and stained the sheet. On the bedside-table was an empty pill-box and a half-empty glass of water. Beatrice had always deplored her habit of keeping supplies of sedatives, obtained by the expedient of going the round of her medical advisers. Her dentist would prescribe them for toothache, her gynaecologist for period pains, her G.P. for insomnia and a psychologist-friend for general need of tranquilisation. Beatrice had never liked to touch her daughter-in-law even while living; and she did not need to do so now to be sure that she had been dead for some hours.*

Disgusted rather than shocked, she looked round for the regulation note— all this was dreadfully like reports in the kind of newspapers she affected to despise, but which she often read on the quiet. She found what she sought— on the dressing-table, of course. The envelope was fastened and addressed to Ossian but Beatrice had no compunction about opening it: the boy's feelings must be spared at any cost. She read:

> Dear Ossian,
> I can't stand any more: you've always made my life a purgatory and since you insisted on bringing Daphnis with us it's been a hell.
> You don't want me; if it wasn't D. it would be someone else, as you've already shown. You mean to go on as you began, with Beatrice's conniv-ance; but I am going to stop. I know this will cause you more relief than regret.
> Charlotte.

This would never do: if it became public a first-class scandal might blow up. The police mustn't find it, not even the French police. Beatrice crumpled the letter and envelope into her handbag and stealthily left the room, locking the door. She crossed the corridor to the lavatory opposite where she burnt the papers with her cigarette-lighter, letting their ashy fragments drop into the pan, and then flushed them away. She could not know and did not suspect that another letter, similar to the one she had destroyed but much more detailed, and addressed to Charlotte's brother Keith, was at that moment flying serenely above the French countryside in a mail-plane. Charlotte, pleading migraine, had tipped the chambermaid to post it immediately after lunch.

When Beatrice hurried down to the office of the hotel-manager to give, discreetly, the alarm, her pallor and trembling were not simulated; but she was still able, with some degree of calm, to consult with him what to do. Luckily it was a fine September evening and most of the other guests were out, so suspicions were not immediately aroused. He agreed, for obvious reasons, with Beatrice in keeping the affair as quiet as possible: fellow-guests were to be told that *Madame Mortimore Jeune* was gravely ill and had been taken to hospital. But doctor and police must be summoned, and at once.

By the time 'the boys' returned, she had answered the officials' questions and Charlotte's body had been removed to the local mortuary. She met her son in the entrance hall, where he and Daphnis were thumbing through a packet of letters which had arrived for them during the day; and she demanded Ossian's attention in private. When, outwardly undisturbed, he entered his friend's room a little later to pass on the news, he found Daphnis already packing his smart cases.

Strangely enough, Daphnis had found among his mail an invitation from some dear friends in Tangier; and with an instinct for making himself scarce when trouble was about, was preparing to move on. One glance at Ossian told him how right he was: any emotion too profound to be superficially demonstrated caused him irritation and disquiet. Brief condolences were all he could spare, for after a good deal of telephoning, during which his blonded curls became ruffled, he found that he could catch an early plane. It was not worth going to bed; indeed there was scarcely time to do so. Instead, he hired a car to the nearest airport and was soon away, a haggard Ossian waving him farewell.

Ossian knew these amusing friends in Tangier and had no wish to figure in their gossip as the disconsolate widower. Daphnis so loathed and despised women that he would even tread deliberately on their heels when walking down a crowded street. Though Ossian had often enjoyed his malicious sallies at the expense of others, he knew how readily they could be turned upon himself. Ossian hoped, somehow, to safeguard for the future his position in what amounted to a select and influential club, to which a glance, an inflexion, a shade of tie or waistcoat might admit or bar admission. Without formal organisation, yet with branches in every country, it gave its members the entry into cultured society wherever they cared to go; and with this, the chance of interesting and profitable employment.

Though he felt the shock of Charlotte's death more than he allowed Daphnis to see, and though he had always felt uneasy at the ban which refused women the lesser courtesies, he could still think with envy of the parties frequented by lithe Arab boys and half-wished to accompany his friend. He did not resent Daphnis' desertion: he would have acted similarly himself in a like situation.

In their set it was understood that self-interest came first: when a relationship grew awkward for any reason, one went on to the next. If loyalty existed (and it was never mentioned, being one of the taboo-words like 'sincerity') it was paid to the cult itself rather than to any individual. Ossian knew by the glaze over Daphnis' pale insolent eyes that their affair was at an end; he could only hope that comments on it would not be too scathing.

Ossian could not quit Beatrice at this juncture, nor did he altogether wish to do so. Like a child, he was more frightened than hurt, but he was badly frightened. He thought with horror of the corpse he had not seen: this was his first brush with death, and it made him conscious of his own advancing years. Had he enjoyed them, for all his pose of gaiety? What was the point of his life up to now; and what of his future?

'Thank God she didn't leave a note,' he murmured. He must go to confession today, without fail. Unable to sleep, he lay half-dressed on the bed in the room which Daphnis had vacated, musing dismally. So little had husband and wife been in each other's confidence of late that he had no idea how Charlotte might have disposed of her property: with luck it would go to the children, but in matters concerning Charlotte one could never be sure. She might have left it to the Church, in spite of her lack of enthusiasm; or to some obscure charity. In any case little enough would filter through to him, he guessed; and the prospect of actually having to earn a living appalled him. At the worst he might even find himself responsible for Hilary's expenses too. And then his friends: he was aware how narrow is the gap that separates a dear boy—or even 'dear girl'—from an old horror; and he was approaching the age when, even with an adequate income, this transition is all-too-easily made. An ageing playboy needs a cheque-book for passport.

Ossian now longed to return to his mother's Kensington flat;* if international contacts failed him, family solidarity might come to the rescue. He was anxious to leave the resort which now held nothing but evil association for him; but he and Beatrice could not depart for another few days at least, since the practical arrangements which death involves were complicated by suicide in a foreign country.

Rumour was already busy and awkward questions were making his life intolerable, when, a day or two later, he caught sight of his brother-in-law Keith mounting the steps into the hotel lounge with a vigorous stride. Of course, relatives had been informed by telegram of the tragedy, but Beatrice had everything in hand so why should . . . ? Ossian had never cared for Keith, and now he remarked with consternation the set of his jaw and his eyes' steely glint. If he disliked him personally, he disliked still more his profession—the law; a bulging brief-case might contain anything. Keith had always supported Charlotte in their disputes and now it looked as though he meant to make trouble. Surely Charlotte, patient during her lifetime, had not by a penultimate action seen to it that he would do so?

x   x   x   x   x

I had all this from Ossian who, whatever his faults, never lacked candour, when he also arrived at our shores.* Unable to endure further the strain of the holiday-resort, he had sought escape in the group of islands off the coast, and I met him, somewhat bedraggled yet still with his 'spoilt boy' air, on the quay while I was waiting for the boat to Cruz-Moquen. During our hastily-snatched conversation there was one thing I did not like to ask him—how had he come there? Attempted suicide was a recurrent drama among his acquaintances: one of them would jump out of a window—and sprain an ankle: another would cast himself into a fire—and singe his beard. Jealousy, the usual motive, would be assuaged at the subsequent reconciliation and fêting of the hero.

Ossian must have done something more effective; had he perhaps swum out to sea one evening until he had gone too far to return, and been picked up by the *Ile-de-Ménec*? Whether this or some other means brought him to us, his story of Charlotte's death revealed much to me; and I remembered the words that Sister Mary Paracelsus must often have had in mind though she never framed them in my hearing: 'Try to find out where you are and where you are going.'

130

13

JOY

She had been thrown up like a piece of flotsam* at the edge of the tide, which, having reached the full, was now beginning to recede from the slope of the strand. From time to time a wave with more force than its fellows still broke over her; and though she was soaking with sea-water, the heat of the sun was strong enough to dry her a little before the next smother of surf flowed up to her. She lay with her back to the ocean, her left side dinting the moist sand and her head pillowed on a heap of gleaming seaweed, which mingled its tendrils with those of her hair.

She had not yet opened her eyes, and the crash of the waves was the only sound perceptible, its rhythm pervading her limbs and mind.

"This is further south than Cruz-Moquen," was her first perception.

Indifferent to changes from wet to dry, from cold to warm, she scarcely breathed, storing impacts but no longer reacting to them. Now, a part of the strand itself she felt the old dichotomies fall away from her—opposition between body and spirit, or the differentiations of time and space no longer had a meaning. The water and air of the place coursed singing through her channels as though these were formed of sand. She subsisted from moment to moment in a state that was not even acceptance, so close was her communion with the elements around her. She lay thus for many hours while the sound of the billows grew fainter with the out-going tide; sometimes she fell asleep, sometimes awoke, but she was without impulse to move.

During a hypnagogic* phase she suddenly rose into the air; made desperate by two persecutors—the old woman and the young man—she was inspired to utter the words that confounded them, in speech that was almost song. As the notes rose and fell, so did she rise from the ground or sink towards it, though never to touch it. This airborne dance-chant not only superseded for her any other art-form: it was an insurge of that spontaneous action which cannot fail of its objective, yet remains unbound.

She took her enemies one at a time and the words which overcame them rose unpremeditated to her lips. For each of them it proved the final shaft when, as they were almost spent, they heard her voice imitating them in a kind of ironic echo.

Reflected as in a mirror, or as though looking back upon her performance from beyond herself, she saw her own face radiant with power and heard the voice issuing resonant with force from the ripe lips. The hair, no longer bleached by salt winds and sunlight or faded by the stress of the years, flowed rich with colour to her shoulders. The robe she wore changed from blue or green to mauve or rose according to the direction of her movement.

As the air-dance soared to its climax at the height of the neighbouring trees, she reached in herself a state of ecstatic union. Below her the figure of the man knelt on the sand to ask a blessing, while his voice floated up to her acclaiming her as a saint. She returned to her sandy couch with a feeling of fulfilment.

The sun began to lose its strength and she opened her eyes, sat up and then dragged herself beyond the tide-mark to the border of the beach where sand had been banked by wind into loose masses. Though she still hardly looked about her, she glanced down at the single garment she was wearing and saw that it was a cotton shift, much torn and weathered. This was her only possession, yet she felt no desire for anything more. She did not even notice the absence of the talisman whose virtue had brought her thus far. Here the sand, untouched by the ocean's recurrences, was warm beneath her; and she again lay down and nestled into it, cherished by the sun's heat which lingered there through the darkened hours.

When daylight again woke her and she looked up at the sky, it was to watch once again the perennial drama of dawn. On the south-eastern horizon a few fiery threads appeared above a bank of blue-grey mist. Light spread upwards from these, kindling the underside of level clouds which, thinning out and widening as they neared the zenith, faded there into parallel bands against a pale background.

Individual forms began to melt and give way to a suffusing colour which, as it deepened, and brightened, was reflected in the sea below. The water was calm, except where it broke round a rocky islet in an oval of surf—not white, but turquoise-green, a flashing contrast to the roseate surface of the water.*

Then, instead of brightening still more, all grew dim as though the sun was being drawn back into the depths below. The bank of cloud upon the horizon darkened; only its crest now shone, illuminated from the back. Due east, lilac clouds parted in gashes of ivory.

Now the fiery crest of the cloud-bank put forth rays of shining mist on either hand; but the sea, grown sullen, would reflect nothing.

Once more as she watched, light receded from the dawn-centre, though the zenith in spite of itself was brightening from moment to moment. At last a rim of fire edged its way above the screen of cloud and a flood of intense colour again spread upward, touching the thread-like strands of vapour to renewed life.

But it was with a difficult birth that the sun emerged,* its orb still obscured by slivers of sea-mist; and scarcely had it freed itself from them when a pall descended from above, engulfing it. A chink of vivid light between two worlds of vapour was all that remained of it.

The zenith-clouds, loosened now into shapelessness, took on an apricot tinge; meanwhile, one of the gashes to the east stretched northward rimmed with gold, the sky behind it changing to silken green. The gold grew pale; the gash extended southward also, its border reaching out above the chink where the sun had vanished, glowing smokily.

Slowly warmth and light triumphed; she took off her one garment, which was so much faded by light and stained by salt water that she could not be sure of its original colour, and gazing into the luminous blue, lay naked in the caress of another day.

"There must have been a wreck,"* she surmised, but did not speculate upon the details of this catastrophe.

Instead, she began to take in her new environment. To the east, the shore stretched away to low cliffs and a promontory of rocks; behind her, sand-dunes made a shelter from the north, while before her the glittering sea lay open. Westward, green herbage came down almost to the water's edge, leading inland to a forest; and it was toward this direction that her first steps took her, when she presently rose and again put on her ragged dress.

"Soon, perhaps, I shall not need even this," was her intuition.

As she wandered along the strand she noticed that the vegetation ahead was unfamiliar to her, but she did not ask herself how far she must have come.

On the sandy stretch by the last reef stood a chapel, so close to the sea that it must have been submerged at the highest tides. Impelled by a forgotten habit, she entered its empty shell. It was windowless except for a slit at the east end above the remains of a stone altar. The interior walls were rose-coloured, but whether on account of a layer of crumbling fresco or because they were lined with a different stone, she did not observe.

Through the cracks in the flagstones of the floor spiralled a mist, drawn upward at low tide from foundations by the sun's heat. She breathed it in as a sibylline fume, leaning for support against one of the walls, her head spinning. With hallucinated clarity came the realisation:

"I am here."

"But who am I that am here?" a question came echoing from the past. The very name of Sister Brigid was forgotten with the Ianua Vitae which she had once thought her home; while Ella de Maine, who had come both before and after, like the alternation of spring- and neap-tides, and all who had shared her experiences, were less than shades. Memory had receded on a tide whose cycle was greater than that of the ocean now spreading outward on her left.

"I am," was enough for her.

Leaving the deserted chapel, she entered the nearest glades of the woodland where, untempted, she picked some glowing fruit from one of the smaller trees and ate it, though she scarcely felt hunger. Presently she dabbled in a spring and tasted this also, but rather for the pleasure of it than to quench thirst. Water, so clear of any legend, custom or dogma refreshed her, as though to banish the Well-Meadow for ever from her mind.

She did not know where she was going nor did she ask. The hum of insects was around her and the calling of birds came to her from the undergrowth; she wondered if other forms of life were sheltered here, but she had no fear of any wild beasts there might be. Human beings would be more formidable but even of them she felt no apprehension.

"This island is uninhabited," came as a conviction from the depths of her being.

She was alone, completely alone, for the first time in her existence. She had a sense of freedom never before experienced, with nothing and no one to inhibit the impulse of the moment. No duties, no rewards, no one to impress, no one to try to love, nothing to pay, nothing to buy; nothing to do but breathe—those derivatives of breath, aspiration and inspiration, forgotten with ambition and toil, and as little worth remembering. The prospect of this state continuing indefinitely did not daunt her, but rather filled her with relief.

"Everything is free and I am free of everything," she mused; then all at once she cried, "I have not left the earth!" and a sound like bird-song broke unheeded from her lips.

The end

NOTES

The Latin epigraph from which Colquhoun derived her title, "Vidi aquam egredientem de templo a latere sinistra," is a slightly modified quotation from the *Vidi Aquam*— scriptural verses traditionally recited during the Easter season in Catholic churches, specifically during the rite of sprinkling with Holy Water. It translates as "I saw water coming from the Temple from the left side." The true text is "Vidi aquam egredi- entem de templo a latere dextro." In substituting the left-hand side for the right, Colquhoun draws attention to a dichotomy that is sometimes present in the routes to enlightenment taught by different occult systems. Following from H. P. Blavatsky's adaptation of the language of Tantra, the left-hand path is sometimes equated with black magic and Satanism. It is more accurate, however, to say that those who take this path are displaying an independence of thought and behavior, in comparison to the more rule-bound conventional approach taken by others. In making this change, Colquhoun is pointing to the unorthodox teaching of the Ianua Vitae Convent and to Sister Brigid's individualistic and sometimes transgressive behavior. Rituals involving the left-hand path commonly involve sexual energies. Given that the reconciliation of the genders lies at the heart of the convent's mission, this allusion may have been intended. In translation, the text from the *Vidi Aquam*, which refers to purification from sin and the bestowal of grace, continues, "I saw water coming forth from the Temple from the right side, alleluia: and all those were saved to whom that water came, and they shall say alleluia." The importance of elemental water to Brigid's spiritual journey becomes increasingly apparent as the novel progresses.

AUTHOR'S PREFACE

41   *the "second-death"* / A theosophical concept referring to a stage in the cycle of life, death, and regeneration. It is explained more fully in the introduction, page 7.

CHAPTER 1: PALE

The chapter title refers to the geomantic figure Albus (Latin; white). It represents peace, wisdom, and purity.

43   *Sister Mary Paracelsus* / In *I Saw Water,* the names of the characters (and settings) reinforce the novel's key themes. The novice mistress's name combines the Christian

with the hermetic. Mary, as the mother of Jesus, has important Catholic associations, and Paracelsus (1493–1541), the Renaissance physician, botanist, alchemist, astrologer, and occultist, is regarded as one of the greatest theoreticians of Western magic. The female and male genders are also linked in her name.

the still-room / Not a room for quiet contemplation but a place for distilling alcoholic drinks. Sister Paracelsus continues the long tradition of brewing and fermenting at religious houses (Benedictine, the liqueur, is perhaps the best-known example). This is also the room where she follows quite a different tradition, the preparation of herbal remedies.

as idle dreams are not encouraged, nor even Wordsworthian wanderings lonely as a cloud . . . / Ironies abound here, as much of *I Saw Water* was produced from Colquhoun's own (non-idle) dreams. Further, Brigid, an individualist vainly trying to lead a communal life, continually reimagines the relationship between nature, memory, solitude, and the self, which William Wordsworth's highly popular poem "I Wandered Lonely as a Cloud" (written 1804) celebrates in the "flash upon the inward eye / Which is the bliss of solitude."

Novices; Postulant / A novice is a prospective member of a religious order whose suitability is being assessed. Acceptance as a novice usually follows a period as a postulant, the first informal step toward admission to the order. The novice participates as fully as possible in the life of the community, joining the professed nuns for work and prayer. A successful novice is then admitted to vows. During the period of their novitiate, novices are under the direct supervision of a novice mistress—in the present case, Sister Paracelsus.

St. Januarius; St. Mazhe / Januarius may have been martyred in the persecution of Diocletian (ca. A.D. 305) and interred in the church at Naples, where his dried blood has seemed to many to exhibit the miracle of liquefaction, particularly in May and September. This phenomenon has been the subject of a number of scientific investigations over the centuries; see *Catholic Encyclopedia,* s.v. "St. Januarius," http://www .newadvent.org/cathen/08295a.htm. "Mazhe" is the Breton "Matthew" (consistent with the Breton setting of the novel). While the liquefaction and bubbling up of Saint Januarius's blood may presage the holy wells later in *I Saw Water,* his feast day of September 19 and Saint Matthew's of September 21 seem the salient detail in the narrator's invocation of them as "the Church's way of marking the Equinox." The narrator sees Mazhe's significance for the seasonal change as greater than his sainthood in the Catholic Church, but Januarius of Naples also evokes the Roman god Janus, the god of transitions and of the doorways to which Colquhoun refers. In this sense, Janus, looking forward and backward and marking transitions, suggests the narrator's and other characters' situation on the Island of the Dead; they are caught in a transitory after-death state, pulled between the details of their lives and a future second death.

A link is also made between change in spiritual affairs and in celestial affairs—the essential unity throughout nature.

Equinox / The autumn equinox generally occurs on September 23, when the equator is in the direct path of the sun, so that day and night are of equal length. A large number of religious feasts and festivals occur around the autumn equinox, a time for harvest and preparation for winter.

44   *Cistercian* / The Order of Cistercians is a Catholic monastic order. It is renowned for its daily austerity and emphasis on physical labor.

'L'enfer, c'est les autres' / "Hell is other people." A line from Jean Paul Sartre's 1944 existentialist play *Huis clos* (commonly translated as *No Exit*). Like *I Saw Water*, Sartre's play depicts characters caught together in an afterlife, but Sartre's characters all know they are dead and are stuck with one another for eternity. Sister Brigid glibly dismisses both the monastic common life of the Cistercians and Sartre's existentialist drama as if they mean the same thing—an undesirable, inescapable social proximity to others—and equates the philosophically dense drama of Sartre (whose works in their entirety were banned by the Catholic Church) with the "ephemeral reading-matter" banned by Ianua Vitae. Whereas the nuns make every effort to retain a "link with a former life" by covertly reading old newspapers, Brigid understands that such a life of confined retrospection is no more than the initial phase of her afterlife.

Ianua Vitae / The name of the convent comes from the Latin proverb *Mors ianua vitae*—"Death is the portal to life"—indicating the cycle of birth, death, and regeneration.

45   *The Parthenogenesist Order* / Parthenogenesis is a form of asexual reproduction found in certain animals (and plants), in which growth and development of embryos occurs in the female without fertilization by a male. Etymologically, the word derives from two Greek words meaning "virgin birth." However, in Christian belief, the virgin birth of Jesus was not a case of parthenogenesis but, like the resurrection, a strictly miraculous occurrence, not explicable as a natural process. The significance of the name of the order, and the nature of its mission, is explained on page 69 of the novel and in its accompanying note.

loden-cloth / A water-resistant material for clothing made from sheep's wool, without removing the lanolin. It is usually green and traditionally used in Austrian clothing.

Black Forest / This reference to the place of origin of the Parthenogenesists is a reminder that Bavaria has many occult associations. It was said to have been the birthplace of Anna Sprengel, Countess of Landsfeldt, the perhaps apocryphal founder of the first temple of the Hermetic Order of the Golden Dawn (ca. 1866) and alleged source of the cipher manuscripts on which the order's rituals were based. Additionally, Theodor Reuss (1855–1923) was active in a number of irregular Masonic lodges in Germany. He attempted to revitalize the Bavarian Order of the Illuminati and went on to found the Ordo Templi Orientis in 1906. Colquhoun was a member of its Nu Isis cell in Britain in the 1950s.

beat-session / The young nurse likely meant dancing to popular music, but Sister Brigid immediately thinks of one of the specialist services available at the local brothel. The reason she draws this startling conclusion becomes clear in chapter 10.

46   *The moment the words were out of my mouth . . .* / In this paragraph, Colquhoun gives the reader some basic information about the Catholic faith and monastic rules. All members of the Catholic Church are encouraged to perform a regular examination of conscience—that is, to reflect on the morality of their daily thoughts and actions. If necessary, an act of contrition should be performed—the saying of a prayer that expresses sorrow for one's sins. The recital of prayers relating to the theological virtues (Acts of Faith, Hope, Charity) results in a partial remission of one's sins. A mortal sin is a deliberate wrongful act of such seriousness that it condemns a person to hell after death.

    Higher standards of thought and action are expected of those who subject themselves to monastic or conventual life. These standards are codified into three "counsels of perfection." They are chastity, poverty, and obedience.

    In the Parthenogenesist Order, The Peerless Guidances correspond to the councils of perfection and The Breaking of Bonds to the act of contrition. Acts of Faith, Hope, and Charity are known much more poetically as The Soaring, The Stretching of Wings, and The Song at the Point of Day, respectively.

47   *'scrannel-pipe'* / A thin voice. Though the phrase has appeared in several poems, it most famously occurs in "Lycidas" (1638), Milton's elegy for a friend who had drowned in the Irish Sea. The allusion hints at Charlotte's death and at Sister Brigid's efforts to make sense of it.

Ella de Maine; Sister Brigid / When individuals enter a monastery or convent, they put aside their old name, along with their old identity and individuality. The new name is chosen to reflect their spiritual aspirations. In her chosen name, Sister Brigid links two separate spiritual traditions. Brigid is the name of an important Irish Catholic saint who lived ca. 451–525, but it also has powerful pagan associations, being identified with one of the Celtic triple goddesses. In *The White Goddess*, Robert Graves highlights the pre-Christian Brigid's connections to poetry and the connections that poets later made to Christianity: "In medieval Irish poetry Mary was equally plainly identified with Brigit the Goddess of Poetry: for St. Brigit, the Virgin as Muse, was popularly known as 'Mary of the Gael.' Brigit as a Goddess had been a Triad: the Brigit of Poetry, the Brigit of Healing and the Brigit of Smithcraft." Graves, *The White Goddess* (London: Faber and Faber, 1948), 346.

Kervin-Brigitte / The origin of the name of this actual hamlet in Morbihan is unclear. Colquhoun undoubtedly selected it because she saw in it the conjunction of the genders. Kervin is a variant of the Irish boy's name Kerwin. There is a large standing stone in a field adjacent to the road that leads to the village.

Healing Chapel, dedicated to Our Lady of the Trees / That trees have a spirit, or possess intelligence or powers such as healing, is an ancient belief once found in cultures the world over. Groves or individual trees may be revered, and the place where an especially powerful tree once stood may retain its spiritual properties. See J. G. Frazer, *The Golden Bough*, abridged ed. (London: Macmillan, 1922), chaps. 9–10. The site of the convent's "wonder-working tree," as with many pagan sites, has, to an extent, been Christianized and acquired associations with the Virgin Mary. This place is particularly exalted, being also the location of a holy well.

Willow / An infusion made from willow bark is a traditional herbal remedy for diarrhea. The watery habitat of the willow forms the link between the tree and the ailment.

48 *palm, cedar, olive and cypress* / According to some traditions, Christ's cross was constructed from these four woods. They signify the four quarters of the globe.

tufa-like / The action of water flowing through limestone dissolves calcium carbonate and then deposits it as tufa, a porous rock.

Sister Mary Cornely / This is an instance of Colquhoun devising a name that combines male and female elements. The sister is named for Saint Cornély (Cornelius), the protector of domestic horned animals. He is celebrated in Morbihan with a Pardon, held on the second Sunday in September. Within living memory, as part of a surviving pagan ritual, cattle were garlanded with flowers and blessed with holy water at Saint Cornély's Pardon. Sister Brigid, it will be recalled, is busy herding cows at the start of *I Saw Water*.

elder-flower-fritters / Elderflowers, either as an infusion or fritters, are a traditional remedy for colds and flu-like symptoms.

Herbal remedies are the pride of our Order . . . / The order, especially in the figure of Sister Paracelsus, embodies a paradox. Sister Paracelsus is at once a nun and a skilled herbalist, but the worldview of the herbalist is not a Christian one. The reason for using particular plants and herbs to treat specific disorders must lie, in part, in empirical observations of their effects, but also in the magical belief that the whole of the created cosmos is linked in a meaningful way. The original sixteenth-century Paracelsus was largely responsible for the codification of this doctrine with respect to natural medicines. Sometimes referred to as the Doctrine of Signatures, the theory holds that since every component part of an individual corresponds with other aspects of nature, then bodily organs will, for example, correspond with certain plants and herbs. The appearance and habitat of a plant will give clues to its medicinal usages. Sister Brigid's subsequent remarks on the ways in which God chooses to show himself should be taken with this in mind.

Through her soubriquet "La Druidesse," Sister Paracelsus is also associated with pagan elements, in particular the fabled Druidical knowledge of natural remedies. Like her Renaissance namesake and pagan forebears, she regards health as having spiritual as well as physical components.

CHAPTER 2: SORROW

The chapter title refers to the geomantic figure Tristitia (Latin; sorrow). It represents pain and suffering.

50   *Ossian* / The most likely source of this name is *The Poems of Ossian,* the celebrated literary forgeries by James MacPherson published in the 1760s, which duped many of the leading literary figures of the time. They were claimed to be translations from ancient Celtic originals. The poetry, like the character of Ossian in the novel, is plausible at first sight, but fraudulent.

Beatrice / In Dante's poem *The Divine Comedy,* a lengthy allegory of the soul's journey toward God, Beatrice is Dante's guide through the spheres of heaven. Yet the explicit naming of Ossian's mother after Dante's Beatrice is highly ironic in that she essentially helps lead Charlotte to destruction rather than spiritual salvation. Her gaudy self-display and spiteful role in her son's marriage set her apart from the innocent object of Dante's courtly love in *La Vita Nuova* and *The Divine Comedy.*

Morbihan / A department (i.e., administrative district) in Brittany. It contains a concentration of megalithic monuments, including the extensive stone rows at Carnac. Ménec is imagined to be an island off its coastline.

Daphnis Burge / Probably named for the legend of Daphnis and Chloe, naive foundlings who fell in love. In early drafts of the novel, Charlotte was to be named Chloe.

mauve list / Charlotte means that most of her and Ossian's friends are homosexual. The color mauve has been associated with homosexuality since the 1890s—the "mauve decade"—when it became popular with figures such as Oscar Wilde and Aubrey Beardsley.

51   *Sandhurst* / The Royal Military Academy Sandhurst is where all officers in the British army are trained. It is situated in Surrey, about thirty miles from London.

52   *Baron Corvo* / Pseudonym of Frederick Rolfe (1860–1913), a writer and eccentric best remembered for his autobiographical fiction, with its homoerotic undertones.

53 *two worlds* / What might, at first sight, appear to be a reference to two of the occult worlds of manifest existence is here no more than an idiomatic expression meaning that Ossian was enjoying all the opportunities available to him. The phrase will take on other, more hermetic meanings as the novel develops (e.g., page 108).

54 *contagion* / The idea that certain physical diseases are contagious is a familiar one, but Charlotte is suggesting that mental states can also infect other people. This is a very old idea that found favor with Jung and other psychoanalysts who used it to explain crowd behavior.

55 *'Death by drowning'* / For most readers of twentieth-century English literature, this phrase will evoke the "Death by Water" section of T. S. Eliot's poem *The Waste Land*. Without pursuing the complexities of the poem, one pervasive theme is the sterility and loss of meaning in modern culture, which has become distanced from its spiritual roots. At the individual level, Charlotte's own life is here revealed as shallow and lacking in spiritual direction. Another theme of the poem, the Adonis myth, concerning the young god whose death was commemorated by the annual "drowning" of effigies and plants in the sea or springs, is of less obvious immediate relevance to this passage, but will become clear when Nikolaz de Kerlescan is introduced in chapter 7. Nikolaz's own death by drowning is dealt with on page 114.

CHAPTER 3: A WOMAN YOUNG

The chapter title refers to the geomantic figure Puella (Latin; girl). It represents peace and passivity. It is the symbol of female sexuality.

56 *second birth* / A reference to the theosophical belief in the evolution of the soul that takes place during the cycles of life, death, and regeneration.

I had chosen the right mother / This is a curious remark for Sister Brigid to make. She means that she regards Charlotte as a guide or mentor for her spiritual journey, despite nurturance not being one of her obvious qualities. Charlotte is impulsive, unstable, and drawn into unsuitable personal relationships, both before her arrival on Ménec and during her stay. Nonetheless, Brigid feels a deep psychological bond with her. A number of their shared paranormal experiences are described in the novel.

esoteric advancement / Esoteric knowledge may be the product of private study or group ritual activity. In the latter, a group of like-minded people seeking the same goals are likely to have a powerful gestalt. When Charlotte and Sister Brigid join the Snake Dance, they both achieve the Light—a state of heightened awareness that is both physical and spiritual.

'hermetic wife' / Perhaps nothing more is meant than that the two were not legally married. However, the phrase can also refer to the sexual union between a magician

and his partner, on either the physical or spiritual planes, thereby achieving an important magical objective: the conjunction of the male and female principles.

Snake Dance / This can refer, generally, to a procession of people who join hands and move forward in a zigzag line or, specifically, to a ceremonial dance of the Hopi Indians of North America intended to ensure rain and an abundant harvest. Colquhoun's primary meaning was the former, but she may also have had in mind the latter. The fact that the dancing floor is the site of an old threshing floor links the dance to the harvest rites, in which the cut and reaped grain is identified with Adonis, the dying and reviving vegetation god. Frazer, *The Golden Bough,* 335–41.

Shiva Nataraja and his Shakti / Shiva is a Hindu god, here in his guise as the Lord of the Dance—the cosmic dancer who performs his divine dance to destroy a weary universe and make preparations for the god Brahma to start the process of creation. Shakti is Shiva's consort.

57 *As it faded . . .* / Although some of the details in the following paragraphs are obscure, the overall meaning is clear. Colquhoun is drawing a distinction between two of the traditional routes to spiritual advancement. In one, knowledge is transmitted from master to disciple following established teachings; in the other, no hierophant (spiritual guide) is required and the aspirant relies on personal mystical insight—the route of self-initiation.

like a fisherman in blue dungarees, emerged from the wilderness / The themes of sterility, healing, restoration, and rebirth run throughout *I Saw Water.* The present phrase suggests the fisher king invoked in T. S. Eliot's *The Waste Land,* which was inspired by Jessie Weston's *From Ritual to Romance* (1920). In her turn heavily influenced by J. G. Frazer's *The Golden Bough,* Weston had posited pre-Christian pagan fertility rites as the origins of the wounded, impotent "fisher king" of the Grail legends, whose body (and lands) must be restored to fertility by the Grail quest.

the trial of the cage of holly-stems / This phrase is probably intended to suggest pagan and Christian tree lore, in which the holly tree carries associations of death and rebirth, in the latter case because of its connections with Christ's crown of thorns. This train of thought leads Colquhoun to Christ as the fisher of men and makes the link with Weston's fisher king.

He then showed us a diagram . . . / The diagram resembles a modification of the Qabalistic Tree of Life, leading to Kether, the "crown" at the top. Those who use the Tree to guide their studies either choose the mystical path, or "way of illumination," that ascends straight up the central pillar, or the occult path that winds up and around the Tree in accordance with a complex series of initiatory steps.

58 *the Blind leading the Blind* / Painted in 1568 by Pieter Brueghel the Elder, *The Blind Leading the Blind* illustrates one of Jesus's parables in the New Testament (Luke

6:39–40): "Can a blind man lead a blind man? Will they not both fall into a pit? A student is not above his teacher, but everyone who is fully trained will be like his teacher."

Ultramontane Order / Ultramontanism is a movement within the Catholic Church in which great emphasis is placed on the prerogatives and powers of the pope, over those of local temporal or spiritual hierarchies, including the local bishop.

Franciscan / A member of an order founded by Saint Francis of Assisi, which upholds strict principles of poverty.

Brother Constantine Jaquasse / The name and character of Brother Jaquasse are based on the seventeenth-century Saint Joseph of Cupertino, who was famed for his simplicity verging on naïveté. He is known to have referred to himself as "the jackass." His feast day is September 18.

59   *radiogram* / A piece of furniture comprising a bulky radio set, often combined with a record player.

Valkyries / Fearsome handmaidens to the Norse god Odin. They decided which warriors should die in battle and conveyed them to Valhalla. The Valkyries are generally depicted on horseback. Colquhoun's allusion probably means no more than that the sisters were domineering and good equestriennes.

60   *statutory twenty minutes* / A deliberate display of power and authority designed to put the visitor at a psychological disadvantage. When writing these paragraphs, Colquhoun must have been thinking of her own unsatisfactory encounters with certain teachers of the esoteric who promised much but delivered little. The phrase also appears in *Sword of Wisdom*, where she details some of these meetings. See Colquhoun, *Sword of Wisdom: MacGregor Mathers and "The Golden Dawn"* (London: Spearman, 1975), 30.

holy oleographs / Oleography is an early form of colored lithography, printed with oil paint on canvas. The process was often used to provide inexpensive devotional images for domestic settings.

61   *aspergilla* / The Latin plural of "aspergillum," a liturgical implement used to sprinkle holy water.

professional mourners / Individuals paid to lament and eulogize the dead.

anchoress / A woman who withdraws from active life for an ascetic life of contemplation. Akin to a hermit.

Les Tourettes / (Old French) The small towers, or turrets.

Turris eburnea . . . / The Latin quotation translates as "Tower of ivory, pray for us. / House of gold, pray for us. / Ark of the Covenant, pray for us. / Gate of heaven, pray for us." It is from the Litany of the Blessed Virgin Mary, a prayer to the Virgin Mary asking for her intercession. It lists many of her qualities, including her exalted nature, holiness, amiability, motherly spirit, and queenly majesty.

62   *Pre-Raphaelite air* / A reference to the Pre-Raphaelite Brotherhood, a group of painters in Victorian England whose paintings often combined religious themes with a realistic and meticulous depiction of nature. The founder was Dante Gabriel Rossetti (1828–1882).

     Mother Ste. Barbe / Another instance of a place name (and gender change) being used for a character. St. Barbe is the site of an alignment of stone rows near Carnac.

63   *Mother Vicaress* / A sister in a nunnery or convent who is lower in authority than an abbess or mother superior.

64   *Public School rejects* / Colquhoun forgets that we are in France and refers to the English educational system, in which "public" schools are anything but. They are not free, highly selective in their intake, and socially divisive. The boys whom Brigid meets have failed the entrance examinations, or their parents may be unable to afford the fees.

     the practice of a craft was itself a way of initiation . . . / Many twentieth-century and contemporary magical societies operate a grade structure in which the member has to acquire or demonstrate a certain level of knowledge or ability before being regarded as suitable for the next stage. Initiation may refer to either a ceremony to mark such a transition or a process designed to confer on the candidate the necessary skills. In more general usage, in preindustrial ages membership in a craft guild was only granted as the result of a long apprenticeship. As a member of several Masonic lodges, Colquhoun would have been well aware that Freemasonry is sometimes referred to as "the Craft."

     ectoplasmic / Ectoplasm is the substance extruded by mediums while in a trance state, indicating that contact with spirits has been made. Here it signals the presence of powerful psychic forces. The cupboard where the bubble-like form appears recalls the "spirit cabinets" used by many mediums in nineteenth-century spiritualism to make their materializations appear more convincing to skeptics.

65   *corbel-heads* / Stone projections acting as supports for roof timbers. They are often carved with human heads or mythological beasts. "Gothick" (usually spelled "Gothic") refers here to the tall, spacious style of church architecture, not to the genre of supernatural fiction.

Gabriel's trumpet / In the New Testament book of Revelation (chapters 8–11), seven angels each sound their trumpet at the Day of Judgment. Gabriel is said to blow the final trumpet, initiating the end of time and the general resurrection.

Michael Penmarch / Penmarch is a peninsula in the southwest of Finistère. In the Breton language, "pen" means headland, and "march" means horse.

66 *windy and open to the sun* / Saint Michael, the Christianized sun god, rules over high rocky crags. Across Europe, churches and chapels dedicated to his memory crown the summits of mountains and pinnacles.

Western Gabriel / In ceremonial magic, each of the cardinal points of the compass is dedicated to an archangel. Magical rituals frequently start by invoking the guardian angels of the cardinal points. Gabriel is associated with the west and with the element water. Michael is associated with the south and the element fire. (Uriel is associated with the north and earth, while Raphael guards the east.)

certain objects of beaten metal / The imagery in this passage is part astrological and part alchemical. Astrologers refer to the sun and the moon, the most important objects in the heavens, as the luminaries. Their conjunction occurs when they appear to be very close together in the sky. The sun is traditionally gendered as male and the moon as female, so Colquhoun is here referring to the unification of the male and female principles. In alchemical writings, this is often referred to as *conjunctio*. A note in the original dream transcription suggests that the instrument may have been constructed to facilitate this conjunction within oneself—the goal of spiritual alchemy.

67 *intercarnate phases* / The periods between embodiments, when the soul exists in a nonmaterial spirit state of existence.

68 *Sister Mary Fursey* / Saint Fursey (d. 650) was an Irish monk who did much to establish Christianity throughout the British Isles. His feast day is January 16. Once again, Colquhoun attaches the name of a male monk to a female character.

Korrigans / In Breton folklore, these are fairy or dwarf-like spirits who are opposed to Christianity. They hate priests, churches, and especially the Virgin Mary. They can predict the future, change shape, and move at lightning speed. They are fond of stealing human children, substituting them with changelings. On the night of October 31 (All Souls' Night), they are said to lurk near dolmens, waiting for victims.

69 *inner truth . . . mystery of Parthenogenesis* / The language here is that of alchemy rather than Catholic theology. The "lunar soul" refers to the female principle of nature, or the Goddess, traditionally associated with the moon, while the sun is traditionally gendered as a male deity. The "radiant Child" is the Magical Child of the

alchemists—the product of the conjunction of the male and female principles. In this way, the opposition between the male and female principles will be resolved and unity achieved. Colquhoun also seems to be suggesting that the male is contained within the female, rather than existing separately. This contrasts with the biblical story of Genesis in which female (Eve) is created from male (Adam).

CHAPTER 4: CONJUNCTION

The chapter title refers to the geomantic figure Conjunctio (Latin; conjunction). It represents a combination of forces, for good or ill.

Many of the events described in this and the following chapter draw upon Colquhoun's knowledge and experience of a Breton religious ceremony, the Pardon. A Pardon is the feast of the patron saint of a church or chapel. It is a pilgrimage of devotion and piety. After a religious service, a great procession takes place around the church, followed by feasting.

The Pardon season begins in March and ends in October. The main Pardon is that of Sainte-Anne-d'Auray in Morbihan. It takes place on July 24, the anniversary of the finding of a statue of Saint Anne by the peasant Nicolazic. Although the date of this Pardon and the dates of the festivals and processions described in the novel are not the same, Colquhoun mentions Saint Anne, while Nikolaz, the name of the heir, must surely be derived from Nicolazic.

70   *Compline or Vespers* / Vespers is the evening church service, and Compline is the final service of the day. Vespers may include prayers for healing and forgiveness.

72   *Bath of Venus* / A number of locations, including Cyprus and Sicily, have holy wells or sacred springs that are known as the Bath of Venus. In *Sword of Wisdom,* Colquhoun asserts that the name is also an alchemical term for the vagina.

Black Madonna of Tenos / Black Madonnas are icons or sculptures that depict the Virgin Mary with dark skin but European features. The icon on the Greek island of Tenos is reputed to possess healing powers and to be one of a number painted by Saint Luke. Images of the Black Virgin are believed by some to be a Christian adaptation of pagan goddesses from the ancient Middle East, thereby representing a repression of matriarchal religions. See Ean Begg, *The Cult of the Black Virgin* (London: Arkana Books, 1985).

73   *Little Pilgrimage* / As Christianity spread through Europe, the Church was either antagonistic to or tolerant of pagan shrines and customs. In general, pagan sites were Christianized in a display of power over the old deities. Sometimes heathen ceremonies were retained in a modified form and invested with new meanings. The events of the Little Pilgrimage—a devotional tour of the convent's major holy wells—take place within a landscape that is partly Christianized but still recognizably pagan. During the pilgrimage, Sister Brigid reflects upon change and continuity—between the form

that worship may take, which is temporary, and the spirituality inherent in a place, which is permanent.

The triple well in the novel has been wholly appropriated by Christianity, to the extent that a chapel has been built over it containing frescos depicting three female Catholic saints. Another well has been partly Christianized, by dedication to Saint Méen, a minor local saint. One spring is unenclosed and has not been Christianized at all: it is here that Sister Brigid has her vision of three goddesses, the pagan tutelary deities of the spring, who form a counterpoint to the Catholic saints memorialized in the chapel. The nearby Monte Ste. Anne is the site of annual ceremonies that continue to commemorate the pagan deity Tanarus, the original dedicatee of the mound. Despite this long tradition, the forces of secularization, represented by the civic workmen who attempt to clear out the wells, are at work, and they need to be resisted.

Brigid later (page 90) notes the bishop's impatience with the rituals performed around the pre-Christian wells. In doing so, she contrasts the historically gendered quality of intuition, regarded as a female strength, with reason, traditionally an attribute of the male.

St. Méen / A Welsh monk who evangelized in Brittany in the sixth century. According to legend, during a visit to the village of Saint-Mere-Eglise, being thirsty, he touched the ground with his staff and created a spring of pure water. The spring remains a destination for pilgrims. His feast day is June 21. There is nothing in the legend to indicate why his healing powers are especially useful for those in psychological distress.

74   *screaming of gulls* / Colquhoun often uses references to birds and birdsong to indicate closeness to nature. See, for example, the final sentence of the novel.

skerry / A small rocky island.

yaffle / A green woodpecker.

feminine trinity / There are a number of significant triplicities in this chapter, many of which evoke in the reader's mind the triple goddess of present-day neo-pagans. The triple goddess—meaning a single Great Goddess with three separate aspects, each representing a phase of human life (e.g., maiden, mother, crone)—may be thought of as roughly equivalent to the patriarchal Trinity of Christianity, in which a masculine god consists of three divine persons (father, son, holy spirit), each being distinct yet consubstantial.

Colquhoun is concerned here with the female aspect of both paganism and Christianity, seen as curative and loving forces, compared with the destructive male triplicity of Ankou and his children, the personifications of death, sorrow, and oblivion. It is significant, also, that Dr. Wiseacre, whose lust for Charlotte effaces "all preoccupations, medical or moral," is physically denied access to the triple wells and their curative properties. Brigid has kept in touch with the old rituals and beliefs, a contact that men have lost.

Ste. Catherine / This is Saint Catherine of Alexandria, martyred in the early fourth century. As a young woman, she had a vision in which the Virgin Mary gave her to Christ in a mystical marriage (hence the proffered ring). She is often depicted in paintings with her symbol, a spiked wheel, the intended instrument of her martyrdom.

75 *Ankou, the god of death* / Refers to the Breton folk belief that death travels about in a cart picking up souls. It is said that if a peasant hears the approach of a cart with a creaking axle at midnight, it is Ankou; when the cart stops before a dwelling, someone within must die. Anken and Ankoun are generally described as Ankou's servants rather than his children. See Frances M. Gostling, "L'Ankou," *Celtic Review* 2, no. 7 (1906): 272–82.

Antiquaries have declared . . . / Rev. William Lisle Bowles, a nineteenth-century antiquarian, proposed that the Hill of Tan is named for the Celtic deity Tanarus, variously said to be the god of thunder or fire, whose symbol is a wheel. In reality, the hill lies near Avebury, in southern England, the site of the largest stone circle in Europe. See W. L. Bowles, *Hermes Britannicus* (London: J. B. Nichols and Son, 1828), 14–15.

76 *The sprays bore clusters of small bells . . .* / By training, Colquhoun was a visual artist. She saw the world through color rather than through character. Here she uses precise descriptions of color to reinforce Sister Well-Meadow's closeness to nature.

Heaven's Queen / The Virgin Mary.

CHAPTER 5: BOUND

The chapter title refers to the geomantic figure Carcer (Latin; prison). It denotes delays and setbacks.

77 *fertility-cycle* / Mrs. Wiseacre, Roli's mother, is middle-aged. The narrator refers to the fact that the likelihood of birth defects, such as Roli's, increases with the mother's age at conception.

78 *Saint Denez* / The site of a passage grave in Finistère.

79 *St. Biniané* / Saint Bibiana (or Viviana) is the patron saint of those who have drunk too much. Colquhoun's spelling of the name is unorthodox, for reasons that are unclear. Her feast day is December 2.

katzenjammer / (German) Hangover.

80 *Dried fish* / A sarcastic reference to the miracle of the loaves and fishes.

red ink on yellowish paper, the rest being in blue on white / Red/yellow and blue/white are important hermetic color combinations. They signify the separated genders, which have to be united if spiritual perfection is to be achieved.

Sister Mary Gildas / Another gender-conflating name. Saint Gildas was a sixth-century English evangelist who died in Brittany. His feast day is January 29.

81   *the day sacred to St. Raphael* / The date, October 24, was correct when Colquhoun was writing. However, the reform of the Roman Catholic calendar of saints in 1969 transferred Raphael's feast day to September 29, to be celebrated together with Saint Michael and Saint Gabriel.

hausfrau . . . three K's / The passage refers to the alleged lack of ambition of German housewives. The three K's are *Kinder, Küche, Kirche* (children, kitchen, church).

Hobbies / A British weekly magazine of the period, primarily for children, focusing on craft activities.

82   *Don't think you can escape me . . .* / The subsequent incorporation of passages taken, almost unedited, from Colquhoun's dreams—the shrinking baby, the materialized hand, Charlotte's highly personal gift—can make the story of her affair with Dr. Wise-acre confusing. Overall, however, the meaning is clear, as Colquhoun contrasts the destructive aspects of physical desire with the ecstasy of spiritual union. Despite their presence on Ménec, the lovers are far from casting off earthly emotions and concerns. While, for his part, Gerhardt behaves unethically with his former patient, the con-summation of Charlotte's sexual passion comes at the price of self-delusion, guilt, and fears of the consequences of an unwanted pregnancy.

83   *Yi-King* / The more usual spelling is "I Ching." This is referring to the *Book of Changes,* which describes a Chinese form of divinatory practice involving sixty-four hexagrams (patterns of six broken and unbroken lines) that can result from the throwing of stalks or coins. There are obvious similarities between this method of divination and the use of the geomantic figures.

     Each hexagram is ascribed a particular number and meaning. As Colquhoun indi-cates, number twenty-seven (named "earth of fire") carries the meaning "nourish-ment." Number six, however, has the meaning "conflict" rather than "inmost sincerity," and "air of moon" should be applied to number fifty-nine. Whether Colquhoun has made mistakes or her changes are deliberate is uncertain.

mandala / A design, deriving from Hindu and Buddhist traditions, used as an aid to meditation. At its simplest, it may be little more than a square containing concentric circles representing the universe, but it is frequently highly elaborate and decorative.

Kerlud / The name of a small hamlet and site of a prehistoric dolmen close to the coast in the Morbihan peninsula of Brittany.

84 *Then it seemed to her that they were joined together . . .* / There is a closely related passage in *Goose of Hermogenes* that starts "as they flew . . . they became permeated with light." Colquhoun, *Goose of Hermogenes* (London: Peter Owen, 1961, 45. The two novels contain many parallels in addition to this example of mystical union. At some point, Colquhoun attempted to itemize the similarities between these novels (and a third, unfinished one entitled *Destination Limbo*). Her list contained twenty-two items, indicating that she was not simply making a record, but was thinking of assigning each of the common themes to one of the twenty-two paths that connect the sephiroth of the Tree of Life diagram.

etheric light / Ether (or aether) is a conjectural substance that appears in the writings of physicists from ancient Greece to Victorian England. Here, Colquhoun gives it the theosophical meaning of light emanating from the etheric body, indicating a kind of energy field that connects the physical body with spiritual planes. Under some circumstances, it is said to form a visible aura.

Jacob's vision / As recounted in the Old Testament (Genesis 28:10–23), Jacob had a vision of a ladder standing on the earth, with its top touching the heavens (28:12). Angels were ascending and descending the ladder, at the top of which stood God himself. The image is of one mystical communication between earth and heaven, or, in the present case, between two individuals on the same plane.

85 *the touch of a cold hand* / There are a number of instances in Colquhoun's writings where she refers to personal experiences of visitors from the astral world contacting her while she was asleep and leaving their mark on her body (see the introduction, page 19). None, however, are as corporeal as this simulacrum of an unarticulated hand that is visible to two people, palpable and cold to the touch. This indicates a substantial attack by Gertrud, who is able to manifest a hand that has greater resilience than ecto-plasm, the usual substance indicating the presence of a spirit that wishes to interact with the physical world. An earlier instance of ectoplasmic manifestation occurs on page 64.

86 *Queen of the Night* / There are a number of meanings here. The most literal is that the pattern on the material reminds the narrator of the starry night sky. Additionally, Colquhoun, a Freemason, would certainly have been familiar with the Masonic themes of Mozart's opera *The Magic Flute,* in which the Queen of the Night is a major character, representing the forces that oppose rationality and enlightenment. The phrase is also frequently used to describe Lilith, a Babylonian demon, later regarded in Jewish teaching as the mythical first wife of Adam. She left him because she saw herself as his equal and refused to be subservient to him. In other traditions she is

Astarte, Aphrodite, or Isis, goddess of fertility. According to the context, therefore, her consort is Adam, Tammuz, Adonis, or Horus.

CHAPTER 6: LOSS

The chapter title refers to the geomantic figure Amissio (Latin; loss). It frequently represents something outside of one's grasp.

87 *Sant Marzhin* / "Marzin" is the Breton form of "Martin." Colquhoun may have been thinking of Saint Martin of Tours, whose feast day is November 11, when autumn wheat seeding is traditionally completed.

88 *chasuble* / The outermost vestment worn by clergy when celebrating Mass.

guilty of dualism / In the preceding paragraphs, which concern the psychological satisfactions of conventual life, Sister Brigid sets out a number of oppositions concerning duty, obedience, and freedom. She alights on the figure of the bishop, whose taste for high living she contrasts with his basic biological functions. In understanding human nature, Brigid warns against the trap of regarding the mechanistic world of matter as distinct from the world of spiritual needs and forces.

Pasion, Ar Bleuniou and Ar Sakramant / The chronology here is difficult to understand, as these are the order's names for the three important traditional Catholic services associated with the Easter season, but the events described take place in November.

89 *Hollsent* / All Saints Day (holl an sent = all the saints). Following tradition, Bretons went to church in the morning and cleaned and tidied the graves of their loved ones in the afternoon. They had their evening meal at home and left the table decked with food for the dead. Because it was forbidden to see the dead feasting, they went to bed early. People would also leave food outside for those of the dead who did not have a home to go to.

the empyrean / Heaven. Sometimes described as the highest part of heaven, a realm of pure fire.

crucifer and thurifer / In Catholic church services, crucifer and thurifer are the titles of two of the lay altar servers who assist the officiating priest. Crucifer carries the processional cross, and thurifer carries the metal censer when incense is used.

Ste. Anne / Although there is no biblical authority, it is generally accepted that Saint Anne was the mother of the Virgin Mary. There appear to be no legends of her visiting France, but she is the patron saint of Brittany. Her shrine is at Sante-Anne-d'Auray, where her annual Pardon is held.

91   *The last of the sunshine . . .* / The evening service that is about to be described celebrates the healing powers of the Virgin Mary. The Latin quotations are from Bible
verses used at the Feast of the Assumption, the service that records the Virgin's ascent
to Heaven in (to use Colquhoun's phrase) a chariot of water. At the height of the ceremony, Roli's parents are given a glimpse of him in an apparently healed state before
he dies and leaves the island.

92   *antiphonal chant* / The alternation of lines between two choirs or, as here, between
male and female voices.

   Quasi cedrus exaltata sum in Libano . . . / The Latin passage is from Ecclesiasticus
24:13–14. It translates as "I was exalted like a cedar in Lebanon, and as a cypress tree
on mount Sion. I was exalted like a palm tree in Cades, and as a rose plant in Jericho."
For several years, Colquhoun kept a magical diary in which she documented her occult
activities and aspirations. In an entry dated August 22, 1953, she recorded the results
of meditating on these verses: "This symbolizes the building up of the androgynous
psychic whole. The masculine element is symbolized by a tree in this case, the feminine
by a locality." One week later, she meditated on the verses again, adding that "the phrase
seemed to subsume for me a raising up above trivial concerns and a touching of the
impersonal." The diary is located at Tate Archive, Tate Britain, London, TGA 929/5/18.

   melismata / The vocal technique of extending a single syllable over several notes,
as used in Gregorian chant or plainsong. When Brigid makes her observations on the
importance of ritual and on the power of language in religious experience, the reader
can be confident that her views are also those of Colquhoun. In a polemical article in
the *Aylesford Review,* a Carmelite publication with literary inclinations, Colquhoun
bitterly regretted liturgical reformation, such as the abandonment of Latin in the
interest of easy comprehension, writing that "a ritual worthy of the name carries its
message to regions of the psycho-physical organism more permanent than those concerned with discursive mentation." Colquhoun, "Liturgical Reformation," *Aylesford
Review* 5, no. 1 (1962): 20–22.

   'the high dream' / An altered state of consciousness, not confined to sleep.

   Rivers of Eden / According to Genesis, a river flowed out of Eden to water the garden. From there it divided and became four major rivers. They are named in Genesis
2:11–14 as Phison, Gihon, Tigris, and Euphrates. The symbolism is that the river out
of Eden nourishes the four quarters of the world with its life-giving waters.

93   *Qui implet quasi Phison sapientiam . . .* / (Latin) "Who fills up wisdom as the Phison,
and as the Tigris in the days of the new fruits. Who makes understanding to abound
as the Euphrates." Ecclesiasticus 24:25–26.

now intensified in death / Roli dies, but does this mean that the healing ceremony has failed? One might ask: What would a successful outcome of such a ceremony be for someone who is on the Island of the Dead? Restoration to full health, as might have been sought prior to arrival on the island, might appear to be regressive in the current circumstances, given that the period between the physical death of the body and the second death is a time of withdrawal until the soul, freed from both physical and astral bodies, leaves them behind to continue on its spiritual path.

CHAPTER 7: THE DRAGON'S TAIL

The chapter title refers to the geomantic figure Cauda Draconis (Latin; tail of the dragon). It is generally unfavorable, bringing evil alongside good.

95 *Festival-octave* / Some major church festivals extend over eight days. The octave is the eighth day (inclusive) after the festival and so falls on the same day of the week as the festival. A week, therefore, has passed since All Saint's Day.

96 *Smug little fool . . .* / The arrival of the heir heralds changes that are both practical and spiritual. He respects neither tradition nor the natural order. He dams the stream and turns it into a stagnant pool. He fells trees and fences the road, denying the nuns access to their traditional pastures. He begins to attack Sister Brigid's beliefs by quoting scriptures against her (his references to the church being founded on a rock and to the gates of hell are from Matthew 16:18).

de Kerlescan / Ménec contains the greatest concentration of megaliths in Brittany, but there is also a significant group of stone alignments at nearby Kerlescan. The *manoir* at Kerlescan would have been the great house where the local landowner lived. It is not unusual for a large landowner to use the name of the locality as his title; hence he is referred to as de Kerlescan. The convent has grazing rights on his estate.

Code Napoléon / The French civil code established under Napoléon I in 1804. The code forbade privileges based on birth, allowed freedom of religion, and specified that government jobs must go to the most qualified.

ancient Celtic usages / Traditional practices and agreements, which lack a proven modern legal basis.

Sant Vran / Colquhoun may have been thinking of the sixth-century saint Veranus, also (but rarely) known as Saint Vran. His miracles included victory over a dragon. His feast day is November 11.

97 *petite amie* / (French) Girlfriend.

What did you mean . . . / The heir regards the teachings of the order as decadent and corrupted. He realizes that it has lost touch with its illumination—direct experiences of its mystical union with God—and points out that its rituals, which once were capable of enabling such union, are now public, watered-down affairs that lack transformative power.

Laval floods, a second Eve, a second Faust, and the Second Coming are images of upheaval, weakness, and horror. Through the taunting of the heir, Brigid realizes that she agrees with what he says. The bonds that tie her to the convent are beginning to slacken. He does, however, offer her a gift—a way forward out of the convent.

98   *a second Eve* / According to Hebrew legend, Eve (Lilith, the Queen of the Night), was created simultaneously with Adam but left the Garden of Eden on her own volition, as she valued her independence. The Eve who was created from Adam's rib (Genesis 2:21–22) is, therefore, the second Eve.

A second Faust / In legend, Faust, or Dr. Faustus, dissatisfied with the limits of traditional fields of study, turned to the occult in his search for ultimate knowledge and power. He made a pact with the devil to acquire this knowledge in exchange for his soul.

The blood-dimmed tide is loosed . . . / From W. B. Yeats's poem "The Second Coming," composed in 1919. According to the Catholic Church, the disposal of the souls of everyone who has ever lived will occur at the same moment, the Last Judgment, which will follow Christ's Second Coming. Yeats, however, believed that history does not take a linear path but follows rhythmic cycles of growth and decay according to shifting solar and lunar influences. He further believed that the Second Coming will be an antithesis of the first, bringing a monstrous subversion of Christ. For Yeats, human souls progress through cycles consisting of incarnate and discarnate phases. This aspect of Yeats's belief is similar to the theosophical framework that underpins *I Saw Water*. In either system, Brigid can expect not the finality of Judgment Day but a series of incarnations as she progresses beyond materiality to absolute consciousness. Yeats was a practicing occultist and had been initiated into the Golden Dawn as a young man. He detailed his theories regarding the cyclical nature of time, much of it revealed through automatic writing, in *A Vision*. See William Butler Yeats, *A Vision* (London: Macmillan, 1925; 2nd ed., 1937).

patronal feast / The occasion on which a parish annually honors its patron saint.

99   *sprigs of rosemary* / Traditional symbol of remembrance.

102   *The Peerless Guidances* / This passage elaborates on the teachings of Ste. Ermengilde, first encountered on page 46 above. At first sight, it corresponds to the familiar separation of hell, earth, and heaven, but the teaching is more theosophical than Catholic, describing the progress of beings as they develop through a number of existential

planes, of which the material human world is only one. The lower world—the world of desire—is called by Ste. Ermengilde The Power to Destroy. The material world is The Holy Welcome, and the highest world, the world of formlessness, is The Scintillating Light. Having already detached confession from psychoanalysis (page 100), Brigid's explanation of the purpose of monastic rule—to make of life a ritual—not only moves away from any Christian notion of the observance as honoring God or committing one's life to the salvation of heaven, but also suggests understandings common in the hermetic revival of the late nineteenth and early twentieth centuries. Colquhoun's cousin, E. J. Langford Garstin, for example, argued that the value of ritual was not in the passing on of conscious information, but rather in a different form of knowledge obtained through the performance itself. See Garstin, "The Value of Ritual," *The Search* 3, no. 4 (1933): 534–42. For Colquhoun's own observations on the subject, see the note to "melismata" above, page 152.

103   *torero* / (Spanish) Bullfighter. The price of liberty—personal, political, and religious— is the theme of this and following paragraphs. Ignacio Sánchez Mejías, a noted Spanish bullfighter, paid for his love of the sport with his life, being gored to death in 1943. The left-wing poets Rafael Alberti and Federico García Lorca each wrote a poem about his death. Lorca's murder in 1936 by Fascists and Franco's censorship of his work contributed to the interpretation of Lorca as a martyr of the Spanish Civil War. For his part, Alberti was exiled for his beliefs, ending his days in Argentina. For matadors, who enter the ring voluntarily, death is an ever-present possibility. For bulls, who have no choice, death is an inevitability. The phrase "the bull that was made for death" occurs repeatedly in Alberti's poem. Colquhoun's source for the line, which she misquotes slightly, may have been the anthology *Transformation 4* (1946), which contained a translation of the poem. The volume also contained several translations by Colquhoun of contemporary French poets, including Breton and Char. See S. Schimanski and H. Treece, eds., *Transformation 4* (London: Lindsay Drummond, 1946).

  S.S. Protus and Hyacinth / Christian martyrs, reputedly brothers, who refused to deny their faith and were martyred ca. 257–59 A.D. The day of their annual commemoration is September 11. Colquhoun conflates this Hyacinth with the Hyacinth of Greek legend, who was killed by the strike of a discus. Apollo refused to allow him to descend into Hades, turning him into a flower instead. Hyacinth, like Adonis, signifies the death and rebirth of nature.

CHAPTER 8: ON MY WAY

The chapter title refers to the geomantic figure Via (Latin; the way). It frequently represents change.

105   *cromlech of Crucuno* / One of the best-known dolmens in Brittany. It is situated in the village center, to the north of Carnac.

December the sixth / Among his many attributions, Saint Nicholas is the patron saint of travelers and sailors. The nature of Nikolaz's death (page 114), therefore, is ironical.

106 *South of Ireland* / The governance of Ireland has been a source of civil and religious unrest for centuries. A settlement of sorts was reached when the largely Catholic south achieved a degree of independence from the United Kingdom, becoming the Irish Free State in 1922. It became the fully independent Republic of Ireland in 1948. Northern Ireland, which is largely Protestant, remains a part of the United Kingdom.

With less surprise than the strangeness warranted . . . / As the ordination of women is forbidden in the Catholic Church, it follows that Mass may only be celebrated by a man. The biblical authority for this is that man was created in the image of God; Christ was also a man, and therefore priests, who act *in persona Christi capitis* (in the person of Christ), must also be male. In an unpublished essay, Colquhoun asserted that the Hebrew word for God, *Elohim*, is feminine, so the creator God must be hermaphrodite. In her view, arguments against the ordination of women must therefore collapse. See the typescript in TGA 929/2/1/67/1.

It is sometimes said that the Black Mass should be officiated by women, but there is no evidence in this passage that Colquhoun was describing a satanic ritual.

Sister Mara / She is capable of splitting and can exist in two places (bilocation) and two guises (Sister Mara and Mary Paracelsus) simultaneously.

108 *rhubarb or gunnera* / Gunnera is a flowering plant, sometimes known as "giant rhubarb." Both are named here for the large size of their leaves.

Sister Mara emerged from a garage . . . / This is one of several instances in the novel in which information is passed in an unusual way: in a clandestine manner (e.g., the note thrown by the fair-haired lieutenant, page 118); in coded form (e.g., the diagram of the branching tree, page 57); or, as here, in a folded leaf.

The transmission of occult knowledge is, perhaps tautologically, a mysterious business. The problem of how to communicate to a restricted audience, perhaps excluding the uninitiated or the merely curious, has confronted authors of magical grimoires and alchemical treatises down the centuries. The reader will be reminded of H. P. Blavatsky's Mahatma letters and the cipher manuscripts from the mysterious Anna Sprengel, from which the early Golden Dawn rituals were derived. Colquhoun herself was faced with the almost nightly challenge of understanding the latent content of her dreams.

nude hermaphrodite / The drawing shows Sister Mara/Paracelsus as having the sexual attributes of both genders. The hermaphrodite is an important symbol in alchemy, indicating not merely the conjunction of the genders but the union of all opposites and the achievement of enlightenment. As with Brigid, Mara has reached the end of her stay at the convent, and both are about to leave.

CHAPTER 9: ACQUISITION

The chapter title refers to the geomantic figure Fortuna Major (Latin; the greater fortune). It represents great good fortune, especially in beginnings, but it can also denote hardship at the outset of an endeavor.

110   *Laveuses de la Nuit* / (French) Literally, Washerwomen of the Night. A Celtic legend, found in Brittany and Scotland, refers to the Midnight Washerwomen—three old washerwomen who go to the water's edge at midnight to wash shrouds for those about to die.

       Fears of the *Laveuses* and their association with imminent death signals the start of a series of events in which the narrator has to undergo certain ordeals before she is able to put aside convent life and its security once and for all. Ella's passage through the cave and subsequent crossing of flowing water represent her descent into the underworld, where she is subjected to temptation and trial by personal ordeal. Physically, she is tested by the baboon-girl and overcomes her by force. Her strength of character is tested when she is offered what appears to be the elixir of life, but she recognizes it as poison. Salvation, in the form of the heirloom, is temporarily out of reach, but she is able to cast aside her old identity and adopt a new one, symbolized as the donning of new clothes.

       Cyclopean blocks / Huge boulders, in this context forming a natural tumble, but this can also refer to unmortared walls in ancient Greece made of stones so large it was once believed that only the legendary race of Cyclopes had the strength to move them.

111   *County Kerry* / Kerry is a county in the southwest of the Republic of Ireland, visited by Colquhoun on several occasions, including when writing her book *The Crying of the Wind: Ireland.*

       I rose shivering . . . / The encounter with the girl in a red sweater occurred in a dream of 1956. The details concerning the *Contes de Jeune* and the Guermes also occurred in the dream. Colquhoun was unable to suggest a waking-life explanation for these names. See the dream transcription in TGA 929/2/1/31/3/26–27.

       Anthropophagi / A mythical race of cannibals first described in antiquity by the Greek historian Herodotus.

112   *At this the girl's face became distorted . . .* / Ella's descent underground and trial by water culminate in her encounter with a shape-shifting entity. In her battle with the baboon-girl, Ella comes face-to-face with her own internal, bestial self. The girl is a parody of woman, reduced to a state of nature, existing only as uncontrolled drives.

113   *Phrynean* / Relating to a prostitute.

susurration / A soft whispering or rustling sound.

ruby / The ruby is a red gemstone with long-standing hermetic associations. The "celestial ruby" is one of the many names for the philosopher's stone. It lends its name to the classic alchemical text *A Brief Guide to the Celestial Ruby,* by Eiranaeus Philalethes, in which it stands for the spiritual wholeness of man before the Fall.

114 *I have some shocking news for you* / Parallels between the heir and Adonis indicate that Colquhoun had the ancient Phoenician god of fertility in mind when writing about Nikolaz. The myth of Adonis—which was brought into general public awareness by J. G. Frazer and has many variants—is a central one in ancient mystery religions. He is a deity of rebirth—particularly venerated by women—whose annual sacrifice by drowning ensures the fertility of crops. Nikolaz, the vigorous, lusty young man, takes over responsibility for the *Manoir* from an ailing uncle. He shakes Brigid from her bucolic spiritual complacency and points out the route for her further spiritual advancement. She succumbs to his attractions and abandons her identity as Sister Brigid. Nikolaz is drowned but bequeaths salvation, symbolized as the heirloom he gave her. Now she is able to abandon her identity as Ella and achieve total impersonal freedom. On Adonis, see Frazer, *The Golden Bough,* 324–47.

115 *Cruz-Moquen* / In reality this is not an island, but the site of a dolmen that has been "Christianized" by the erection of a cross on top. Many megalithic sites have attracted myths concerning sex and reproduction. Local folklore at Cruz-Moquen relates that women who wished to become pregnant should raise their skirts to the dolmen at full moon. Full moon is stipulated because this is when the powers of the lunar goddess are at their peak and those of the male solar god are at their weakest.

116 *catechumen* / Someone preparing for baptism or confirmation.

Tuba mirum . . . / The Latin passage translates as "Wondrous sound the trumpet flingeth; / through earth's sepulchers it ringeth; / all before the throne it bringeth." The lines are from the *Dies Irae* (Day of Wrath), a hymn that describes the Day of Judgment. The last trumpet summons souls before the throne of God, where the saved will be delivered and the unsaved cast into eternal flames.

117 *ether* / The theosophical substance that connects the physical with the higher planes (see the note to "Etheric light" above, page 150). Here Colquhoun indicates that it can be the medium through which emotional states are transmitted from person to person.

Ite, missa est / Translates as "Go, the Mass has ended." These are the concluding words of the Catholic Mass. They are addressed to the congregation, informing worshippers that the rite has finished.

CHAPTER 10: RED

The chapter title refers to the geomantic figure Rubeus (Latin; red). It is an unfavorable figure, representing passion, deception, violence, and vice. As Ella's grip on her identity loosens and her psychological vulnerability increases, the chronology of the narrative also becomes loose and confused. Played out as a memory of her novitiate, her struggle with physical and emotional weakness is allegorized as a struggle between nuns and invading soldiers for possession of the convent. The combat is intensely personal and invasive, as Brigid is subjected to a sadistic attack that has strong lesbian overtones. Nonetheless, she manages to keep her secret intact.

118 *occupation by the armed forces* / France was overrun by the German army during World War II (1939–45), and the Brittany peninsula became home to a large occupying force. It housed important bases intended for launching attacks on England.

119 *Madame Lacoste* / The sadistic brothel keeper shares her name with the Château de Lacoste, one of the residences that belonged to the Marquis de Sade, a notorious libertine.

120 *epicene type* / Men who are effeminate or lacking in masculinity. This can refer to behavior, personality, and/or appearance.

121 *talismanic virtue* / A talisman is an object that has been endowed with magical power. In this instance, the heirloom has acquired its properties not through consecration but through its association with Nikolaz.

CHAPTER 11: SAFEGUARD GOING OUT

The chapter title refers to the geomantic figure Fortuna Minor (Latin; the lesser fortune). It represents transient success that is dependent upon outside help. It is a figure of change and instability.

123 *cornemuse* / French bagpipes, traditionally associated with Celtic piping and the music of Brittany. The reference invokes the connection to the shrill dirges of the rites of Adonis and to the return of the corn crop recounted by J. G. Frazer. Its connection here to the sailors and fishermen also echoes one of the images counterbalancing the aridity of modern life in T. S. Eliot's *The Waste Land*—the music and conversation of the fishmen around Magnus Martyr in part 3 of the poem.

Brésil-Peulven / Brésil may be a Gallicized spelling of the mythical island of Brasil (or Hy-Brasil), which lies off the west coast of Ireland. It is said to be perpetually swathed in mist and cannot be reached. Peulven is the site of a standing stone in Finistère.

Locqueltas / A district in Morbihan. The home of the Nikolaz family, beside the artificial lake, establishes a further link between the heir and elemental water.

Leaving the port of Ménec behind me . . . / The narrative from here to the end of the chapter originated as a dream-inspired short story entitled "The Novice," which Colquhoun incorporated into *I Saw Water*. See the unpublished typescript in TGA 929/2/1/31/1/104–5. In her notes, Colquhoun referred to the episode as "the Coven." A coven is the Wicca equivalent of a Masonic lodge, or a Golden Dawn temple. The episode suggests a failed attempt by Brigid (now Ella) to be accepted into another spiritual community, having left the convent.

totem-beasts / A reference to the traditional belief that all people are guarded and watched over by an animal spirit or totem beast, which joins them at the time of their birth.

124   *rousse . . . Rossetti* / Dante Gabriel Rossetti (1828–1882) was an English poet and painter and founder of the Pre-Raphaelite Brotherhood, a group of painters whose works often combined religious themes with a realistic and meticulous depiction of nature. His most famous model, Lizzie Siddal, had luxurious red hair.

herb of grace / One of the common names for *Ruta graveolens,* or common rue, an herb with a number of medicinal and culinary uses. There are similarities between this meal and the Adonia festival of ancient Greece, held in memory of the annual death of Adonis, for which women would prepare herbs and salad leaves. These were not eaten but rather cast upon the waters.

CHAPTER 12: BEARDLESS

The chapter title refers to the geomantic figure Puer (Latin; the boy). It refers to male energies, primarily aggression but also sexuality.

126   *or at least unenforced* / To the Parthenogenesists, gender differences represent a duality to be overcome. Many magicians believe that the conjunction of male and female at the moment of sexual climax signifies progress, however brief, toward that goal. By contrast, in the lives of Ossian and Charlotte, when sex occurs it is homosexual (illegal in the United Kingdom at the time the novel is set and a sin in the eyes of the Church), illicit, or used manipulatively, or it is withheld altogether. Such is the measure of the journey they have still to make.

127   *Key in lock on inner side . . .* / Colquhoun had in mind the suicide of her cousin Edward Garstin, who took an overdose in a locked room and left just such a note pinned to the door. Garstin was responsible for much of Colquhoun's early exposure to the occult. He was the author of two treatises on alchemy and edited an occult journal, *The Search,* for several years.

she had been dead for some hours / In the novel, Charlotte's story is told in reverse. Her suicide takes place on the day before her arrival on Ménec—that is, on the day before the events described in chapter 1 occur. In this way, Colquhoun suggests the cyclical nature of death, rebirth, and life.

129 *his mother's Kensington flat* / Kensington is a part of London that includes Hyde Park and Knightsbridge. It has its dingy parts as well as its wealthy ones. Colquhoun might still have had Garstin in mind, as he lived here with his mother in a run-down area.

130 *I had all this from Ossian . . . when he also arrived at our shores.* / It is possible that Ossian, too, committed suicide after the scandal of Charlotte's suicide caused Daphnis and his circle to abandon him; Charlotte's lawyer brother, Keith, seems likely to have cut Ossian off from Charlotte's money. As the narrator states a few sentences earlier, "An ageing playboy needs a cheque-book for passport." Socially ruined, past his prime, unsuccessful as a designer, and without the safety net of Charlotte's money, Ossian's flight to another group of islands may be postmortem.

CHAPTER 13: JOY

The chapter title refers to the geomantic figure Laetitia (Latin; joy). It indicates happiness.

131 *She had been thrown up like a piece of flotsam . . .* / The process of shedding personal identity continues as the second death approaches. Divested of all clothes and possessions, Ella's sense of self also decays: she is no longer the first-person narrator but the impersonal "she." This occurs in the intertidal zone, the point where land and water meet and the antinomies are resolved. In a series of images of change and transformation, Ella now casts off her earthly form: "'I am,' was enough for her" (page 134).

hypnagogic / The transitional state between wakefulness and sleep, often a period of altered perceptions.

132 *the roseate surface of the water* / May allude to Homer's famous epithet, which appears frequently in the *Odyssey*: "child of morning, rosy-fingered dawn." Ella is here headed toward her rebirth. But the roseate water and the fiery cloud bank also invoke the rites of Adonis explored by J. G. Frazer in chapter 32 of the 1922 edition of *The Golden Bough,* where the runoff from spring rains are said to stain the river Adonis red, and represent the blood of Adonis, gored to death each year by the boar on Mount Lebanon.

133 *it was with a difficult birth that the sun emerged* / While atmospheric and optical mirages involving sunrises (green flashes, for example) do occur over ocean waters, Colquhoun's vivid painterly description of the second sunrise and gold dawn (referencing the Hermetic Order of the Golden Dawn) here reinforce Ella's impending

second death and subsequent rebirth. The "chink of vivid light between two worlds of vapour" suggests the fleeting remnants of Ella's connection to her previous life.

There must have been a wreck . . . / May suggest Ella's "first death," but more generally ties together the theme of death and rebirth supported by allusions to Frazer, Eliot, Milton, and Nikolaz's death. But, tellingly, Ella no longer remains attached to her past, as she "did not speculate upon the details of this catastrophe."

OTHER SELECTED WRITINGS

MUIN

(September 2–30)

I am the month of Muin, month of the vine
Exhilaration is mine through the garland of fruit
Draped from the right shoulder across the swell
Of a belly like Primavera's; yet mine of early
Fall is the realm. On the head too are grapes
And vine-leaves wreathing my autumn-coloured hair
My robe the bluish mist of a sky pregnant
With the first heavy dews.

How calm I am! Yet is there perhaps hidden
An anger that gives authority to my poise?
I drank from the horn-cup and swam into a trance
So deep that only attraction amethystine
Recalls me, after a voyage through gates of horn.

I come now to bless and renew dreams that are true

THE TREE-ALPHABET AND THE TREE OF LIFE

Following up the essay on *Barddas* (No. 3, *The Druid*) it may be suggested that Einigan, the first man, is equivalent to Adam Qadmon in the Qabalah, his alphabet corresponding to the first ten Numbers (i.e. the Sephiroth) on the Tree of Life.

The 'three rods' which Menw saw growing out of the mouth of Einigan after death are the three Vertical Pillars—Mercy, Mildness and Severity—of the diagram. The second alphabet, that of Menw, is the oldest Tree-Alphabet, the Boibel-Loth, or Birch-Rowan, consisting of sixteen letters and their augmentations, and corresponds to the Paths (Netibuth) which link the Sephiroth. By leaving the first three Netibuth unassigned, the fact that their disposition forms the Awen is revealed at the top of the diagram. This is the Divine Name which Menw did not teach in public.

Both alphabets can be conveniently placed on the Tree of Life by marking the Sephiroth with Einigan's APCETILROS alphabet in Roman capitals, following the order of the descent of the Mezla, and the Netibuth with the Boibel-Loth in Ogham. Thus A = Kether, the World of Archetypes (Atziluth) while P and C are Chokmah and Binah which together form the World of Creativity (Briah).

The secrets of these two worlds or planes of existence remained secret; the letters from C to S lie below the Abyss, being concerned with manifestation, and comprise the Worlds of Formation (Ietzirah) and Materiality (Assiah).

The Netibuth are twenty-two in number, one for each letter of the Hebrew alphabet; the first three of these compose the Awen, the next sixteen are assigned to the Tree-alphabet while the remaining three record some of its augmentations.

When Beli arranged the Boibel-Loth, 'he left the ten cuttings secret,' that is, he did not expound the Sephiroth, whose mysteries were known only to the Bards; but he taught the knowledge of the Netibuth, as being nearer to ordinary consciousness, to the people.

DANCE OF THE NINE OPALS

When a picture comes directly from the unconscious, it is almost as difficult for the artist as it is for the spectator to say what it means. Imagine seeing a full-grown tree for the first time, without having any idea of its history or function! When unknown forms arise, they appear as any natural form might when seen for the first time; this is, in fact, what they are—forms from a super-nature which is only beginning to be explored. It is important to record these 'rocks and stones and trees' of the supersensual life.

This painting, it seems to me, comes from some hinterland of the mind, some border-line region, since elements drawn from both actual and potential worlds are to be found in it. It is built from several impacted strata of material and meaning:

1) Various druidic stone-circles known to Cornish folk-lore as 'Nine Maidens' (ni mên = 'holy stones'). Legend says that the circle is composed of girls turned to stone for dancing on (at) the Sabbat, and can be restored to natural shape if embraced at midnight when the moon is full. The monument is a petrified 'Hexentanz'; it is here seen as one of the 'psychic zones' of the country-side, one of its 'fountains out of Hecate.'

2) A Celtic solar festival or fertility-rite; the Maypole's streamers are replaced by coloured 'lines-of-force' connecting the stones with the central fountain and with each other.

3) The nine planets of traditional astrology, including Pluto and Vulcan, revolving round the cohesive and dynamic force of the solar system.

4) Apollo, symbolised by the sun-burst in the centre of the ring, 'leading his choir, the Nine.'

5) The common chord, symbolised by the three tints—one of them basic—in each stone, carried through an octave, including the first two accidentals. The 'music of the spheres.'

6) Kether ('the crown') mitigating the nine lesser sephiroth—often represented in cabalistic tradition as a tree of life.

7) A supernatural flower with nine petals and fiery pistil.

8) The nine moons of pregnancy with perpetual solar impregnation.

9) The opal signifying by its combination of colours the animal, vegetable and mineral worlds. By its connection with the Zodiacal Libra, it links the whole morphological system with the idea of a balance between static and dynamic forces.

This is a list of the painting's inspirational starting-points, as far as I have been able to analyse them. Some of the interpretations of its forms I noticed myself, others were pointed out to me; others still, doubtless, remain to be discovered. But however much one may try to explain a painting, in the end it must carry its message direct to the unconscious of the spectator through his senses by means of its forms and colours.

PILGRIMAGE

Most of the 'great' religions and the esoteric groups that echo them state that the ultimate ground of being is One: for mono-theists there is 'one God,' for adherents of more esoteric associations, 'the One.' Usually no reason is given for these assertions, as though they stated a truism needing no support. Yet observable fact would seem to contradict them: multiplicity is more in evidence than any fancied unity and for proof one has only to look around (or indeed, within).

Illumination is therefore contingent on being in one of the many right places at the right time. This necessitates pilgrimage: ideally the devotee becomes a perpetual pilgrim, a 'noble voyageur' without permanent base.

Over the earth's surface are to be found localities which the ancients called 'Fountains out of Hecate.' To tap these chthonic power-centres it is essential to be near them at the times when they erupt as geysers of energy. Certain places have an affinity with certain times—of the day, of the week, of the year, of the cycle. Many of these are still to be discovered, or rediscovered; mythology and folklore provide clues, calendrical observances being especially useful. One's own hunches about the atmosphere of certain places are often worth following up. Short of becoming a wandering 'venerable,' it is important to live (or at least occasionally to stay) near one of these 'Fountains.' In this way one can gradually come to know the seasons when its stream of power wells up most strongly. One can immerse oneself in it, even if one lacks the knowledge to direct it to other purposes.

I am aware of centres whose power can be classified under elemental Water and Earth (to use Rosicrucian terms)—and here the power seems to 'rise.' Probably there are others situated some distance above the ground which are allied to Fire and Air and whose power 'showers down.' Earth-centres often mediate their force through caves—sometimes artificial—and subterranean 'faults'; Water-centres through underground streams, blind-springs,* holy wells, haunted rivers and lakes.

The power of any centre varies with the seasons, and these in turn are influenced by the positions of Sun and Moon, the Zodiac, the Planets and the Fixed Stars—a lore needing much research. The earth's surface and the atmosphere above it can be envisaged as a chequer-pattern: the Places, demarcated by horizontal lines, being 'fixed' while the Times, represented by verticals, are in a state of perpetual motion following the dance of the heavenly bodies. When a cross is formed by its appropriate vertical passing over a particular horizontal, this marks the moment when the pilgrim should aim to be present. One might call it a shuttle service which indicates both the origin of calendars and their necessity. Incidentally, it shows why any arbitrary change in a calendar, however 'reasonable,' often encounters popular resistance stemming from the collective unconscious.

What does the pilgrim do, once arrived? Perhaps nothing, beyond holding himself in a state of expectancy; but anything that produces a state of readiness to absorb the forces presenting themselves will be a help. Ritual—ancient or modern, traditional or self-devised—may do this but entire passivity may be equally effective. What is likely to be of no effect at all are the meetings in unconsecrated places and at (esoterically speaking) haphazard times, which some of the churches are now offering as an alternative to traditional ceremony.

THE NIGHT SIDE OF NATURE

May not the same obscure forces impelling the depths of the human psyche operate also to shape certain phenomena of external nature? The investigation of this question is one of the chief problems which imaginative biology must set itself to solve. A genuine alchemical science of life must celebrate an extension, even to absurdity's limits, of that approach to nature known inaptly as the 'pathetic fallacy' and under this name already explored in part by Romantic poets.

Modern psychology finds that the type-qualities of the normal person are, in the neurotic, morbidly intensified: indeed, that neurosis consists in this intensification. Three main categories of the sick soul are indicated, and these agree, except in their undisguised vividness, with the chief normal character-patterns.

There is first the individual who may grow into the 'manic-depressive' type of neurotic and finally plunge completely into some kind of 'folie circulaire.' Next there is the being whose inner life is thronged with phantasies of persecution and who may develop into a 'paranoiac' and finally into the megalomaniac, or psychotic who is completely dominated by delusions, mainly of grandeur. Finally, there is the enclosed, self-regarding, narcissistic type who may become a 'schizophrene' and at last—the split between the claims of inner and outer life becoming complete—may reach a state that used to be called 'dementia praecox.' Needless to say, there are cases on the borderline between two of these typical categories, and others that show symptoms of all three; there is perhaps scarcely one pure example of any. The scheme should therefore be regarded simply as a diagram; and the same variety and lack of rigid definition must be expected, when the field of the human unconscious is compared with the corresponding manifestations of the external world.

If the mutual reflective power of microcosm and macrocosm may be assumed, and the sequence of like effect upon like cause, then the same forces* which give rise to symptoms in the human psyche are the agents of equivalent effects in the larger nature. The 'anima mundi'* subsumes all human types, and sometimes it would seem itself to be a sick soul. An interesting line of research would be the predominance of one or other of the three chief forces in any given place or period of history, with its interaction between internal and external climatic conditions.

The motto of the 'manic-depressive' nexus is that figure of speech known as the *oxymoron*, the linking in a single phrase of two contraries, each containing the germ of its opposite.* In nature it includes all cyclic manifestations; seasonal change and its cause in the duality of night and day; sleep and waking; the phases of the moon, recurring comets, tides and tidal waves; rut, menstruation and birth-pains; fevers and other recurrent maladies; the peristalsis of the intestines, the systolic action of the heart, breathing, growth in so far as it can be shown to proceed from alternate effort and calm.

Here too should be placed the idea of reincarnation, or rather of that rhythm of incarnate and discarnate periods which the psyche undergoes in its cycle of development. Such notions take their place as theories, even if they cannot be shown to connect with discoverable fact. And here must be assigned the idea common to several philosophers (Vico, Blake, Spengler, Gentile, Yeats) that the whole universe is cyclic in structure.

In the life of the emotions this phase is characterised by ambivalence, the psyche's alternating roles of lover and loved, tyrant and victim. It holds those aspects of life which are most feminine, all that ancient astrology symbolised by the moon; and this may make woman's traditional 'fickleness' and 'love of change' more comprehensible. In his work *Psychology*, Edward Glover notes among his patients a preponderance of women, and of feminine men, in the 'manic-depressive' group; and it is easy to see from woman's physical constitution why this should be so.

Observations, still of life though hardly of 'nature' in the narrow sense, may be added, as for instance the boom-and-slump of financial markets, and the fluctuations of trade, fashion and taste in general.

The motto of the 'paranoiac' group is *exaggeration* as a figure of speech.

> Why, man, he doth bestride the narrow world
> Like a colossus,

and it may be surmised that the forces that urge the human 'paranoiac' towards his 'folie de grandeur' impel corresponding phenomena in the macrocosm. The grandiose in nature—heroic or mock-heroic—shares the same category with the man who thinks he is Napoleon and the man who actually is Napoleon. Here belongs all gigantism whether natural, like that of the 'Big Trees' of California, or freakish, like the effects of hyper-pituitary action.

Exterior power, whether real or fancied, can only be wielded and retained by force; there is no 'paranoia' without phantasies of persecution. This group therefore is concerned with aggression, and to it belong all structures with that objective, such as teeth, claws, predatory beaks, spines, prickles and piercing fins. It must also associate itself with defence and the prevention of attack, and so adopts various forms of natural camouflage and 'protective colouring.' And since it cannot be without the delusions that follow upon a swollen ego, whatever contributes to illusion must be classified with it, as mirage, 'ignis fatuus,'* the double image. Indeed it is provided with little more than these by way of background; it tends to move away from seasons, weather and basic vegetation— mainly under the 'manic-depressive' dominion—and to approach the animal kingdom and those parts of the vegetal realm which most resemble animals in structure and function, namely the parasites, symbiotics, fungi and carnivorous plants.

The 'paranoiac' must prey upon other beings and be in its turn preyed upon; profoundly, it concerns itself with the necessity for this kind of life. In the emotional life it is the sado-masochistic nexus. Glover notes among human 'paranoiacs' a preponderance of men; and, as can well be seen, the class includes every gradation of the hero-type, all that was anciently symbolised as solar.

In the body politic, it may be related to warfare and revolution; to politics in general, the sphere of leader and demagogue and of those upon whom such are imposed; to conspiracy and intrigue, the secret society or brotherhood felt as menace. It rules also the sublimated forms of combat such as the chase, sport and competitive games; and all those tools and weapons, chiefly of metal, by which men substitute beak and claw. From this angle the universe is seen as an arena of perpetual struggle, as for instance in the Zoroastrian system.

The 'schizoid' takes for motto the figure of the *synecdoche,* the naming of the part for the whole. It is marked by that symptom of division which leads to every kind of fetishism. The 'schizoid' personality or thing is, as its name implies, notable for a splitting, superficial or deep, discovered either in the psyche itself or in its sense of separation from the rest of the cosmos and inability to make effective contact therewith. This separation is not an eminence *per se,* yet it tends to mark out the being from immediate surroundings and isolate it in a kind of vacuum. Here one finds riven rocks and blasted trees, all effects of landslides, earthquake, storm and volcanic eruption, of violences without apparent purpose. One thinks of Glover's 'schizophrenic' patients with their intense yet pointless volubility, their 'flight of ideas,' so different from the logical and almost-convincing stories of conspiracy produced by his 'paranoiacs.' Or in gentler mood, budding and fruition may be found here, the infinitesimal splitting of cells to engender new life, and all in morphology that differentiates the part from the whole. Again, that which cuts off by concealment should be noted and hence the mists, clouds, fogs, vapours—whatever can form an occluding veil. The type expresses itself best through landscape, the fundamentals of life, the organic setting.

Its characteristic emotional life may be symbolised by any solitary figure, virgin or anchorite or Narcissus in contemplation, the seeming offspring of parthenogenesis. It is the type of hybrid and hermaphrodite—the split in the psyche is usually the division into male and female related as a discord. The task is to replace this unresolved duality by a genuinely androgynous whole, the fruitful relation of man and 'daimon,' '*conjunctio.*' One remembers that 'Mercury of the Sages' which is said to partake of the character of both sun and moon.

Socially considered, all pursuits demanding analysis should be included as 'schizoid,' as instance many branches of science and philosophy, literature and organisation. (Fully realised, as the perfected androgyne, it also embraces whatever demands the completest synthesis.) Here originate not only 'cataclysmic' theories, whether religious or scientific, of the beginning and end of the world, but myths such as the 'Fall of man.'

A duality is found in all these three fundamental types, so that in none can be found a true expression of Advaitin* philosophy. In the first the duality is cyclic, in the second algolagnic,* in the third internal and continuous, so that all find their image in what is piebald or parti-coloured, in magpie and orchid, in alexandrite and tourmaline.

WEDDING OF SHADES

When the body becomes crystalline
It is the Bath of Venus
*

I think of him
And right and left my hands
Are full of rosy fire
*

I arrive like a ghost
I move like a roe
Eyes say nothing
Lips are blind
But the air tingles
*

A clear red
I bask in
Red of a wound
Red of health
His radiation
*

I that love clothes
Have to go naked
Not even my thigh
A jewel can wear:
The night-side of nature
Is my domain
Where darkness demands
The tryst unadorned
*

The were-tiger's wounds show on the daylight body:
With no embrace there are bruises on my thighs
*

Enclosed by distance
As by a tower
I yield in trance
To a glowing shower—
Origin
Of bloom on the skin
*

I am the untrodden path
Turning far back
That leads beside daylight
Unspoken word unlit moon
Flower unbreathed-on submerged plant
Star unreached-for
Crown of pearls

DIVINATION UP-TO-DATE

For the past seven years a group of researchers in what they call 'Advanced Study in Psychology' has been experimenting in new methods of pre-cognition. Led by a Harley Street specialist, they keep in touch with important universities in England and throughout the world. Their work is a logical extension of the field originally pioneered by Freud, continued by Jung, and enlarged upon by Rhine.*

There is no link with 'psychical research' as ordinarily understood. The group works by examining records of dreams, doodles, automatisms and other spontaneous material; and has made a number of accurate predictions from these. Upwards of sixty dreams occurring in one week have to be considered before a forecast is made: a single dream is seldom in itself clearly indicative. Rather it is an element in a general pattern, to be traced throughout the dreams of the different group-members. Any disturbance in this patterning must be carefully noted. Some dreams are realistic, many more symbolic; and the phenomenon of the 'shared dream' has been observed between two or more members of the team. Material that would mean little to the layman yields up its message to the interpretation of an expert.

The group has been particularly successful in obtaining warning of disasters which are meaningful to the community in general. It seems that usually such incidents must be amenable to modification through human agency, as for instance, travel accidents by land, sea or air, or the explosion of thermo-nuclear weapons. Happenings which come into the legal category of 'Act of God' tend not to be foreseen: for example, the typhoon in Japan this autumn which caused extensive floods and capsized a ferry with the loss of a number of American servicemen, besides many other casualties, did not appear in the premonitions. But there is no hard-and-fast rule—or if there is it has yet to be discovered—for the earthquake at Orleansville,* Algeria, on the night of September 9th was indicated some days previously.

A tentative theory suggests that something akin to the instinct of self-preservation forces its way out of the collective unconscious and into the personal unconscious when danger threatens. Probably everyone receives the warning, but very few can understand it. Telepathic communication may also play a part, but this is by no means proved.

Oneiromancy is not new: it was already old in the days of the *Somnium Scipionis,** having been practised from the earliest times, though often in an 'underground' manner. What is new is the scientific attention now paid to it. And almost anything, from coffee-grounds to the entrails of a beast, has in the past been used for divinatory purposes. Again, what is new is the careful recording of spontaneous material with its meaning and verification. University degrees are given in Psychological Medicine and Parapsychology by various faculties, and some members of the group hold such degrees. But one wonders whether, today as yesterday, the actual method is only important in so far as it excites the mantic capacities of an individual or a group?

Cassandra* was fated always to prophesy truly and never to be believed; has her mantle now fallen upon a small group that meets in Harley Street? Let us hope that no means, however peripheral, of safe-guarding life and property (to say nothing of prestige) will be ignored by those responsible for public safety.

LES GRANDES TRANSPARENTES

Are they in the form of crystals with colour
Reflected in ruby or sapphire, are their wings
Soft with the tints that bird-plumage may borrow;
Or are they more like the runnels
Of life in wood, and concentric?
Cloud are they, netted, unknit,
Never the same for an instant?

They are all. Medusa-like, tenuous
Yet sharp too, coming almost to touch
Almost to surface with edges, almost to sight.

They are both here and there, they penetrate all ways
They go both north and south, they are past and to come
They pierce all directions at once, they move and are still
They are the profound tilt, the absolute angle
To things that we know.

Perhaps they have face that can smile;
Or were they once imaged
Grand and unbending in background of gold?

And if they should call, can we answer?

LOVE-CHARM II

I write with the unfading ink
Used for a declaration
A record not to be falsified.

I invoke the parts of the body
In their planetary connections
From the head dedicated to Mars
To the feet in Jupiter
Zenith to nadir
I assign them all to Venus' work
Until we possess one another.

Sigils of the grimoire you I recall

Constructing the pantacle of protection
I make the gestures, speak the words

I call on left and right
I call on north and south
I call on night and day
I call on the two halves of the year
I conjure into Venus' pantacle, there to stay
Until we possess one another.

I summon from the collective dream
Symbols of the magian world
To do my will under Venus' sign:

I summon salt and sulphur
I summon mercury and gold
I summon diamond and ruby
I summon lymph and blood
I summon serpent and lion
I summon white tincture and red
I summon the tree bearing moon and sun as fruit
I put you under Venus' reign
Until we possess one another.

The vessel is ready:
Phoenix, here the alembic
Alchemy's fire-bird, light the furnace here!

Venus, bring a happy conjunction
At an auspicious hour
Bring the word and the touch
Bring coalescence of colours
Bring the coruscating sphere
Bring the night of gold.

RED STONE

Acid sharpness Adam aduma
soul alzernand almagra altum
ram quick gold gold cancer

cadmic altered gold camerith bile
ashes ashes of tarta corsufle body
chibur red body right déeb
body properly speaking dehab summer
iron form of man form brother
fruit cock's comb cock gabricus
gabrius gophrith Ethiopian grain
gum red gum hagaralzarna man
fire fire of nature infinity youth
hebtri stone kibrit red stone
golden litharge Indian stone
Indrademe stone lasule stone
red litharge light morning Mars
marteck male red magnesia
metros mine neusis oil of Mars
incombustible oil red oil

olive perpetual olive orient
father a part starry stone
Phison king réezon
residence redness ruby
salt red salt germ
sericon sun sulphur
red sulphur quick sulphur tamané
theriae thelima thion
theta toarech vare
vein blood poppy
red wine wine virago
yolk of egg red vitriol chalcitis
colchotar cochineal glass
zaaph zahan zit
zumech zumelazuli

THE ZODIAC AND THE FLASHING COLOURS

Basic to much that was taught in the Order of the Golden Dawn is the doctrine that colour applied to certain objects and allied with certain mental praxes may be the instrument of a change in consciousness. Though nowhere definitely stated in its instruction papers, this teaching is nevertheless implicit in their contents. According to it, colour provides an avenue into 'worlds' or spheres-of-being other than that recognised by everyday perception.

The Golden Dawn (or rather, its unknown superiors) evolved from the spectrum an elaborate colour scale, of which a design, the Rose of Twenty-Two Petals, manifests the completed symbol. The following list of zodiacal attributions is drawn from this design:

1	Red	Aries
2	Red-Orange	Taurus
3	Orange	Gemini
4	Amber	Cancer
5	Lemon Yellow	Leo
6	Apple Green	Virgo
7	Emerald Green	Libra
8	Peacock Blue	Scorpio
9	Blue	Sagittarius
10	Indigo	Capricorn
11	Violet	Aquarius
12	Magenta	Pisces

For the last, the Order's decree was Crimson, but Allen Bennett, one of its more advanced members, in a note entitled *Of Flashing Sounds* (*The Monolith,* vol. I, no. 2)* replaced this with the more apposite Magenta. I adopt this, and the terms Lemon Yellow instead of Greenish Yellow, Apple Green for Yellowish Green, Peacock Blue for Green-Blue, as being more vivid.

The sigils of the zodiacal signs should be painted each in its appropriate colour upon a background of its spectral opposite. Thus Aries is bright red on a ground of emerald. The pigments must be luminous but not transparent and must be evenly applied. The exact shade of each must be found so as to make a complete contrast with its opposite. Order papers suggest that enamel paints be used or coloured paper to give the required tone-intensity and evenness of surface. So it came about that a magical Order was advocating the methods of *collage* and op-art more than fifty years before such procedures filtered through to the art-circles of Europe.

Having made a sigil according to these instructions, look fixedly at it for a few moments and its two colours will seem to 'flash' one against the other as if with a life of their own. In fact it constitutes what the Order called a 'flashing tablet,' sending a signal from the material world to the world of formation. That the practice of gazing at such a tablet would today be designated a mild form of self-hypnosis is not significant: if pursued, it may involve the inquirer in unanswerable questions about the validity of subjective impressions. What is important is that the process may initiate a change in consciousness.

A set of zodiacal signs thus represented forms a helpful item of equipment in a personal temple or sanctum. Meditation on each sign in turn can prove a fruitful source of knowledge, and will at least stimulate speculation. Meantime, even a cursory glance at the completed set demonstrates some suggestive parallels in symbolism.

It is at once obvious that the series divides naturally into two halves at Libra which, being represented by an emerald sigil on a red ground, inverts the 'flashing colours' of its zodiacal opposite, Aries. Similarly, Scorpio inverts those of Taurus, and so on. In this way are opposite signs both linked and distinguished.

The colours of the sigils move from Aries to Pisces through spectral gradations: from bright red to magenta; the same colours in their grounds from Libra to Virgo.

Arranged as a clock-face, the zodiac forms an elegant diagram that stresses the inherent polarity of its constituents. Aries is placed at the zenith, and twelve o'clock, Libra at the nadir and six, Cancer at three and Capricorn at nine. Taurus at one o'clock faces Scorpio at seven, Gemini (appropriately!) at two faces Sagittarius at eight, with Leo at four and Aquarius at ten, Virgo at five and Pisces at eleven.

The colours of the Four Elements being red (Fire), yellow (Air), blue (Water), and indigo (Earth)—with their flashing opposites of green, violet, orange and amber—it would seem by the colours attributed to them that Aries and Libra, respectively Cardinal Fire and Cardinal Air, have a special overall affinity with elemental Fire. Leo and Aquarius, respectively again Kerubic Fire and Kerubic Air, have a corresponding affinity with elemental Air; as do Sagittarius and Gemini, Mutable Fire and Mutable Air, with the element of Water. Again, Capricorn (Cardinal Earth) and Cancer (Cardinal Water) correspond with elemental Earth.

All these links are stressed by the colour and ground-colour of each sigil but it must be noted that according to the Rose, the colours assigned to the Elements are not identical with those of any sign in the Zodiac. Air is described as 'bright pale yellow,' Water not as the blue of Sagittarius but as 'deep blue,' Fire as 'glowing orange-scarlet' and Earth as a group of four colours difficult to represent diagrammatically. However, as a near approximation, the reds may be aligned with Fire, the yellows with Air and the blues with Water. As for the attribution of indigo to Earth, it is the colour ascribed to the 32nd Path of Ietzirah and Earth is also attributed to this same Path.

To the Signs of the fiery triplicity belong the primary colours—red, yellow and blue; to those of the airy triplicity the secondaries, orange, green and violet. But the triplicity of Earth seems to fall outside this sequence with red-orange, apple green and indigo instead of the tertiaries—russet, citrine and olive, which would result from a simple mixing of two each of the secondaries. No more can the watery triplicity, with amber, peacock blue and magenta, take its place in this classification.

The Planets may be paired in the same way as the Signs, by reference to their flashing colours:

Red	Mars	Emerald Green	Venus
Red-Orange	Pluto	Peacock Blue	(?)
Orange	Sol	Blue	Luna
Amber	Uranus	Indigo	Saturn
Yellow	Mercury	Violet	Jupiter
Apple Green	(Isis?)	Magenta	Neptune

The Golden Dawn colour scales included the five traditional planets with the Sun and Moon, but now the more recently studied Uranus, Neptune and Pluto may be added. The late Dr. W. B. Crow suggested tawney (which approaches amber) for Uranus and magenta, already attributed to Pisces, for Neptune. Red-orange seems suitable for Pluto, but as the trans-Plutonian planet Isis is still astronomically half-discovered, the ascription to it of apple green is guess-work. However if Madame Blavatsky was right to claim in *The Secret Doctrine* that our solar system contains ten planets besides the Sun and Moon, there is still another to be revealed and may prove to be suited to the remaining peacock-blue.

While the foregoing considerations should be given due weight when judging a natal map, the best use for a zodiacal or planetary 'flashing tablet' will always be as a meditation glyph.

THE OPENINGS OF THE BODY

In Madame Blavatsky's *The Secret Doctrine* there is a diagram showing the relationships and correspondences that exist between the various openings or 'gates' of the human body. Seven of these openings are situated in the head; the remaining three, situated below the waist, are related to three of the previous seven, but in this correlation, the three openings of the upper body are inexplicably ignored. Only ten openings in all are mentioned—and these evidently with reference to the female body as in the male there would be nine—and a symbolic connection with the Sephirotic Decad of the Qabalah is traced.

Madame Blavatsky nowhere defines what she means by an 'opening,' the eyes are not openings in the sense of 'holes' so that by this definition two of the seven openings of the head would be excluded. One may mention also (while noting that it is excluded from Madame Blavatsky's list) that the navel is only an opening before the birth of the embryo; after birth it is but the scar of an opening, though generally concave in form. Again, the nipples are openings only under certain conditions. But one may also err on the side of caution if one does not mention various gland-openings: for instance, those of the glands of Bartholin in the female and of the Cowper in the male, and of the innumerable sweat ducts and sebaceous glands in both sexes. However, an opening may be defined rather as a 'nerve centre' or 'zone of sensitiveness,' a passage for the giving and receiving of stimuli. Madame Blavatsky may have had something like this in mind, though her omission of the torso-openings is still unexplained. One must not be led away by the term 'nerve centre' into any attempt to relate closely these visible openings of the physical body with the *Chakras* of Tantric metaphysics.

In fact there are thirteen main openings in the female and twelve in the male, and the greater number present in the female body may indicate a more highly-evolved and specialised structure than that of the male. It does not need much ingenuity to relate the twelve openings of the male to the signs of the zodiac; the thirteen of the female may be adapted to receive that *Mezla* or 'influence' which is said to stream downward from the thirteen strands of the Beard of Macroprosopos.

The distribution of these openings needs much study in research and meditation. The first six are arranged in couples of two: the eyes, the ears, the nostrils; then there is a single opening, the mouth, completing the seven gates of the head. The next two are also a couple, the nipples, then follows the navel, completing the ternary of the torso or upper body. In the lower body are three single and separate openings; the urethral and vaginal orifices and the anus, which make up the final ternary, complete only in the female.

The questions of the relative position of these gates, the linking of their functions, the proportion of their distance from one another and the duplication of certain among them, raises many problems. Since their diagram cannot be made to fit with any exactitude the pattern of the Sephirotic Tree of Life, the attribution to the Zodiac in the case of the male, and to the 'Magnanimity' in that of the female, seems more appropriate than Madame Blavatsky's theory.

How may the openings receive those 'thirteen streams of magnificent oil'?

SANCTIFYING INTELLIGENCE

Sphere of Saturn
Root of elemental water
Understanding the Queens a female image

Star-sapphire pearl civet myrrh cypress
Silver belladonna opium-poppy
Left cerebrum larynx
Plane circle oval diamond triangle
Philosophical salt Jupiter as metal

Water and earth woman as queen of heaven
Yoni outer robe of concealment
Silence angelic Thrones
Compassion vision of sorrow

THE TARO AS COLOUR

This design for a Taro pack is both personal and traditional. It renders the essence of each card by the non-figurative means of pure colour, applied automatically in the manner of the Psycho-morphological movement in Surrealism. The pack is traditional in following instructions drawn from the texts of the Hermetic Order of the Golden Dawn. It is, however, distinct from the figurative pack evolved in the Order's early days by MacGregor Mathers and his wife Moïna, for the use of their students. The more advanced among the latter received the initiated titles of the cards which illustrate their character as meditation-glyphs. The title acts as 'Mantra' to the design's 'Yantra.' The employment of the Taro in divination and, still more, in commercial fortune-telling is thus seen as decadence.

The 22 Major Arcana are inseparable from the rest of the pack, i.e. from the 4 Court Cards and the 9 Decanate Cards in each of the 4 Suits. Basic to all is the concept of the Four Elements: Air (Swords, pale yellow), Water (Cups, deep blue), Fire (Wands, scarlet) and Earth (Discs, indigo). Four family groups appear, each dependent from one of the Aces or Roots of Power. Each Ace attracts to itself one card from among the Major Arcana as its 'Shakti' or formative energy to co-operate with it in manifestation. For example, the Ace of Swords (central colour, pale yellow) is entitled the Root of the Powers of Air and captures The Fool, entitled The Spirit of Aether, the Air card of the Major Arcana. Together they produce the Court Cards: the Prince of Swords (central colour, pale yellow), the Queen (deep blue), the King (scarlet) and the Princess (indigo). These represent respectively Air-of-Air, Water-of-Air and Earth-of-Air.

The Decanate Cards depend in their turn from the Court Cards: the numbers 6 & 9 of Swords from the Prince, the 3, 5 and 8 from the Queen and the 2, 4 and 7 from the King. Only the number 10, the Earth number, depends from the Princess. Number 1 is identical with the Ace, partaking of the nature of both Court Cards and Decanate Cards. The same scheme applies in the other three suits, the Ace of Cups, Root of the Power of Water, capturing The Hanged Man (the Water Arcanum), the Ace of Wands capturing The Angel (the Fire Arcanum) and the Ace of Disks, The World (the Earth Arcanum). The remaining 18 Major Arcana arrange themselves according to their occult titles into four groups which seem to have Elemental affinities:

1. The Four Magi: The Juggler, The Priestess, The Hierophant and The Hermit, together with the Princesses (Earth).
2. The Five Daughters: The Empress, Strength, Justice, Temperance and The Star, together with the Queens (Water).
3. The Five Lords: The Emperor, The Wheel, The Devil, The Tower and The Sun, together with the Kings (Fire).
4. The Four Children: The Lovers, The Chariot, Death and The Moon, together with the Princes (Air).

After I had completed the pack I saw some slides showing nebulae in outer space and the birth of stars. These recalled my designs and confirmed my conviction of their cosmographic function.

NOTES

MUIN

From *Grimoire of the Entangled Thicket* (Stevenage: Ore, 1973). The eight poems in the volume form part of a series of twenty-two: one each for the thirteen-month Celtic lunar calendar, plus nine for the pagan festivals that mark the year's progression. The poems and accompanying drawings date from 1972, described by Colquhoun in her introduction as "an important year for devotees of the Silver Crescent," because in that year the thirteen months of the calendar coincided exactly with their new moons. In addition to the eight poems published in the *Grimoire,* a further four are in typescript at Tate Archive, Tate Britain, London, TGA 929/2/2/1/1. No others have been traced.

THE TREE-ALPHABET AND THE TREE OF LIFE

The typescript is in TGA 929/2/1/66. The essay was written in 1966 in response to an article in the third issue of *The Druid.* No subsequent issues of the periodical have been traced, so this may be its first appearance in print.

DANCE OF THE NINE OPALS

Unpublished. The typescript is in TGA 929/2/1/17. A letter, in TGA 929/1/1847, dates the essay to 1942.

PILGRIMAGE

Sangreal 2, no. 1 (1979): 29–31. The editors described *Sangreal* as the "journal of the mysteries of Britain." The aim was to unite the Western mystery tradition with the legends, history, and folklore of Britain. It was published quarterly between 1978 and 1982.

    blind-springs / Springs of water that do not break the surface. Their presence may be detected by dowsing.

THE NIGHT SIDE OF NATURE

The Glass 8 (1953): [8–12]. *The Glass* was a literary journal that appeared between 1948 and 1954 and published pieces "of an imaginative or introspective character" (editorial). Colquhoun's essay had been refused by *The Bell* in 1944 (see TGA 929/1/136–7). She took her title from the book of the same name by Catherine Crowe, first published in 1848.

Crowe's intention was to argue the case for the serious investigation of hauntings, dop-pelgängers, presentiments, and other supernatural happenings.

the same forces / Spirits if you will, or the 'grands invisibles' of André Breton. [Author's note.]

'anima mundi' / (Latin) The soul of the world. An ethereal spirit, sometimes con-ceptualized as a vital force, said to be diffused throughout all nature.

germ of its opposite / 'Does the fish soar to find the ocean, / The eagle plunge to find the air.' [Author's note.]

'ignis fatuus' / (Latin) Foolish fire. Will-o'-the-wisp, or ghost lights, caused by the spontaneous combustion of marsh gases in swampy places.

Advaitin / Refers to a school of Hindu teachings that concern the inseparability of God, the world, and the self.

algolagnic / Sadomasochistic.

WEDDING OF SHADES

Unpublished. The undated typescript is in TGA 929/2/2/2/5/2.

DIVINATION UP-TO-DATE

London Broadsheet 2 (1955): [4]. The *London Broadsheet* was a short-lived (1954–55) peri-odical in which Colquhoun had a regular column entitled "Between Heaven and Earth." This is one of those columns.

Rhine / J. B. Rhine founded the Parapsychology Laboratory at Duke University in 1930 and conducted the first systematic investigations into clairvoyance and telepathy.

earthquake at Orleansville / The earthquake in 1954 killed more than one thousand people. It is said that many domestic pets deserted their homes the previous day.

Somnium Scipionis / (Latin) *The Dream of Scipio* is a volume written by the Roman author Cicero. It describes a fictional dream of the Roman general Scipio Africanus, which foretold his successful destruction of Carthage in 146 B.C.

Cassandra / In Greek mythology, Cassandra had been granted the gift of prophesy by Apollo, but because she refused his sexual advances he ordained that her predic-tions would never be believed.

LES GRANDES TRANSPARENTES

The Bell 8, no. 6 (1944): 537. *The Bell* (1940–54) was an Irish magazine of literature and social comment.

LOVE-CHARM II

In P. Owen and M. Levien, eds., *Springtime Three* (London: Peter Owen, 1961). The com-panion piece, "Love-Charm I," was published in *Osmazone* (Örkeljunga, Sweden: Dun-ganon, 1983).

RED STONE

The typescript is in TGA 929/2/2/2/5. This is one of a series of eleven poems that together make up the "Anthology of Incantations." Six were published in the surrealist periodical *TRANSFORMACTION* in 1971 (no. 4, pp. 20–21), and this is probably the date of their composition. A further two appeared in *Osmazone.* "Red Stone" has not previously been published.

THE ZODIAC AND THE FLASHING COLOURS

Hermetic Journal 4 (1979): 5–7. The *Hermetic Journal* appeared between 1978 and 1992 and published articles mostly on alchemical subjects.

> *The Monolith* / This was the journal of the Order of the Cubic Stone. The order followed the tradition of the Golden Dawn and taught a system of Enochian magic. Volume 1 appeared in 1967.

THE OPENINGS OF THE BODY

Quest 4 (1970): 26–27. *Quest* is a quarterly journal that first appeared in 1970, edited by Marian Green. It has no relation to *The Quest,* edited by G. R. S. Mead, which ran from 1909 to 1931. Colquhoun first offered this article for publication in 1950 to Antony Borrow, editor of *The Glass* (see TGA 929/1/162).

SANCTIFYING INTELLIGENCE

This poem is from "The Decad of Intelligence," a sequence of ten poems completed in 1979 and previously unpublished. The typescript is in TGA 929/2/2/2/5.

THE TARO AS COLOUR

Sangreal 1, no. 2 (1978): 31–33. This essay was originally written as a catalog note for Colquhoun's exhibition at the Newlyn Gallery, Penzance, in 1977, at which her newly completed pack of Taro cards was shown for the first (and only) time.

PUBLISHED WORKS BY ITHELL COLQUHOUN

1930
"The Prose of Alchemy." [Article on imagery in alchemical writings.] *The Quest*
21:294–303.

1939
"The Double Village." [Imaginative prose. An extract from *Goose of Hermogenes*.] *London Bulletin* 7:23. Reprinted in *Les enfants d'Alice: La peinture surréaliste Anglaise 1939–1960,* exhibition catalog (Paris: Galerie 1900–2000, 1982), in French translation; *Surrealism in England, 1936 and After,* exhibition catalog (Canterbury: Herbert Read Gallery, 1986), 67–68; M. Remy, ed., *Au treizième coup de minuit: Anthologie du surrealisme en Angleterre* (Paris: Éditions Dilecta, 2008), 103, in French translation; and M. Remy, ed., *At the Thirteenth Stroke of Midnight: Surrealist Poetry in Britain* (Manchester: Carcanet Press, 2013), 66.

Untitled autobiographical statement. [With b/w photo of the artist.] *London Bulletin* 8–9 (February): 10.

"The Moths." [Imaginative prose.] *London Bulletin* 10. Reprinted in *British Surrealism 50 Years On,* exhibition catalog (London: Mayor Gallery, 1988), 62; M. Remy, ed., *Au treizième coup de minuit: Anthologie du surrealisme en Angleterre* (Paris: Éditions Dilecta, 2008), 99–100, in French translation; and M. Remy, ed., *At the Thirteenth Stroke of Midnight: Surrealist Poetry in Britain* (Manchester: Carcanet Press, 2013), 63.

"What Do I Need to Paint a Picture?" [Brief explanation of her artistic techniques with four photographs of the artist.] *London Bulletin* 17:13. Text reprinted in P. Rosemont, ed., *Surrealist Women* (Austin: University of Texas Press, 1998), 114.

"The Volcano." [Imaginative prose. An extract from *Goose of Hermogenes*.] *London Bulletin* 17:15–16. Reprinted in *Surrealism in England, 1936 and After,* exhibition catalog (Canterbury: Herbert Read Gallery, 1986), 67–68; M. Remy, ed., *Au treizième coup de minuit: Anthologie du surrealisme en Angleterre* (Paris: Éditions Dilecta, 2008), 103–4, in French translation; and M. Remy, ed., *At the Thirteenth Stroke of Midnight: Surrealist Poetry in Britain* (Manchester: Carcanet Press, 2013), 64.

"The Echoing Bruise." [Imaginative prose. An extract from *Goose of Hermogenes*.] *London Bulletin* 17:17–18. Reprinted in *TR* 2, no. 1 (1979): 96; M. Remy, ed., *Au treizième coup de minuit: Anthologie du surrealisme en Angleterre* (Paris: Éditions Dilecta, 2008), 104–6, in French translation; and M. Remy, ed., *At the*

Thirteenth Stroke of Midnight: Surrealist Poetry in Britain (Manchester: Carcanet Press, 2013), 65.

1941

"Uxor Spiritualis." [Short story.] *Life and Letters Today* 31, no. 52: 207–10.

1942

"Nature Note." [Imaginative prose.] In *The Fortune Anthology,* edited by J. Bayliss, N. Moore, and D. Newton, 29. London: Fortune Press.

1943

"Triad." [Imaginative prose.] *Poetry Quarterly* 5:31.

"Everything Found on Land Is Found in the Sea" [imaginative prose; an extract from *Goose of Hermogenes*] and "The Water-Stone of the Wise" [poetic statement concerning spiritual alchemy]. In *New Road,* edited by A. Comfort and J. Bayliss, 196–98, 198–99. Billericay, Essex: Grey Walls Press. "Everything Found" reprinted in TRANSFORMACTION 4 (1971): 16–18 (titled "Sublimation"); *Surrealism in England, 1936 and After,* exhibition catalog (Canterbury: Herbert Read Gallery, 1986), 67–68; *Angels of Anarchy and Machines for Making Clouds: Surrealism in Britain in the Thirties,* exhibition catalog (Leeds: City Art Gallery, 1986), 82–83; P. Rosemont, ed., *Surrealist Women* (Austin: University of Texas Press, 1998), 168–70; M. Remy, ed., *Au treizième coup de minuit: Anthologie du surrealisme en Angleterre* (Paris: Éditions Dilecta, 2008), 100–101, in French translation; and M. Remy, ed., *At the Thirteenth Stroke of Midnight: Surrealist Poetry in Britain* (Manchester: Carcanet Press, 2013), 67–68. "Water-Stone" reprinted in *Surrealism in England, 1936 and After,* 67–68, and Rosemont, *Surrealist Women,* 170–80.

"Public Art." [Essay on the importance of art in public buildings.] *Tribune,* November 12, 18.

1944

"Aged Six." [Poem written when the author was six years old.] *View,* ser. 4, no. 2: 52.

"Les Grandes Transparentes." [Poem.] *The Bell* 8, no. 6: 537.

"Public Art." [Essay. A condensed version of the article of the same name from the previous year.] *World Digest,* February, 65–66.

"Possibilities for True Fresco." [Essay with three b/w drawings by the artist. The first in a series of articles on the applications and techniques of traditional fresco painting.] *Illustrated Carpenter and Builder,* March 17, 283–84.

1945

"True Fresco." [Essay.] *Illustrated Carpenter and Builder,* January 19, 59.

"True Fresco—2." [Essay.] *Illustrated Carpenter and Builder,* February 9, 154.

"True Fresco—3." [Essay.] *Illustrated Carpenter and Builder,* February 16, 186.

"Preparation of Gesso Panels for Decorative Painting." [Essay with six b/w illustrations by the artist.] *Illustrated Carpenter and Builder,* September 7, 986, 988, 990.

1946

Response to questionnaire. In *Le savoir vivre*. Brussels: Le Miroir Infidèle. Reprinted
in P. Rosemont, ed., *Surrealist Women* (Austin: University of Texas Press, 1998),
214.

"Echoes of Voodoo." [Imaginative prose. An extract from *Goose of Hermogenes*.] *Jazz
Forum* 1:21.

Translations of the French poems "Sunflower," by Breton; "Tom-Tom II," by Césaire;
"There Are No Pointless Jests," by Georges Henein; and "To Live Among Such
Men," by Char. In *Transformation 4*, edited by S. Schimanski and H. Treece,
97–100, 109. London: Lindsay Drummond.

1947

Translations of three poems by Mallarmé: "Languor," "Wreathed in Storm-Clouds," and
"The Old-Clothes Woman." In *A Mirror for French Poetry*, edited by C. Mack-
worth, 64–67. London: Routledge.

1948

"The Myth of Santa Warna." [Prose poem written to accompany a suite of watercolor
paintings.] *The Glass* 1:[21–22].

Translations of two poems by Mallarmé: "Mes bouquins refermes sur le nom de
Paphos" [retains the original French title] and "Anguish." *Adam: International
Review*, December, 16–17.

1949

"The Mantic Stain." [Essay. The first explanation of surrealist automatisms in English,
illustrated with b/w examples of automatic works.] *Enquiry* 2, no. 4: 15–21.
Reprinted, without the illustrations, in P. Rosemont, ed., *Surrealist Women* (Austin: University of Texas Press, 1998), 220–24.

Translation of the poem "Siesta of a Faun," by Mallarmé. *Poetry Review* 40, no. 4:
240–43.

1951

"Children of the Mantic Stain." [Essay. A revised and expanded version of "The Mantic
Stain," with different b/w illustrations.] *Athene* 5, no. 2: 29–34. Reprinted, without the illustrations, in *The Dark Monarch: Magic and Modernity in British Art*,
exhibition catalogue (St. Ives: Tate, 2009), 99–105.

"An Aspect of Popular Taste." [Essay on decoration and folk art.] *Athene* 5, no. 3: 51.

"Little Poems on Hidden Themes." [Poetic sequence.] *The Glass* 7:[6–7].

Untitled extract from *Goose of Hermogenes*. *The Glass* 7:[15–18].

1953

"The Brand Caliburn," "Magical Sequence," "The Wax Image," "Divination," and
"Amulet" [five poems]; "Roads of the Moon" [short story]; and translations
of the poems "Little Song I," "Little Song II," and "The Flowers" by Mallarmé.

In *Springtime,* edited by G. S. Frazer and I. Fletcher, 29–32, 95–99, 107–9. London: Peter Owen.

"The Night Side of Nature" [essay in which Colquhoun makes a modern-day case for animism]; "Diagrams of Love" [poetic sequence]; and cover drawing. *The Glass* 8:[8–12, 20–21].

"Little Poems on the Theme of the Way" [poetic sequence] and responses to a questionnaire concerning the nature and importance of mythology. *The Glass* 9:[18, 24–25].

1954

"The Head that Is Not," "The Visit," and "Rune." [Three poems.] *The Glass* 10:[8].

Translations of the French text "An Island Field," by Éduard Glissant, and the French text "The Conflagration" and poem "Third Vision in the Room," by Romain Weingarten. *The Glass* 11:[15–17, 33–35].

"Warning" and "Epitaph." [Two poems.] *Grub Street* 3:10.

Two untitled poems. *Grub Street* 4:10.

"Heaven and Earth" [article on G. B. Gardner and witchcraft] and "Alchemical Satire," "Lost Horus," and "Sent Away" [three poems]. *London Broadsheet* 1:[2–3].

1955

"Divination Up-to-Date" [brief nonfiction on the predictive power of dreams] and "My Sister and I" [poem]. *London Broadsheet* 2:[1, 4].

"Portrait of a Magician: Austin Osman Spare" [brief nonfiction] and "The Lamia" [poem]. *London Broadsheet* 3:[1, 4]. "Portrait of a Magician" reprinted in *The Borough Satyr: The Life and Art of Austin Osman Spare,* exhibition catalog (London: Fulgur, 2005).

"The Dying-Kick of the Dying-God" [nonfiction exposition of Thelemic Aeonics] and "Stretch Out" [poem]. *London Broadsheet* 4:[2, 6].

"Unidentified Flying Objects" [brief nonfiction] and "I See" [poem]. *London Broadsheet* 5:[3, 4].

"The Goat Without Horns." [Short story.] *Other Voices* 1:1.

The Crying of the Wind: Ireland. [Topographical book with twenty-two line drawings and dust jacket design by the author.] London: Peter Owen.

"The Symbol of the Seven Sisters" and "Vanishing Islands of the West." [Two extracts from *The Crying of the Wind: Ireland.*] *Irish Digest,* November, 13–15.

1957

The Living Stones: Cornwall. [Topographical book with twenty-one line drawings and dust jacket design by the author.] London: Peter Owen.

Preface to *English Masterpieces, 700–1800,* edited by H. W. Herrington. London: Peter Owen.

"The Bell-Branch" and "Moyslaght" [two poems] and "Coronach for Iona" [poetic suite]. *Clan Colquhoun Society Newsletter* 3:[2, 5–6]. Colquhoun was the official Clan Colquhoun bardess.

Review of *The Secret Lore of Magic,* by Idries Shah. *Prediction,* December, 51.

1958

"Corolla's Pinions" and "Serenade of Zicava" [two extracts from *Goose of Hermo-
   genes*]; "Epithalamium," "Elegy on the Hermetic Order of the Golden Dawn,"
   and "Little Poems from Cyprus" [three poems]; and translations of the poems
   "Lament of the Look-Out Man on a Polar Midnight" by Laforgue, "The Cob-
   bler" by Mallarmé, and "Song of the Highest Tower" by Rimbaud. In *Springtime
   Two,* edited by P. Owen and W. Owen, 36–50. London: Peter Owen.
"Sarn Elen." [Poem.] *Aylesford Review* 2, no. 3: 94.
"The Crown and the Kingdom: The Qabalah." [The first of a four-part series of articles
   on aspects of the Qabalah "designed for the student who wishes to know more
   about the roots of occult tradition."] *Prediction,* May, 39–41.
"The Crown and the Kingdom: The Ten Sephiroth." [Article.] *Prediction,* June, 36–37.
"The Crown and the Kingdom: The Twenty-Two Paths." [Article.] *Prediction,* July,
   39–41.
"The Crown and the Kingdom: The 400 Desirable Worlds." [Article.] *Prediction,*
   August, 37–40.

1961

Goose of Hermogenes. [Novel with dust jacket design by the author.] London: Peter
   Owen. Reprinted in 2003 with a biographical sketch of Colquhoun by Eric Ratcliffe and personal reminiscences of her by the publisher, Peter Owen.
"Love-Charm II" and "The Three and the Nine." [Two poems.] In *Springtime Three,*
   edited by P. Owen and M. Levien, 103–5. London: Peter Owen.

1962

"L'Isle de la fleur Nocturne." [Imaginative prose. Translated into French by Paule
   Mévisse.] *Fantasmagie* (Brussels) 9:16–17.
"Liturgical Reformation." [Essay in which Colquhoun presents her highly critical views
   on changes to the Roman Catholic liturgy.] *Aylesford Review* 5, no. 1: 20–22.

1963

"La goélette 'Étoile du soir.'" [Short story. Translated into French by Serge Hutin.]
   Soleils (Paris) 4:53–55.

1968

"Moyslaght" and "Swannenbrunn." [Two poems.] *Ore* 12:7.
"Island of Mystery." [Essay on a visit to St. Helens, an uninhabited island in the Scilly
   Isles, that gave rise to an experience of synchronicity.] *Prediction* 34, no. 4:
   21–22.
"The Church with a Crooked Spire." [Essay on a personal experience of a time warp.]
   Prediction 34, no. 7: 11–12.
"The Light of the Cross." [Essay on carved Cornish crosses.] *Prediction* 34, no. 9: 6–8, 44.

"Still Mythical Ireland." [Nonfiction, with five sketches by the artist. The first in a series of articles on travel destinations for the impecunious.] *Times Educational Supplement,* September 20, 537–39.

1969

"The Revealer." [Poem.] *Cornish Review* 12:12. Reprinted in A. M. Kent, ed., *The Dreamt Sea: An Anthology of Anglo-Cornish Poetry, 1928–2004* (London: Francis Boutle, 2004), 73.

"The Thirteen Treasures of the Isle of Britain." [Nonfiction concerning geographical links with the numinous.] *Prediction* 35, no. 6: 12–14.

"Meditation Begins at Home." [Brief essay offering practical advice for the beginner.] *Prediction* 35, no. 8: 9–10.

"In the Light of Cornwall." [Article giving advice on inexpensive holidays in Cornwall, with three b/w drawings of Cornish scenes by the artist.] *Times Educational Supplement,* January 27, 153–54.

"Magna Mater." [Article giving advice on visiting Malta.] *Times Educational Supplement,* October 10, 35–37.

1970

Review of the verse drama *Holman,* by Brian Pearce. *Ore* 14:30–31.

"The Interlace." [Article concerning the meaning of Celtic designs.] *Quest* 1:12.

"The Openings of the Body." [Article concerning the esoteric functions of body orifices.] *Quest* 4:26–27.

"Relics of Romanticism in Czechoslovakia." [Article.] *Times Educational Supplement,* January 16, 44.

"Wisdom Tradition of the Gael." Part 1, "The Green Diamond." [The first of two articles on mystical locations in the British Isles and their otherworldly inhabitants.] *Prediction* 36, no. 4: 20–22.

"Wisdom Tradition of the Gael." Part 2, "The Danaan Tree of Life." [Article.] *Prediction* 36, no. 5: 20–22.

"Land of Legend and Ancient Peace." [Essay concerning visiting Brittany.] *Times Educational Supplement,* October 9, 41–42.

1971

"Bergie and Zan." [Biographical article on MacGregor Mathers and his wife, Moïna.] *Prediction* 37, no. 1: 24–26.

"A Walking Flame." [Article on MacGregor Mathers.] *Man, Myth, and Magic* 80:2257–58.

"Cornish Earth." [Glossary of Cornish words and phrases compiled by the author.] *Cornish Review* 18:57–66.

"Two Pupils and a Master." [Article on Yeats and Crowley as pupils of their master, Mathers.] *Prediction* 37, no. 10: 12–14. Reprinted in D. Küntz, ed., *The Golden Dawn Legacy of MacGregor Mathers* (Edmonds, Wash.: Holmes, 1998).

"Kurt Schwitters en Angleterre." [Article.] *Fantasmagie* 29:20.

"The Two Silurists." [Essay on Thomas Vaughan, the Welsh alchemist, and his brother Henry, the poet.] *Prediction* 37, no. 7: 22–24.

"Aperçu sur l'origine du collage." [Brief article on Moïna Matherss's part in the origin of collage.] *Fantasmagie* 31:28.

"Incantations." [Six poems from a series of twelve: "Feminine of Magnesia," "Fire," "Sputum Lunae," "Lac Virginis," "Caput Mortem," and "Dissolution."] *TRANSFORMACTION* 4:20–21.

"Here" and "Ruis" [two poems; "Ruis" is from the Celtic tree-alphabet sequence] and review of *Selected Poems of Gertrud Kolmar,* translated by David Kipp. *Ore* 15:21, 32, 36–37.

"Imbolc" [poem from the Celtic tree-alphabet sequence] and reviews of *Letters from John Cowper Powys to Glyn Hughes,* edited by Bernard Jones; *The Cranwell Lectures,* by J. J. Williamson; and *Evolution to Democracy,* by John Creasey. *Ore* 16:20.

"Rubbish into Art." [Essay on the use of collage in education with two b/w illustrations of Merz collages by the artist.] *Times Educational Supplement,* December 10, 33.

"Berlin Is an Island." [Essay on visiting Berlin on a tight budget.] *Times Educational Supplement,* January 1, 20–21, 26.

1972

Review of *City of Revelation,* by John Michell [in which Colquhoun queries the accuracy of his numerological calculations]. Supplement, *Ore* 17:2–4.

"In Search of Faculty X." [Review of Colin Wilson's book *The Occult.*] *Prediction* 38, no. 1: 9–10, 14.

1973

"On the Portrait of 'S'rioghail mo rhream'" and "The Tree Month Duir." [Two poems.] *Ore* 18:4–5. "The Tree Month Duir" reprinted in *Grimoire of the Entangled Thicket* (Stevenage: Ore, 1973), 8. "On the Portrait of 'S'rioghail mo dhream'" reprinted in Eric Ratcliffe and Wolfgang Görtschacher, eds., *Veins of Gold: "Ore," 1954–1995* (Salzburg: University of Salzburg, 1997), 21.

Reviews of *Avebury,* by Richard Burns, and *Warrior of the Icenian Queen,* by Eric Ratcliffe. *Ore* 19:27.

"The Chain Poem." [Article with examples of this collaborative surrealist technique.] *TRANSFORMACTION* 5:22–23.

Grimoire of the Entangled Thicket. [Poetry chapbook with eight illustrations and cover design by the artist.] Stevenage: Ore. Reprinted, without the illustrations, in A. M. Kent, ed., *The Dreamt Sea: An Anthology of Anglo-Cornish Poetry, 1928–2004* (London: Francis Boutle, 2004), 73–75.

"Banners from the Sky." [Article on luminous portents.] *Prediction* 39, no. 1: 23–24.

"The Spear of Destiny." [Review of the book of the same name by Trevor Ravenscroft.] *Prediction* 39, no. 5: 18–19.

1974
"Song of the Chalice Bearer." [Poem from the Celtic tree-alphabet sequence.] *Ore* 20:7.
Review of *The Savage God: A Study of Suicide*, by A. Alvarez. *Ore* 20:55.

1975
Sword of Wisdom: MacGregor Mathers and "The Golden Dawn." [Monograph detail-
ing Mathers's role in the history and significance of the Hermetic Order of the
Golden Dawn and Colquhoun's reflections on her personal experiences with the
order's magical legacy.] London: Spearman.
"Egypt and the Nile." [Practical advice on visiting Egypt on a budget.] *Times Educational Supplement*, January 3, 23.

1976
Introductory essay [containing an account of Colquhoun's artistic development]
in *Ithell Colquhoun: Surrealism, Paintings, Drawings, Collages, 1936–76*. Exhibition catalog. Penzance: Newlyn-Orion Galleries.

1977
Review of *A Sun-Red Mantle*, by Eric Ratcliffe. *Ore* 22:37.

1978
"The Taro as Colour." [Essay explaining the occult color scheme underlying Colquhoun's Taro designs.] *Sangreal* 1, no. 2: 31–33.

1979
Review of *The Ancient Wisdom*, by Geoffrey Ashe. *Ore* 23/24:46–47.
"Pilgrimage." [Article counseling visitors to chthonic power centers.] *Sangreal* 2, no. 1: 29–31.
"The Zodiac and the Flashing Colours." [Article explaining how to paint the signs of
the zodiac in their appropriate magical colors.] *Hermetic Journal* 4:5–7.
"Colour and the Two Sigils." [Article discussing the importance of painting magical
sigils in their correct colors.] *Hermetic Journal* 4:8–9.
"Memoir of E. J. L. Garstin." [Essay on Garstin, a noted alchemist and Colquhoun's
cousin.] *Hermetic Journal* 6:11. Reprinted as the foreword to *Rosie Crucian
Secrets: Their Excellent Method of Making Medicines of Metals Also Their Laws
and Mysteries*, by Dr. John Dee, edited by E. J. Langford Garstin, 7–10 (Welling-
borough: Aquarian Press, 1985).
"Notes on the Colouring of the Homer's Golden Chain Diagram." [Article in which
Colquhoun gives her views on the correct colors of the *Aurea Catena Homeri*.]
Hermetic Journal 6:15–17.
"Mr. Test and the Strawberry Blondes." [Short story inspired by a visit to the collection
of ships' figureheads in the County Museum, Enniscorthy Castle, Wexford,
Ireland.] *South West Review* 6:68.
"Onset of Winter" [poem also in Arabic translation] and "Red" [poem]; "Little Poems
from Egypt" [poetic sequence]; and "The Echoing Bruise" [essay; first published

1939]. *TR* 2, no. 1: 94–96. The journal also contains reproductions of six paintings and drawings by Colquhoun.

1980

"Lamorna." [Extract from *The Living Stones: Cornwall.*] *Wood and Water* 1, no. 7 (Samhain): 11.

"An Avon Well." [Essay on a visit to a holy well.] *Wood and Water* 1, no. 7 (Samhain): 19–20.

"My Star," "Leaf of Grace," and "Question and Answer Foursome" [three poems] and "Notes on Automatism" [article]. *Melmoth* 2:28, 30, 31–32.

1981

"Fearn" and "Uath." [Two poems.] *Ore* 27:6. Both reprinted in Eric Ratcliffe and Wolfgang Görtschacher, ed., *Veins of Gold: "Ore," 1954–1995* (Salzburg: University of Salzburg, 1997), 21–22.

"Women in Art." [Letter commenting on references to her work in a previous issue of the journal.] *Oxford Art Journal* 4, no. 1: 65.

1982

"Coronach for Iona." [A suite of six poems and seven drawings. The drawings record a visit to the island of Iona, made in August 1981; the poems are earlier, first published in 1957.] *New Celtic Review,* Lammas, 4–5.

Review of *The Narrows,* by David Jones. *Ore* 29:39–40.

"Uath." [Poem.] *New Celtic Review,* Beltane, 5. First published in *Ore* 27 (1981).

1983

Osmazone. [Poetry chapbook with drawings by the artist. Limited edition of two hundred copies.] Örkeljunga, Sweden: Dunganon.

"A Dream." [Essay reflecting on holy wells.] *Wood and Water* 2, no. 6: 3.

"Uath." [Poem.] *Wood and Water* 2, no. 7: 3. First published in *Ore* 27 (1981).

2007

The Magical Writings of Ithell Colquhoun. [A compilation of texts and notes by Colquhoun from a collection of her personal papers.] Edited by S. Nichols. Raleigh, N.C.: Lulu Enterprises.

2011

"The Torso Laughs" and "A Visit to Tally Ho!" [Two passages on Ataturk, son of Aleister Crowley, from an unfinished biography of Crowley, ca. 1977, with a preface by Michael Staley.] *Starfire* 2, no. 4: 173–94.

"The Habit of Perfection." [Poem misattributed to Colquhoun. Interleaved between pp. 176 and 177 is a holograph poem, transcribed by Colquhoun, with a sketch between each of the stanzas. The poem was written by Gerard Manley Hopkins, not by Colquhoun, although the sketches are by her.] *Abraxas* 2.

INDEX